Disability in the Arab World

Interdisciplinary Perspectives

Disability in the Arab World

Interdisciplinary Perspectives

Edited by
Monika Baar and Amany Soliman

LEUVEN UNIVERSITY PRESS

This publication has received funding from the KU Leuven Fund for Fair Open Access, and ERC Consolidator Grant (*Rethinking Disability: The Global Impact of the International Year of Disabled Persons (1981) in Historical Perspective*, contract Nr. 648115), and the Open Book Collective (see www.lup.be/obc)

erc

European Research Council

Published in 2025 by Leuven University Press / Presses Universitaires de Louvain / Universitaire Pers Leuven. Minderbroedersstraat 4, B-3000 Leuven (Belgium).

ISBN 978 94 6270 485 5 (Paperback)
ISBN 978 94 6166 700 7 (ePDF)
ISBN 978 94 6166 701 4 (ePUB)
https://doi.org/10.11116/9789461667014
D/2025/1869/42
NUR: 741

Typesetting: David G. Hanna
Cover design: Daniel Benneworth-Gray

GPRC
Guaranteed
Peer Reviewed
Content
www.gprc.be

This volume is dedicated to the memory of Rudolf de Jong (1958–2024),
director of the Netherlands-Flemish Institute in Cairo from 2012 to 2024

Contents

Acknowledgments

This volume benefited from the European Research Council (ERC) Consolidator Grant *Rethinking Disability: The Global Impact of the International Year of Disabled Persons (1981) in Historical Perspective*, contract Nr. 648115, which was carried out at Leiden University from 2015 to 2022. The volume received initial input from the Cleveringa conference: Interdisciplinary Approaches to Disability: The MENA Region in the Modern Period, which took place in Cairo on 25–26 November 2018 and for which Rudolf de Jong, director of the Netherlands-Flemish Institute in Cairo offered intellectual, moral, and financial support. Thanks are also due to Paolo Sabbatini, director of the Italian Cultural Institute in Cairo in 2018, who offered to host the conference, and to the Embassy of the Netherlands in Cairo, which contributed financially to the event. Last but not least, we would like to thank Georgia Katakou for assisting us with the preparation of the manuscript for publication.

Introduction

Monika Baar

The field of disability studies

According to the most recent estimate of the World Health Organization about 16 percent of the world's population lives with a disability and approximately 80 percent of them are assumed to reside in the Global South.[1] These are, however, rough calculations: because disability is a heterogeneous and unstable category, it is difficult to provide statistics about its prevalence worldwide. It can be congenital or acquired later in life; it may be a physical, cognitive, or mental condition; and it can have a variety of causes: genetics, accident, illness, advanced age. Its impact is not merely at the individual level, as it affects the family and wider society. Moreover, it is also a matter of global governance and of policymaking, and it is also an issue of legislation for international and national organizations alike. The benefits and relevance of disability as an analytical category have become recognized much later than those of the comparable categories of class, race, gender, and ethnicity: the emergence of the interdisciplinary field of disability studies dates to the 1980s.[2] Although in recent times the field has gained in visibility, it is yet to be integrated into mainstream academic discourses. This goal has a certain urgency, because the inclusion of disabled citizens into academic research can also help to reinforce the process of societal inclusion.

The concept of disability may appear to be timeless and fixed, but if a historical and anthropological dimension is adopted to its study, its varying understandings across time and space become eminently visible. One trait that seems to occur universally is that the condition is framed as a degree of difference and/or deviation from the norm. Disabled people often become labeled and stigmatized, for example by being associated with certain features, such as inferiority, incompetence, and amorality. They are also frequently getting the blame for their own condition. The result is often exclusion from society, which is motivated by the desire for sameness and the rejection of difference.[3] This marginalization may even become self-fulfilling expectation for the disabled person, which may lead to withdrawal from society.[4]

Anthropologists have been at the forefront of addressing different regional, social, and cultural contexts and relating these to global frameworks. By doing so, they aim to denaturalize disability: to indicate that its understanding is contingent and constantly changing. They explore how different notions of personhood, family, community, and morality influence perceptions of disability across the globe.[5] The need to pay attention to these different contexts goes in parallel with the necessity to explore differences that occur across time: to what degree was the lived experience of disability and its societal perceptions in the past different from that of our own age? Moreover, is it possible to identify a condition retrospectively and to establish its continuity across different time scales? Can we, for example, legitimately claim that the state what the medieval Muslim scholar Abu Zaid al-Balkhi described as restlessness, which is accompanied by profound sadness, is identical with the syndrome that we call depression today?[6] There are two fundamental viewpoints in this debate. The universalist position presupposes a biological foundation, which makes it possible to assume and detect such continuities overtime. The relativist position implies that a certain condition is always historically and culturally determined, which makes it impossible to consider experiences in the (remote) past and the present as constant.[7]

There exist various interpretative models of disability in academic literature. While all of them yield intellectual gains, they also have limitations, and they can best be regarded as ideal types. The first one of these, the moral model (also known as the religious model), renders meaning to disability by attributing it to a certain character, certain deeds, or to karma. It can be the result of some wrongdoing committed by the person concerned or by their ancestors and it can carry shame, blame, and stigma. Alternatively, congenital and acquired disability may be seen a as a life challenge and sign of exceptionality, or a sign of being chosen by God. Understandings of disability in the premodern period often, but not always and not exclusively, drew on the moral model.[8]

Another framework is the medical model that considers disability an individual pathology and tragedy, thus, an undesired condition in need of remedy. In this model, medical and rehabilitation experts are assigned the power to decide who is disabled and who is not and what treatment is necessary. The goal of the treatment is "to fix" the body (or mind) by bringing it as close as possible to the norm. When it comes to watersheds in the history of disability, the processes of modernization and secularization are typically deemed to have brought about fundamental transformations.[9] As the argument goes, with the advent of capitalism, people whose impairments rendered them economically unproductive were identified with idleness and immorality. The ideology of individualism asserted the personal responsibility of the self-reliant individual, and thus saw disabled people in need of assistance or care as a burden on society.

Political activism led to transformations and eventually to the change of the status quo from the 1980s onwards. Vibrant disability activism in several countries gave rise to the emergence of the social model, which redefined disability from a medical into a sociopolitical category.[10] According to this interpretation, disability is a social construct, and its roots are not to be found in the individual body, but in societal discrimination. The individual's physical, sensory, or cognitive difference constitutes an impairment, but the disability itself is caused by negative dismissive attitudes. The removal of psychical barriers is therefore not in itself sufficient; it needs to happen in parallel with the removal of negative societal stereotypes, discrimination, and oppression. The social model provided the vantage point for the development of new, inclusive attitudes, and it also instigated a new social movement that regards disability as one aspect of a person's identity, comparable to class, race, gender, ethnicity, and sexuality.

The cultural model does not perceive disability as a health issue that could be assessed in an impartial manner, neither does it treat the condition in terms of a medical pathology or social discrimination. It breaks with the impairment–disability division of the social model because it focuses on biology and culture alike "as factors remaining in mutual relations, also in conflict."[11]

This model is concerned with the differences that influence perceptions of (dis)ability and its lived experience across cultures and it considers the individual subjectivities of disabled and non-disabled persons interdependent. It acknowledges that disability intersects with other dimensions of identity, such as race, ethnicity, gender, and sexuality.

The fourth, human rights-based understanding of disability, which was influenced by the social model but is not identical with it, views disability as a natural and indispensable dimension of human diversity.[12] It affirms that all human beings, irrespective of their (dis)abilities, have certain rights that are inalienable. One of the most notable international developments in the recent four decades has been the integration of disability into the framework of human rights, culminating in the adoption of the first binding treaty, the United Nations Convention on the Rights of Persons with Disabilities (CRPD) in 2006 (although not every country has ratified it). The rights-based approach requires a new way of thinking: rather than just ensuring mere survival of disabled people, it acknowledges the right to a quality of life. According to the convention, "persons with disabilities include those who have long-term physical, mental, intellectual or sensory impairments which in interaction with various barriers may hinder their full and effective participation in society on an equal basis with others."[13]

Disability in the Arab world

Until very recently the study of disability—its theoretical underpinnings, its methodology, and its geographical coverage—has remained dominated by anglophone scholarship: the above-mentioned interpretative models are also products of this tradition. This means that the "prototypical" disabled person is assumed to reside in affluent democratic countries or perhaps belong to the urban elites of developing countries. There is insufficient reflection on this shortcoming in academic literature and this situation poses difficulties for research on the Arab region and more generally on the Global South. This is paradoxical not only because a major part of the disability community resides in this part of the world, but also because the reliance on the existing insufficient frameworks can lead to the misinterpretation or marginalization of experiences.[14]

Under these circumstances, our knowledge remains rather fragmentary and further inquiry is necessary to broaden its temporal and spatial horizons. Among the existing publications on the premodern period, the monograph *Disability in the Ottoman Arab World, 1500–1800* by Sara Scalenghe deserves special mention.[15] Focusing on societal attitudes, it demonstrates that premodern Ottoman, Arab, Muslim society "tended to include rather than exclude, victimize, or stigmatize impaired and non-normative bodies."[16] The book's overall verdict is that attitudes to disabled people were "relatively benign" thanks to intentions in Ottoman Arab society to create an equilibrium "between the rights and duties of the individual and the interest of the community."[17] At the same time, in her article that reviews the emerging field, the same author warns against the idealization and romanticization of their conditions, also because in some cases impairments were rooted in violence.[18]

Regarding the premodern Arab world, studies drawing on the analysis of theological and legal accounts indicate that, from a theological point of view, disabled people could be regarded as "people with afflictions," whereas from a legal point of view as "people with excuse" from some of their religious duties. Other designations included "strange and different people" and those with "damaged" or "blighted" bodies.[19] The latter could include, as Kristina Richardson showed, blue eyes, boldness, and bad breath.[20] The Chrisitan concept of original sin is absent from Islamic theology, hence impairments were not interpreted in terms of a divine judgement. Instead, conditions such as blindness, deafness, and mental illness could be explained by having recourse to the humoral medical tradition. According to this, the cause of these conditions was that the body's humours, which determined a person's temperament, were out of balance: either in excess or in deficit.[21]

Another subject that requires further investigation is the impact of major political transformations, such as colonization and modernization, on the concepts and the lived experience of disability in the late Ottoman and the colonial period in the nineteenth century and early twentieth. These transformations brought about new understandings of citizenship based on productivity and new educational and medical systems based on Western notions of bioethics and eugenic thought. They also gave rise to an ideology that saw the Arab region as a lower stage of civilization, giving rise to the "development paradigm." Under these circumstances disability became an area for colonial intervention, in which governments, charities, non-governmental organizations (NGOs) and religious organizations placed themselves in the role of benefactors.[22]

There is no doubt that the violence, occupation, environmental damage, and unhealthy working conditions resulted in the large-scale production of disabilities. At the same time, it is important to avoid the pitfall of homogenizing and standardizing colonial experiences as invariably negative. Doing so would lead to the portrayal of disabled people as voiceless and passive subjects, who could be only recipients of services and charity in a subordinate situation, but never actors being capable of autonomous thinking and acting.[23] This would entirely ignore the agency to act and think in ways that go against the expectations of colonial power. [24] It is also crucial to avoid the simplifying lens that sees developments through the dichotomy of "the local" and "the foreign," because such an approach ignores the interactions between the two.

The First Arab Decade of Disabled Persons (2003–12) catalyzed discussions on the relevance, interpretation, and application of human rights in the Arab region. One discrepancy is that the human rights framework implies a normative family structure that values individual autonomy and does not take into consideration the interdependence of extended families that are prevalent in the Middle East.[25] In these settings care and support of disabled family members is typically undertaken by women who do not embark on paid work. Since such care work is usually not performed against their own wishes, this kind of support can in fact be seen as a welcome aspect of the interdependence between disabled and non-disabled people, something that is commonly ignored in the disability studies literature.[26]

Another aspect of the human rights framework revolves around the power of language, including the question of how to translate various concepts and words into Arabic. The creation of an inclusive language around disability has been one of the prominent goals of disability activists in the English-speaking world. This involves the use of first-person language, in which the focus is on the person and not on the disability, thus a switch from "disabled person" to "person with disabilities." But when such an attempt of politically correct usage is undertaken in the Arabic context, the outcome will not be necessarily identical, because, as Molly Bloom has pointed out, "the embodied sense of disability and the social relationships into which disabled people are figured are different."[27] As these instances demonstrate, research into disability in the Arabic world and beyond requires intervention at all levels, ranging from micro to macro, and it necessitates a truly interdisciplinary engagement.

This volume

Taking these research directions on board, the aim of this book is to contribute to ongoing and emerging scholarly engagement with disability in the Arab region. Given the enormous scientific lacuna and the fragmented nature of existing knowledge, a comprehensive account would not be possible at this stage. Instead, through our case studies we would like to join those handful of pioneering scholars who have shown that disability in the Arab region merits research in its own right. Some of the chapters are based on presentations during the conference *Interdisciplinary Approaches to Disability: The MENA Region in the Modern Period*, which was organized by the research team of the ERC project Rethinking Disability at Leiden University in Cairo in November 2018. Others were added when the plan to publish this volume started to emerge. The volume has an interdisciplinary character and includes contributions from representatives of various fields: psychology, sociology, history, linguistics, and development studies. Some focus on the contemporary period, while others adopt a historical dimension and the common denominator between them is interwovenness of these two perspectives. While the volume acknowledges the significance of the medical context in the study of disability in the Arab world, it seeks to expand existing mainstream frameworks by including the social and human rights perspective. The understanding of the human rights perspective is not restricted to the conventional legal aspects. In addition to discussing conceptual issues, the chapters examine the applicability of the human rights context in an Arab cultural and religious context. They also examine issues of transmission, translation, circulation, and interpretation, paying attention to both conventional and new media. In the second part of the volume, the essays discuss historical themes, including the history of public assistance in the colonial and postcolonial states, the history of humanitarian intervention in religious and global contexts and Pan-Arab engagements with disability in a human rights perspective.

Our volume seeks to provide fresh perspectives and hopefully it can contribute to the narrowing of the existing knowledge gap on disability in the Arab world. Several other topics will require attention in the future. The pre-modern period would, for example, benefit from studying the way in which issues of physical and sensory impairments were addressed in classical Arabic literature, for example by eminent scholars such as Ibn ʿAdiyy, al-Jāḥiẓ and Ibn Fahd al-Makkī. Another crucial topic is the relevance of religion in everyday life. While it may not have a significant role in affluent and secularized countries, it is a core element of Muslim society and according to the tenets of Islamic faith vulnerable members of society should receive assistance. In these situations, charity and compassion cannot be dismissed as undesired, patronizing attitudes that stand in the way of independence, nor can it be automatically assumed that the disabled person's desire is such independence. This is especially the case because in the absence of an active welfare system, often no alternative exists to this type of care. This is not to deny, however, that disability in the Arab world can be considered a taboo, leading to stigmatization and marginalization and the human rights framework. Finally, more research would be necessary on the lived experiences of disability in the Arab world both in the past and the present, if possible, relying also on ego-documents. Especially the voices and perspectives of Arabic women would merit better representation. In the hope that these desiderata will resonate with the interest of future researchers, it remains for us to return to our current volume and offer an outline of its contents.

The first chapter by **Bouchra Yahia**, *Islamic Psychology: A Religious Perspective on Human Nature Based on the Theories of Ibn Sīnā and Al-Ġazālī"*, relates to a growing field within the larger discipline of psychology of religion that examines a wide spectrum of topics related to human nature, psychological structures, and mental health from an Islamic perspective. While discussing medieval knowledges, it establishes a connection with contemporary medical needs. It does so by re-examining and re-evaluating mainstream psychology by using primary and secondary Islamic sources with the intention to establish a framework that is in accordance with religious ground rules. It discusses a conceptual framework of psychology from a Muslim viewpoint centered on the concept of the soul (nafs). It explores the meaning of Islamic psychology through studying the theories of Ibn Sīnān (also known as Avicenna) and Al-Ġazālī (Algezelus), with the objective of establishing more insight into the religious viewpoint of human nature and its practical implications with regard to mental health and illness. The main aspect is the multidimensional view of humans, being the psycho-medical, psycho-philosophical, and psycho-spiritual dimensions, respectively addressing the body (*jism*), soul (*nafs*), and spirit (*rūḥ*). With Ibn Sīnā offering a detailed structure of the soul by placing a great deal of emphasis on inner senses and bodily as well as cognitive processes, Al-Ġazālī's spiritual approach focuses on a constant dynamic between four concepts: the *qalb*, *rūḥ*, *nafs*, and *'aql*. The chapter argues that understanding of Islamic psychology can lead to new approaches to treatment in the present that more closely align with the Muslim worldview.

Heba Fawzy El-Masry's chapter *A Sociological Understanding of Intralingual Translations of the Concept of Disability on Twitter in Egypt* shows that disability is labeled in Egypt by different Arabic words and phrases that function as intralingual translations of the same concept within the same culture. A sociological approach to studying these intralingual translations reflects the power of cultural heritage, which portrays disability in a negative light, and its influence on the widespread perception of disability in Egypt. The chapter tests Bourdieu's theory of translation in intralingual translation and in web analysis. It explores the influence of popular culture on the widespread perception of disability by analyzing discourse about disability on Twitter. It assesses efforts to combat the association of disability with negative meaning components within the domain of language use. Although the same terms are now used in Arabic to label the same concept related to disability, the different perceptions about them translate into different usages of the same words by the state on the one hand and by common people who are influenced by *doxa* (a society's taken-for-granted, unquestioned truths) in the Egyptian society on the other. The roots of *doxa* about disability lie in the Egyptian cultural legacy, which is reflected in proverbs, some religious beliefs, and even films, and that can be investigated in light of a sociology of translation that adapts Pierre Bourdieu's conceptual tools into a theory that helps in understanding the influence of social patterns on the *habitus* (the set of skills and social resources that govern how people engage with the world) of the ordinary people as reflected on Twitter.

Riham Debian's chapter *Into Arabic: UNCRPD'S Rights Discourse and the Politics of Interpretation* deals with the discourse shift in the inclusion politics as manifested in the articulation of the United Nations Convention of Rights of Persons with Disabilities (UNCRPD 2006) and its cultural transposition and translation through languages and across the North/South divide. The chapter reads the UNCRPD (2006) and its Arabic translation to examine the politics of naming, its effect on the framing of person with disabilities (as object of charity versus subjects with rights) and its ramification with respect to the developing social policies/practices of inclusion. The chapter seeks to conceptually engage with the Recognition/Acknowledgement paradigm to investigate the type of inclusion represented in the Source Text and its transposition in the Target Text. To this end, the chapter opens a repertoire between Political Philosophy, Critical Discourse Analysis, and Translation Studies to structure its framework from the theoretical literature on the politics of recognition. The chapter utilizes Fairclough's three-dimensional model (2013) as a tool of analysis to examine the discursive event embedded in the production and dissemination of UNCRP, its implication with respect to both the politics of interpretation in the Source and Target Texts, and the discursive and socio-cultural practices across the civilizational divide.

Imene Zoulikha Kassous in her chapter *Exploring the Inclusivity of Disability Related Language in a Multilingual Research Context: A Case Study of the Algerian Context* focuses on a country that signed the Convention on the Rights of Persons with Disabilities (CRPD) in 2007, ratified it in 2009, and started communicating with the Office of the United Nations High Commissioner for Human Rights (OHCHR) Committee of the United Nations Human Rights Office in the course of 2015. Many relevant documents have been published recently in this area in three different languages: Arabic, French, and English. Indeed, Algeria is known for its multilingual context due to its historical encounters with Arabs and French in addition to the demands of globalization. In this respect, the purpose of this analysis is to demonstrate the inclusivity of the current language use in Algeria in relation to disability and the extent these documents maintain inclusive language that respects and accepts everyone regardless of their differences while promoting equal opportunities. The selection of the material was based on a restricted timeline (2015–20) and the search was performed in all three languages on international and Algerian database platforms. Findings have demonstrated that there is an instability in the use of terminology, including awkward translations from other languages into Arabic as well as the use of problematic and offensive terms.

Gildas Brégain's contribution addresses *The Transformations of Policies for the Blind in Algeria and Tunisia in the Twentieth Century (1918–1987)*. It focuses on North Africa, where blindness has long been a category with a particular social status. Since the twelfth century, some blind people had the opportunity to integrate into Koranic schools and mosques, and become reciters of the Koran at ceremonies, or become Imam. Thanks to this, a small minority of blind people were able to rise socially, and differentiate themselves from the majority, who had to rely on begging, family assistance, or community solidarity. This chapter addresses the gap on this topic in academic literature by analyzing and comparing the policies of assistance to the blind in two North African countries during the twentieth century during the colonial and post-independence period: Algeria and Tunisia. It also examines the circulation of experts, ideas, and materials between these two countries, where since colonial times the authorities chose to divide government work by creating a sector of public action specifically dedicated to the blind. The chapter discusses the public action that included the creation of an administrative agency responsible for the issue, the allocation of specific social and economic benefits, and the funding of educational or vocational training institutions.

Maria Chiara Rioli in her chapter *Disability, Humanitarian Diplomacy, and the Roman Catholic Church in Modern Palestine* discusses an instance of religious humanitarianism: the mission of the Dorothean nuns who arrived in Palestine from Italy in 1927 and opened the Effeta school for deaf Palestinian children in 1971. This happened in the spirit of the Second Vatican Council, which led to a shift from the conversionist attitudes to the desire to share life with the people. Based on extensive archival material, the chapter explores the history and practices toward deaf children carried out by the Dorothean nuns, in a region that often experienced violence. Through the case study the chapter shows the international circulation of medical and rehabilitation ideas and practices, and it reveals that Catholic humanitarianism in the Middle East was embedded in political and diplomatic relations between Israel, Jordan, the Vatican, Italy, and since the 1990s, the Palestinian authority. By pointing to the cooperation between the Effetha school and the Palestinian authorities, it also nuances the idea that at the end of the twentieth century secular and Catholic forms of welfare toward disability run separately.

Majid Turmusani discusses the *Challenges and Opportunities for the Implementation of CRPD in the MENA Region: Insights from Iraq and Qatar.* All ESCWA (United Nations Economic and Social Commission for Western Asia) countries of the MENA region have ratified the UNCRPD treaty and became state parties to the convention. As duty bearers, they continue to assume their obligations (legal and moral) in providing support for their citizens with disabilities. While this constitutes an unprecedented opportunity to ensure the rights of persons with disabilities in the region, such progress is being hampered by certain structural, attitudinal, and policy barriers and not least by lack of data and evidence on disability. In this chapter case studies are being presented on how disability rights are being fulfilled through inclusion practices in two countries of the region: Qatar and Iraq. In Qatar, progress has been achieved on several aspects of social and economic development and is being ranked high on the Human Development Index. The infrastructure and services are well developed in this country following universal design principles to a great extent. Inclusive technology is particularly developed in Qatar, and it targets people with disability under current e-accessibility policy (SCICT, 2011) developed under Ministry of Transport and Communication. In Iraq, the pioneering project of the United States Agency for International Development (USAID), "Access to Justice" program, is strategically situated to strengthen partner's capacity (that is, civil society and government) through creating dialogue between partners and enhancing respect for human rights.

Amany Soliman and Monika Baar show in the concluding chapter, *Conclusion: Pan-Arab Engagements with Disability from the 1980s until Recent Times* that while the idea of a collective identity, shared heritage, and connected futures was always present in the Arab mindset, a momentum for joint Arab civil society action on the rights of persons with disabilities only emerged in the late 1990s. The chapter identifies the United Nations's International Year of Disabled Persons in 1981, the creation of of the Arab Organization for Persons with Disability in 1998 and The Arab Decade for Persons with Disabilities (2004–13) as milestones in the creation of a common framework. Using archival material from the Archive of the League of Arab States, it shows how cooperation with Arab civil society toward the emancipation of people with disabilities in Arab societies emerged amid frustrations about the failure of joint action and how it intersected with massive political, security, and social challenges in the Arab world. The epilogue points to the tragic coincidence that the launch of the Second Arab Decade for Disabled Persons in 2023 coincided with a new cycle of violence in the Middle East, leading to an enormous increase in maimed bodies. It therefore concludes that disability scholars have an ethical imperative to call for the cessation and prevention of violence all over the world.

Notes

1. This volme uses both the designation "disabled people" and "people with disabilities," the first one typically referring to historical contexts and the second to contemporary ones. While in recent human rights documents "people with disabilities" has become mainstream, not everyone prefers this option.
2. Kudlick, Catherine J. (2003). "Disability History: Why We Need Another 'Other.'" *The American Historical Review*, 108(1), 763–793.
3. Stiker, Henri-Jacques (2019). *A History of Disability*. Ann Arbor: Michigan University Press, 13.

4. Grinker, Roy Richard (2019). "Autism, 'Stigma,' Disability: A Shifting Historical Terrain." *Current Anthropology*, 61 (Supplement 21), 55–67.

5. Bloom, Molly (2020). "Toward a Disability Anthropology of the Middle East and North Africa." *Hespéris-Tamuda LV*, 4, 275.

6. Bulut, S., Hajiyousouf, I., and Nazir, T. (2021). "Depression from a Different Perspective." *Open Journal of Depression*, 10(4), 168–180.

7. Rees, O. and Crowley, J. (2015). "Was There Mental Trauma in *Ancient Warfare*? PTSD in Ancient Greece." *Ancient Warfare*, IX(4), 70–74. Rees represents the universalist position and Crowley the relativist position.

8. Retief, M. and Letšosa, R. (2018). "Models of Disability: A Brief Overview." *HTS Teologiese Studies/ Theological Studies* 74(1), 2.

9. Ibidem., 3.

10. Shakespeare, Tom (2010). "The Social Model of Disability." In Davis, Lennard J. (ed.), *The Disability Studies Reader*. New York: Routledge, 266–273.

11. Snyder, S.L. and Mitchell, D.T. (2005). *Cultural Location of Disability*. Chicago: University Chicago University Press, 9; Waldschmidt, A. (2017). "Disability Goes Cultural: The Cultural Model of Disability as an Analytical Tool." In *Culture, Theory, Disability*. Bielefeld: Transcript Verlag, 19–27.

12. Degener, Theresia (2016). "Disability in a Human Rights Context." *Laws* 5, 3(35). https://doi.org/10.3390/laws5030035

13. https://www.un.org/disabilities/documents/convention/convoptprot-e.pdf

14. Meekosha, H. (2011). "Decolonizing Disability: Thinking and Acting Globally." *Disability and Society*, 26(6), 667–682.

15. Scalenghe S. (2014). *Disability in the Ottoman Arab World, 1500-1800*. Cambridge: Cambridge University Press, 2014.

16. Ibidem., 112.

17. Ibidem.,134.

18. Scalenghe,S. (2019). "Disability Studies in the Middle East and North America: A Field Emerges." *International Journal of Middle Eastern Studies*, 51, 112.

19. Laes, C. (2018). *Disability and the Disabled in the Roman World. A Social and Cultural History*. Cambridge: Cambridge University Press, 170–171.

20. Richardson, K. (2012). *Difference and Disability in the Medieval Islamic World: Blighted Bodies*. Edinburgh: Edinburgh University Press.

21. Arikha, Noga (2007). *Passions and Tempers: A History of the Humours*. New York: Ecco.

22. Cleall, E. (2024). "Disability and Postcolonialism." *Postcolonial Studies*, 27(1), 1–16. https://doi.org/10.1080/13688790.2024.2322252

23. Brégain, G. (2016). "Colonialism and Disability: The Situation of Blind People in Colonised Algeria." *Alter: European Journal of Disability Research/Revue européenne de recherche sur le handicap*, 10(2), 148–167.

24. Merle, I. (2004). "Les Subaltern Studies: Retour sur les principes fondateurs d'un projet historiographique de l'Inde colonial." *Genèses*, 56(3), 141.

25. Hagrass, H. (2005). "Definitions of Disability and Disability Policy in Egypt." In Barnes, C. and Mercer, G. (eds.), *The Social Model of Disability: Europe and the Majority World*. Leeds: The Disability Press, 148–162.

26. Ibidem.,154.

27. Bloom, Molly (2020). "Toward a Disability Anthropology of the Middle East and North Africa." *Hespéris-Tamuda LV*, 4, 276.

References

Arikha, Noga (2007). *Passions and Tempers: A History of the Humours.* New York: Ecco.

Bloom, Molly (2020). "Toward a Disability Anthropology of the Middle East and North Africa." *Hespéris-Tamuda LV,* 4, 273–291.

Brégain, G. (2016). "Colonialism and Disability: The Situation of Blind People in Colonised Algeria." *Alter: European Journal of Disability Research/Revue européenne de recherche sur le handicap,* 10(2), 148–167.

Bulut, S., Hajiyousouf, I., and Nazir, T. (2021). "Depression from a Different Perspective." *Open Journal of Depression,* 10(4), 168–180.

Cleall, E. (2024). "Disability and Postcolonialism." *Postcolonial Studies,* 27(1), 1–16. https://doi.org/10.1 080/13688790.2024.2322252

Degener, Theresia (2016). "Disability in a Human Rights Context." *Laws* 5, 3(35), 1–24. https://doi. org/10.3390/laws5030035

Grinker, Roy Richard (2019). "Autism, 'Stigma,' Disability: A Shifting Historical Terrain." *Current Anthropology* 61 (Supplement 21), 55–67.

Hagrass, H. (2005). "Definitions of Disability and Disability Policy in Egypt." In Barnes, C. and Mercer, G. (eds.), *The Social Model of Disability: Europe and the Majority World* (pp. 148–162). Leeds: The Disability Press.

Kudlick, Catherine J. (2003). "Disability History: Why We Need Another 'Other.'" *The American Historical Review.,*" 108(1), 763–793.

Laes, C. (2018). *Disability and the Disabled in the Roman World. A Social and Cultural History.* Cambridge: Cambridge University Press.

Meekosha, H. (2011). "Decolonizing Disability: Thinking and Acting Globally." *Disability and Society,* 26(6), 667–682.

Merle, I. (2004). "Les Subaltern Studies: Retour sur les principes fondateurs d'un projet historiographique de l'Inde colonial." *Genèses,* 56(3), 131–147.

Rees O. and Crowley J. (2015). "Was There Mental Trauma in Ancient Warfare? PTSD in Ancient Greece." *Ancient Warfare,* IX(4), 70–74.

Retief, M. and Letšosa, R. (2018) "Models of Disability: A Brief Overview." *HTS Teologiese Studies/ Theological Studies,* 74(1), 1–8.

Richardson, K. (2012). *Difference and Disability in the Medieval Islamic World: Blighted Bodies.* Edinburgh: Edinburgh University Press.

Scalenghe, S. (2014). *Disability in the Ottoman Arab World, 1500–1800.* Cambridge: Cambridge University Press, 2014.

Scalenghe, S. (2019) "Disability Studies in the Middle East and North America: A Field Emerges." *International Journal of Middle Eastern Studies,* 51, 109–134.

Shakespeare, Tom (2010). "The Social Model of Disability." In Davis, Lennard J. (ed.), *The Disability Studies Reader.* New York: Routledge, 266–273.

Snyder, S.L. and Mitchell, D.T. (2005). *Cultural Location of Disability.* Chicago: University Chicago University Press.

Stiker, Henri-Jacques (2019). *A History of Disability.* Ann Arbor: Michigan University Press.

United Nations. Convention on the Rights of Persons with Disabilities and Optional Protocol. https:// www.un.org/disabilities/documents/convention/convoptprot-e.pdf

Waldschmidt, A. (2017). "Disability Goes Cultural: The Cultural Model of Disability as an Analytical Tool." In Anne Waldschmidt, Hanjo Berressem and Moritz Ingwersen (eds.), *Culture – Theory – Disability. Encounters between Disability Studies and Cultural Studies* (pp. 19–27). Bielefeld: Transcript Verlag.

CHAPTER 1

Islamic Psychology: A Religious Perspective on Human Nature Based on the Theories of Ibn Sīnā and Al-Ġazālī

Bouchra Yahia

Abstract

This chapter relates to a growing field within the larger discipline of psychology of religion, which examines a wide spectrum of topics related to human nature, psychological structures, and mental health from an Islamic perspective. While discussing medieval knowledges, it establishes a connection with contemporary medical needs. It does so by re-examining and re-evaluating mainstream psychology by using primary and secondary Islamic sources with the intention to establish a framework that is in accordance with religious ground rules. It discusses a conceptual framework of psychology from a Muslim viewpoint centered on the concept of the soul (nafs). It explores the meaning of Islamic psychology through studying the theories of Ibn Sīnā (also known as Avicenna) and Al-Ġazālī (Algezelus), with the objective of establishing more insight into the religious viewpoint of human nature and its practical implications with regard to mental health and illness. The main aspect is the multidimensional view of humans, being the psycho-medical, psycho-philosophical, and psycho-spiritual dimensions, respectively addressing the body (*jism*), soul (*nafs*), and spirit (*rūḥ*). With Ibn Sīnā offering a detailed structure of the soul by placing a great deal of emphasis on inner senses and bodily as well as cognitive processes, Al-Ġazālī's spiritual approach focuses on a constant dynamic between four concepts: the *qalb, rūḥ, nafs*, and *'aql*. The chapter argues that understanding of Islamic psychology can lead to new approaches to treatment in the present that more closely align with the Muslim worldview.

Keywords: Psychology of religion, Islamic psychology, mental health, Ibn Sīnā, Al-Ġazālī

Introduction

Although psychology and religion are concerned with many similar issues, they have long been formally separated due to the secularization of modern society. This, however, seems to have created a lacuna for those whose religion plays a key part in their lives. One reaction to this has been a growing awareness, particularly among Muslim academics and psychologists, of the importance of developing insight into the relationship between Islam and psychology.[1] Over the past few decades, research into the psychological aspects of Islamic teachings has led to a growing number of debates and publications in this field. This had led to the development of an "Islam and psychology movement," based on sources from the Islamic tradition and with spirituality and religion at its core.[2]

In this chapter, I will present an alternative paradigm of psychology by discussing an Islamic perspective based on the works of two traditional Islamic scholars, Ibn Sīnā and Al-Ġazālī. Both scholars lived and worked during the early years of Islam, when the young religion was still in a formative stage and science was primarily studied within a religious context—a stark contrast with today's approach. While psychology was not a separate discipline during their time, these two prominent scholars wrote on various subjects closely related to psychology and their works still carry a weight of importance in Muslims' understanding of their religion to this day. Therefore, I will discuss their viewpoints related to mental well-being and illness in their time, particularly by focusing on their perspective on the condition that could today be diagnosed as (clinical) depression. Hopefully, this religious viewpoint will shed light on an alternative view on psychology and offer more insight into its practical implications and current relevance.

Psychology in the West

There are two characteristics that frame the Western paradigm of so-called conventional psychology, and that are important to take into consideration within the context of this chapter. The first one is the secularization of modern society. This essentially means the rejection of religious ideas and organizations as legitimate sources in the face of scientific and other knowledge. Within this context, this means that religious ideas have no influence on ideas developed within the field of psychology and, therefore, are not considered to be an authoritative source of knowledge or information. This automatically means that empiricism and scientific evidence are the ultimate source of knowledge and method of research.[3] All psychological schools of thought in the Western world are secular in nature; the Islamic psychological model that I will be discussing here is, obviously, not.

The second characteristic is the parochialism of Western society within so-called mainstream psychology. In short, this means that almost all psychological approaches are drawn up within a Western context and applied as a general rule to the rest of the world. The vast majority of studies are conducted in the Western world, particularly in the United States, which also produces the most researchers. Extensive research concludes the following:

> The universe of social and organisational behaviour that is being sampled is almost entirely restricted to studies done within less than a dozen of the more than 200 countries in the world, constituting little more than 10% per cent of the world's population.[4]

Western Europe and the United States are over-represented among this small group of countries.

This last quotation touches upon a sensitive subject within psychology as a social discipline. Some norms and values of this Western tradition of psychology do not always align with ones in so-called non-Western cultures, especially in areas where it concerns the influence of religion and culture in people's lives. This sentiment can pose a practical problem, particularly for Muslim communities in the West when facing psychological issues.

Extensive research among Muslims from different cultural backgrounds in the Netherlands showed that a vast amount of them question Western psychological treatments, instead preferring alternative methods by so-called religious healers.[5] Similar conclusions were drawn in a British study of London Bangladeshis.[6] In the United States, one of the most significant barriers for seeking treatment among Muslims is the limited availability of Islamically integrated mental health services.[7] Though more comparable research is necessary, these conclusions indicate a persistent issue in the care of Muslim patients with mental disorders in the West that needs to be addressed. One reaction to this has been the "Islam and psychology movement."[8]

Islam and psychology

Insights into the relationship between Islam and psychology began to develop in the late 1970s and have steadily progressed over the years. Many obstacles in this field are yet to be overcome, including the formulation of an agreed-upon definition and theoretical framework. In a broad sense, "Islam and psychology" refers to "the interdisciplinary field that explores human nature in relation to Islamic sources and which uses this knowledge to bring human beings into their best possible state, physically, spiritually, cognitively, and emotionally."[9]

Whereas Islam and psychology can be seen as the umbrella term in this discussion representing the wider movement, the term Islamic psychology does not yet have a consensual definition but commonly refers to "Islam's version of psychology."[10] This latter term usually translates to Arabic as *'ilm al-nafs*, which literally means "the study of the self." This form of psychology acknowledges the element of spirituality within psychology, and how this ties in with our sense of self and mental state. In the remainder of this chapter, I will use the term "Islamic psychology" exclusively, as the objective is to describe an Islamic-based system of ideas with regard to the definition of the self, and its considerations on mental health and illness.

So far, research in the field of Islamic psychology has drawn from different sources. However, a significant influence on Islamic psychology has been provided by early Muslim scholars, traditionally working in the first few centuries after the Prophet Muhammad's death. These first centuries of Islam were a scientifically fruitful period with financial encouragements from the Muslim authorities to expand on their knowledge. This was attributed to the expansion of the Islamic empire and direct contact with other civilizations, particularly the Greek. This prompted a translation movement where ancient Greek texts were translated to Arabic. Starting with Galenic medical treatises and advancing to Greek philosophy, Muslims started integrating Greek scientific knowledge into their medical education and built upon this science with their own theories. This period, which gave impetus to Islamic scholarship, has become known as the Islamic Golden Age: an era of great academic endeavours in the Muslim world that is traditionally seen as stretching from the eighth to the thirteenth centuries.[11]

Many scholars who lived and worked during these early years of Islam are largely responsible for shaping the Muslim understanding of a wide variety of topics. Their influence stretches so far that the current interest in Islamic psychology is seen by some researchers as a revival of these early scholarly works.[12] Living and working in an Islamic environment, they were pioneers in combining the Greek philosophical and scientific tradition with the theological principle that God is the ultimate creator of all things.[13] In other words, their current appeal could be attributed to the adherence of these scholars to scientific methods in their research while simultaneously not compromising on their Islamic worldview and upholding Islamic values. In today's post-colonial Islamic world, many Muslims paint a nostalgic picture of the Golden Age: as one with a thriving Islamic society, where science flourishes *through* faith instead of *despite of* it, and where the dominant views of the West and secularism were virtually non-existent.[14]

To establish a psychological framework with Islamic integrity, it is important to understand human nature from an Islamic point of view. Islamic conceptualizations of our "self" and what defines who we are as humans are central to this understanding. One method for doing this is by focusing on scholarly works, which in this case will be from Ibn Sīnā and Al-Ġazālī. Both scholars have made an indispensable contribution to the development of Islamic philosophy and wrote extensively on subjects closely related to psychology, with the primary motive of understanding creation. As will become clear, they together represent a comprehensive notion of the main elements of Islamic psychology, which can broadly be divided into psycho-medical, psycho-philosophical, and psycho-spiritual dimensions. The remainder of this chapter will focus on these elements and how their theories translate into practice.

Ibn Sīnā

Abū 'Alī Al-Ḥusayn Ibn Sīnā (980–1037), known in the West as Avicenna, was born in Bukhara (in present-day Uzbekistan) and is primarily known as a Persian philosopher and physician. During his lifetime, he worked as a physician to several courts, and, inspired by Greek thinkers such as Aristotle and Plato, produced many works, the two most important of which are *The Book of Healing* (*Al-Shifā'*), and *The Canon of Medicine* (*Al-Qānūn fī al-Ṭibb*). The latter is a medical encyclopaedia that became an authoritative textbook in medieval European universities.[15] As a physician, Ibn Sīnā wrote about the human body and practiced what is now known as Arab-Islamic medicine: a scientific form of medicine, consisting of a combination of Islamic principles and the medical heritage of the Greeks. As a philosopher, he wrote about the human soul and his main contributions in this regard consist of his elaborations on the body–soul relationship, motivation, sensation, perception, and, ultimately, human nature in general. Much like his Greek predecessors, Ibn Sīnā considered medicine as a branch of philosophy. This meant that every theoretical medical discussion is essentially rooted in Islamic philosophical concepts, one of the most important ones being the duality of man: the active presence of soul and body and the relationship between these two. This close connection between medicine and philosophy in Ibn Sīnā's writings means a complex conceptual network about health and sickness as will become clear.[16]

Psycho-medical dimension

The premise of traditional medicine as practiced by the Greeks and later the Muslims is that every human being consists of a body (jism), soul (nafs), and spirit (rūḥ). The interaction between these three divisions takes place in the spaces of the body.[17] In other words, health and illness revolves around the dynamic between these three divisions and how they relate (or connect) to one another. Contrary to the modern medical paradigm, understanding this dynamic is more important in the process of healing than understanding the healing of shapes (that is, physical parts of the body). Another important building stone of Arab-Islamic medicine is the humoral theory. In short, this theory asserts that the human body consists of four humours: yellow bile, blood, phlegm, and black bile. From birth, every person has a certain balance and unique ratio between these four juices, which determine their so-called temperament. Any disturbance of this balance makes a person sick and must be restored when healing.

These premises form the foundation of the medical paradigm that medical practitioners, such as Ibn Sīnā, worked within in diagnosing and treating illnesses. There was only one way to be healthy, which was having a balanced temperament, and illness meant disturbing this temperament in any way. Nevertheless, despite the seemingly major differences with the modern medical paradigm, this paradigm constitutes the front-runner of modern medical practice.[18]

Psycho-philosophical dimension

In the chapter "De Anima" from his work *Al-Shifā'* (The Healing) Ibn Sīnā' describes the soul, that is, the *nafs*, from a philosophical point. According to Ibn Sīnā, the soul is what distinguishes living beings from non-living beings and is made up of three respective stages: the vegetative soul, the animal soul, and the human (or rational) soul. He continues to describe these stages with the vegetative being the lowest one, meant to feed itself, grow, and reproduce, and the animal soul being more developed as it possesses two faculties: the faculty of movement and the faculty of perception. The faculty of movement contains feelings of attraction (lust) and repulsion (anger), and subsequently acting upon them, which are seen as the most basic emotions of every animal and human being. The faculty of perception is of an observing nature and possesses external and internal senses. The external senses are the common five senses of sight, hearing, smell, taste, and feel. The internal senses on the other hand provide in the processing, understanding, and classifying of information and experiences.[19] Without elaborating too much on these technical terms, it is important to know that their main function is to sense and anticipate on the *intentions* of subjects, thereby representing the cognitive part.

The third and ultimate stage is the human soul, where human beings have an intellect (*'aql*) at their disposal. This intellect can be subdivided into a practical part and a theoretical part. The practical intellect encourages humans to take certain actions and has the function of encouraging ethically acceptable behavior in people. This practical intellect is partly in contact with the animal soul that forwards the signals of repulsion and attraction to the practical intellect. Based on these signals they receive, people develop appropriate feelings, such as shame or sadness, and react accordingly. The practical intellect is the place where general principles on which morality are based are formed, with some help of the theoretical intellect. According to Ibn Sīnā, moral character can be innate and instinctive, but it can also be due to a strong dominance of the practical intellect over behavior by basing all its choices on rational and moral principles.[20]

Lastly, the theoretical intellect is the highest form of intelligence and is related to receiving, acquiring, mastering, and producing knowledge. Where the practical intellect is concerned with everyday behavior and bodily functions, the theoretical intellect focuses on deeper forms of knowledge and understanding. Ibn Sīnā describes the human soul as a being with two faces: one, the practical intellect, is outward-looking and deals with everyday behavior and bodily functions while the other, the theoretical intellect, turns inward and tries to arrive at a deeper understanding of the world, the universe, and oneself. Every human being is born with a potential theoretical intellect, which develops and unfolds over the course of life until it is finally able to think, reason, and produce knowledge for itself. Since the potential intellect cannot perfect itself on its own, Ibn Sīnā argues that there must be another form of intellect, which is always present and supports the human intellect to manifest itself. This is what he calls the Active Intelligence, or God.[21]

Al-Ġazālī (1058–1111)

Born in the Persian province of Khorasan, Abū Ḥamīd Muḥammad ibn Muḥammad Al-Ġazālī (1058–1111) is one of the most renowned scholars in Islamic history. He is known as an Islamic jurist, theologian, and mystical thinker, and has written authoritative works on many subjects. His most famous work is his magnum opus *Iḥyā' ulūm ad-dīn* (The Revival of the Religious Sciences), where he deals extensively with almost all spiritual aspects of life. As a Sufi, a practitioner of mystical Islam, Al-Ġazālī was mainly focused on his spiritual connection to God and adhering to an ascetic lifestyle. Sufism (*taṣawwuf*) is the general indication of a mystical development in Islam, which has its origins in the early Islamic period.[22] Its supporters, so-called Sufis (*ṣūfī*), are known by their asceticism. An important aspect of Sufism is to focus on the inner experience of faith in order to create a stronger connection to God. It is important to keep in mind that Sufism should not be seen as a separate religious movement or cult with a clear starting point. More so, it is a part of Islam in which one strives for a higher religious experience by emphasizing the spiritual.[23] Psychology is an important part of Al-Ġazālī's works due to themes that are central to Sufism, such as the eternal struggle with oneself, spiritual growth, and development of the soul. This ultimately led Al-Ġazālī to develop a "psychology of man."

Psycho-spiritual dimension

In *Iḥyā' 'ulūm al-dīn* (Revival of the Religious Sciences), Al-Ġazālī's objective is to "enlighten the soul" to attain a perfect state by elaborating on virtually all spiritual aspects of life. Al-Ġazālī places the human (or rational) soul between what he calls the animal and divine realms. Depending on how an individual develops, the soul may ascend to the divine or descend to the animal. Al-Ġazālī also compares the *nafs* to a closed place with two doors: one door is open toward the spiritual world of the angels and the other door is open towards the body and the material world.[24] With this last example, he ultimately positions the *nafs* as the psychological part of human beings, and throughout his work, he emphasizes that it needs both sides (physical and spiritual) to be able to develop further in this world.

In the "Revival," he devotes an entire chapter to what he calls *'Ajā'ib al-qalb* ("The Miracles of the Heart"), where he explains his views on the religious psychology of man. Four concepts are central to this understanding and represent the inner make-up of man: *qalb*, *rūḥ*, *nafs*, and *'aql*. Every concept has two meanings: the first meaning belonging to the visible and material world, and the second belonging to the invisible and immaterial world.[25]

Qalb can be translated as the "heart" and literally refers to "the conical organ" located in the chest, as well as to a "spiritual and divine substance" (*laṭīfa rabbāniyya rūḥāniyya*) that is in direct communication with the physical heart. In this second sense, the *qalb* is the perceiving and intuitive part of man that penetrates to the true essence of things. The concept of *qalb* is central to the management of the soul and can be regarded as the central governing body of the soul. It is an intuitive and cognitive ability with a directing function. The *qalb* is at the center of perception by governing man's instincts (internal) and actions (external). A person can be driven by desire to reach a goal, but these feelings of desire must be kept in check by wisdom, knowledge, and reflection. Without these restrictions, Al-Ġazālī is convinced that man is lost to his lusts.[26]

Rūḥ can be translated as "spirit" and refers first to a kind of primary life pneuma—the starting point of which is in the physical heart and from whence it flows to the rest of the body. The second meaning is again a "spiritual and divine substance" that penetrates to deeper truths and represents a knowing aspect of man. As for the *rūḥ*, this represents a bodily function that is equivalent to some form of biological life force on the one hand, and, on the other, refers to what is perhaps the most abstract and sacred part of man. This explanation is motivated by a Qur'anic verse stating that, upon the creation of man, God breathed in him from "His *rūḥ*" after which man came to life.[27] For religiously motivated reasons, Al-Ġazālī does not elaborate much on this concept. He refers to a Qur'anic verse that says: "They question you about the *rūḥ*. Say: The *rūḥ* belongs to the commandment of my Lord. You have been given nothing but very little knowledge."[28] In Al-Ġazālī's understanding, man has not been given the capacity to grasp this concept and, therefore, it is not worth the try.[29]

Nafs, the soul or "the self," first refers to that part of man that contains our primitive instincts, such as hunger and anger, and is similar to the animal soul. In the second meaning, the *nafs* represents a deeper consciousness of man ("spiritual and divine substance"), which depends on its changing state and comes in three different forms: *an-nafs al-ammāra bi-s-sū'*, *an-nafs al-lawwāmah*, and *an-nafs al-muṭma'inna*.

Unlike the *qalb*, the *nafs* is more connected to the animal soul. The *nafs* is more sensitive to external conditions and fluctuates in state. To clarify the understanding of this term and, more importantly, to avoid confusion, *nafs* is more accurately translated as "the self" in this context. When the *nafs* indulges in its primitive urges and lusts, Al-Ġazālī speaks of *an-nafs al-ammāra bi-s-sū'* ("the self who commands evil"). The opposite of that is *an-nafs al-mutma'inna* ("the quiet self"). The latter knows how to defend itself well against temptations and thus represents a state of calm and contentment. In between is *an-nafs al-lawwāma* ("the accusing self") who is engaged in a struggle against its basic urges but has not (yet) reached a tranquil state.[30] Considering the previous example, this suggests that when the *qalb* is in strong connection with wisdom, knowledge, and reflection, there is sufficient control to obtain *an-nafs al-muṭma'inna*. If not, the *nafs* falls into a state of *al-ammāra bi-s-sū'*. According to Al-Ġazālī, the *nafs* is constantly going back and forth between good and evil, and it is everyone's responsibility to develop one's character in such a way that the *nafs* is under control. At the same time, Al-Ġazālī believes that there is but a temporary victory over these basic urges. Thus, Al-Ġazālī considers humans to be in a constant state of conflict with themselves and their primary instincts of lust and anger.

The *'aql*, or ratio, on the one hand refers to the possession of knowledge and ability to reason, and, on the other, to the ability to perceive and understand the true meaning of things in the form of a "spiritual and divine substance." Al-Ġazālī does not elaborate much on the 'aql. This concept represents the rational and intelligent part of man as well as the means of obtaining and understanding knowledge. In addition, the 'aql also has the ability to derive the deeper meaning of things that are hidden in knowledge.[31] This concept continually reappears throughout the rest of his work as being a quality that has enabled man to think and make informed decisions.

What these four concepts above illustrate are the four components that make up the human soul. The schema serves as a spiritual anatomy of the human soul as it were, and reflects a deeper reality of the human core, beyond what is visible. Although Al-Ġazālī defines each concept in the same way, what he seems to describe is that these four concepts together refer to the make-up of the soul and at the same time the soul itself. In other words, they cannot be detached from what we call "the soul" as separate components, but they represent the soul both together and individually. It is a complex construction that is non-comparable to any Western counterpart.

Furthermore, a remarkable resemblance can be seen between Al-Ġazālī's three stages of the *nafs* and Sigmund Freud's psychodynamic theory.[32] Both are based on an internal struggle between immediate gratification ("id" and *an-nafs al-ammāra bi-s-sū'*), a stage of negotiation and consideration ("ego" and *an-nafs al-lawwāma*) and a higher variant in which the good is clear and indisputable ("superego" and *an-nafs al-muṭma'inna*). The Arabic terms used by Al-Ġazālī in this case are taken directly from the Qur'an to represent the most fundamental struggle in the human self and are therefore based on Islamic revelation. It is striking that the essence of his psychodynamic theory bears such close resemblance to an Islamic scholar based on the Qur'an.

Additionally, there is a nuance to add to this comparison, namely that the three stages of Freud develop in man from childhood and are present from then on (to a certain extent) while in constant conflict. The stages of the *nafs* of Al-Ġazālī, on the other hand, refer to a (temporary) state of the soul. The three stages of the *nafs* are not independently operating actors, like the id, ego, and superego are in Freud's theories, but are the result of underlying mechanisms and feelings. In that sense, one could argue that the two theories are complementary to each other. For example, when the id predominates, the soul is in a state of *an-nafs al-ammāra bi-s-sū'*.

In the same manner, the remaining concepts can also be linked respectively. Nevertheless, for both Freud and Al-Ġazālī, this tension between the different stages is a constant in life and a state of peace or *an-nafs al-muṭma'inna* is always the goal, but this state is ultimately of temporary duration.

General conclusions on the *nafs*

The foregoing displays a general overview of what Ibn Sīnā and Al-Ġazālī refer to when they discuss the *nafs* and how they view the basic nature of man. While this is not an exhaustive schema of their views, it does however give an insight into the way they think about man and how they incorporate religious values in their work. Before proceeding, some general conclusions could be made so far.

From an Islamic point of view, man is comprised of three dimensions: the physical body (*jism*), the self or soul (*nafs*), and the spirit (*rūḥ*), suggesting that man leads a physical, metaphysical, and spiritual existence, all of which are intertwined. The *nafs* may be considered the most important dimension—finding itself in the middle of an aspect that is lower than itself ("the body") and an aspect that is higher than itself ("the spirit").[33] For both scholars, there is a perpetual tension between these visible and invisible forces at hand, and they both stress the importance of finding a balance between them. Ibn Sīna argues that the soul is the first reality of man: it is where the existence of man begins, and it is the part that is immortal as the material body perishes upon death, but the soul continues to live on. The soul and the body are so closely intertwined that a deteriorated physical condition could be caused by the soul—a concept known today as psychosomatic illness.[34]

There is a complicating factor in the multidimensional use of words in the Arabic language that needs to be addressed. Concepts regarding the soul such as used by Al-Ġazālī for example are so context dependent that English equivalents for the terms are often deficient in meaning, mainly because of the close connection to the religious context in Arabic. An important example here is the word *nafs* that so far in this chapter has been translated as "soul" or "the self" but can also refer to the "psyche." The word "psyche" originally means soul in Greek but, over time, has come to take on the meaning of the "mind" in English, thus evolving into a more neutral and secular term. In contrast, the translation of *nafs* can be either "psyche" or "soul."[35] The same word is used in both spiritual and scientific contexts and there is no Arabic synonym separating the secular from the religious. The term *nafs* is thus an example of the strong inter-weaving of the psychological and spiritual dimensions within an Islamic context.

Furthermore, both scholars emphasize the importance of ethically moral behavior as defined by their religious values. Ibn Sīnā stresses an innate God-consciousness and states that it is incumbent upon the soul to acknowledge the existence of God and to obey Him. Therefore, one is subject to God-imposed obligations, which include praying several times a day, fasting, and partially giving away one's property. The purpose of performing these acts is to discipline and enrich the soul for the purpose of gaining a greater understanding of God. This would distract man from his physical desires and eventually lead to a realization of true potential in existence.[36] This is even more pertinent in Al-Ġazālī's writings who, as a Sūfī, encourages "disciplining the soul" and describes character traits that are important to cultivate to this end, such as wisdom, courage, mod-eracy, and justice.[37]

Characteristics of what we know now as the cognitive and behav-ioral schools can be seen in this emphasis on control over thought pro-cesses and the importance of so-called good and healthy behavior, which, of course, in this case would be as informed by the religious tradition. Earlier, similarities between Freud and Al-Ġazālī were also pointed out. By no means is this a suggestion that Freud was influenced by Islamic tra-dition or Al-Ġazālī, nor is it a statement of ascribing Islamic roots to the schools of cognitivism or behaviorism. However, it is an indication of the parallels between the theories of these Muslim scholars and the theoreti-cal underpinnings of more recent psychological schools.[38]

In the remainder of this chapter, I will explore how their theories translated to practice by discussing the meaning and treatment they gave to a common mental illness in their time.

Melancholia and (clinical) depression

In the early Islamic centuries, there was medical and societal recogni-tion for the existence of mental illnesses. Special provision was given to the mentally ill as Islamic hospitals included separate psychiatric wards from the ninth century onwards.[39] These wards were specifically meant for the research and treatment of mental illness while facilitating special care for those suffering from these illnesses[40]—one example of which being melancholia: a condition similar to what we know today as (clinical) depression and that can be described as "the original concept of depressive illness."[41]

Following the current definition as outlined in the DSM-V,[42] depression, otherwise known as major depressive disorder or clinical depression, is a serious mood disorder whereby one experiences "persistent feelings of sadness and hopelessness and loses interest in activities they once enjoyed." Current treatments for mental disorders focus on bringing about changes in thinking, behavior, or physical processes. The condition that most closely resembles this contemporary disorder is *mālīḵūliya* ("melancholia," derived from the Greek *melaine chole*, meaning "black bile"). This common medical term evolved in Europe into what we know today as clinical depression—the term that has dominated ever since. This was one of the best described and most treated mental illnesses, distinguishing it from current diagnoses of psychosis and neurosis. The main reason for this is that it was relatively common, but also fairly harmless and quite treatable, which prompted doctors to address it more often.[43] According to statistics from the World Health Organization, depression is one of the leading causes of disability worldwide, making it as relevant today as it was ten centuries ago.[44] Seen as this condition is as prevalent now as it was during their time, the rest of this chapter will be devoted to how Ibn Sīnā and Al-Ġazālī defined and treated melancholia through their respective specialism.

Ibn Sīnā's definition

In book four of his *Canon of Medicine*, Ibn Sīnā describes melancholia as

> the change of beliefs and thinking from the natural course to corruption, fear, and ruination because of a black bile temperament. This temperament oppresses the spirit (*rūḥ*) of the brain from within and terrifies it by its darkness, as the external darkness oppresses and terrifies.[45]

Working from the Galenic paradigm that heavily influenced Arab-Islamic medicine, Ibn Sīnā has a physiological approach to melancholia and thus attributes the disorder to a surplus of one of the four temperaments, namely the black bile, and its negative effect on the rest of the body. He describes it as a physical process, in which the increase and/or so-called burning of black bile affects the brain as well as the affected person, darkening their thoughts, both literally and figuratively.

In addition to this surplus, the other determining factor in melancholia is the *rūḥ*. The *rūḥ* in this case is understood as the pneuma—giving life to the rest of the body as soon as it comes into contact with some part of it. Ibn Sīnā devoted a chapter in the *Canon* to the meaning of this word and how it affects the body. The starting point of the *rūḥ* is at the heart (*qalb*) from which it flows to the rest of the body and makes contact with organs. After establishing this contact, these organs become able to perform their function. For example, the ability to see is only active after the *rūḥ* has reached the lens of the eye just as hearing only works after the *rūḥ* touches the auditory nerve. According to this definition, the *rūḥ* gives life to organs and their functions.[46] Ibn Sīnā argues that an excess of black bile is disastrous for the influence of the *rūḥ*. Black bile is characterized by cold and dryness—both of which bring the *rūḥ* into a state of confusion and, as actual life force, disrupts the rest of the connections in the body. One of the reasons why a weakening of the *rūḥ* leads to mental disturbances is because the *rūḥ* is protector of reason and rationality (*'aql*) in man. Ibn Sīnā describes the *rūḥ* as "a luminous substance. It's a ray of light. [...] Light is in harmony with the breath (i.e. rūḥ), darkness in discord with it."[47]

As a physician, Ibn Sīnā largely approaches melancholia from what we now know as a (neuro-)biological and cognitive point of view. He divides the causes of depression into two categories: physical and psychological. On the one hand, bodily processes take place resulting in a surplus of black bile that disturbs the temperament. This morbid surplus constitutes a pressure on the *rūḥ* whose functions weaken and is therefore no longer able to offer sufficient protection to the rational ability. Consequentially, the person in question becomes vulnerable to distressing and intrusive thoughts, such as painful events and death, which in turn are intensified by bad events. It is these factors that influence a person with a weakened *rūḥ* and keep it in a depressed state, eventually pushing one into a state of melancholia.[48] In conclusion, Ibn Sīnā considers the most important defect to take place in the body through a disturbance of the physical balance, which then results in a clouding of the normal train of thought, after which pessimism and dejection prevail.

He identifies symptoms of incipient melancholia to be negative thoughts about past events, irrational fears, hypersensitivity, difficult living conditions, preference for loneliness, negative prospects, and poor health. As melancholia develops, insomnia and a negative self-image start developing. At the most advanced stage, other symptoms become self-hatred, worry about death, and a development of obsessions. Ultimately, these symptoms also work through in external appearance in the form of dark circles around the eyes.[49]

In his works, Ibn Sīnā also addresses the fact that some doctors in his time attribute melancholia to the influence of evil spirits, so-called jinn. He responds to this with the following:

> [W]hether melancholia is caused by the jinn or not is a remote question. If it were caused by the jinn, it happens by changing the temperament to black bile, for melancholia's cause is the dominance or black bile. Thus, the cause of that black bile may be jinn or something else.[50]

Without categorically dismissing the presence and influence of jinn in the physical world, their effect on one's mental well-being could only be established by affecting their physical qualities, that is, manipulating the black bile, and thereby poisoning the human being, thus defining the problem solely as a physiological issue. While exorcism of jinn by physicians and religious healers was a known practice in his time, Ibn Sīnā emphasizes that any influence from jinn can solely be regarded as an indirect cause. Melancholia was a disturbance of the black bile, and jinn could only cause melancholia by manipulating this bile, thereby remaining loyal to his medical foundation.

Treatments

With regard to treatment, Ibn Sīnā prescribes treatments consisting of enforcing stimulating environmental factors to change the patient's mood. For example, the patient should be placed in an environment where it is neither warm nor cold and where the air is filled with pleasant spices. For the cold and dry element of the black bile, it is important that they are cheered up so that the heart is warmed and strengthened. Therefore, the patient should spend a lot of time in daylight, preferably surrounded by cheerful people or with good friends to clear their mind. One must have enough activities and sleep and make plans. Confidence is seen as a source of happiness, and this can be achieved by overcoming (relatively) minor difficulties and learning to cope with disappointment.[51]

Some of his other treatments focus on recovery of the temperament and strengthening the *rūḥ*. There used to be a form of antidepressants that had an uplifting or numbing effect on the body and were thus meant to reduce depressive symptoms. These were grouped under the general denominator of *muffariḥ an-nafs* ("rejoicement of the soul").[52] Specific resources to this end and mentioned by Ibn Sīnā include, for example, wine ("nourishing"), pearl and silk ("restoring shine and light"), camphor and rose water ("warming"), and sweet aromas, such as amber or musk ("invigorating"). These could be used individually or in combination and are all aimed at strengthening the *rūḥ* to defend itself against the harmful effects of the black bile.[53]

It is not clear how these treatments were put into practice. Ibn Sīnā does not describe how the intake of pearl and silk, for example, takes place. In addition, it is striking that Ibn Sīnā considers wine as medicine, because of the ban on alcohol consumption in Islamic tradition. He does not explain this contradiction further, but it is quite possible that Ibn Sīnā refers to a type of grape drink with a slightly intoxicating effect known as *nabīḏ*. This drink was allowed for medicinal purposes according to some Islamic views as long as it was taken in moderation.[54] A moderate ingestion of wine could increase happiness and joy according to Ibn Sīnā because it stimulated the *rūḥ* and blocked "heavy" thoughts, making it an effective remedy for melancholia. In any case, the use of these agents was mostly in combination with one of the foregoing measures of more psychological nature, adding to it that it is easier to cure melancholia when it is in its early stages than when it has progressed.[55]

With these treatments, Ibn Sīnā recognizes the role of psychological processes and is a proponent of the idea that psychological changes also produce physical changes. The same way of reasoning can be seen later in the cognitive school of thought. There is a similar recognition for the cognitive process and the effects it can have on one's well-being. The most notable example of this is Ibn Sīnā's encouragement to allow melancholic patients to achieve small victories to increase self-confidence and self-esteem as a stepping stone to good health. Much the same slant is used in cognitive behavioral therapy in which negative thinking patterns must be broken through positive thinking and acting. Other parallels can be drawn with current neurobiological approaches in the form of the use of antidepressants that are meant to restore disturbances in the body.

Al-Ġazālī's definition

As a Sufi, Al-Ġazālī has a different conception of melancholia than Ibn Sīnā, which starts with his use of the term "disease." In "The Revival," Al-Ġazālī distinguishes between diseases of the body and diseases of the soul. In the former, a limb or other part of the body is not functioning properly, but in case of diseases of the soul, the full potential of the soul is not properly utilized, that is, not turning in the direction of the Creator, which is its primary purpose for creation. Al-Ġazālī mentions worship and the search for (divine) knowledge as the only thing that distinguishes man from animals. When the soul is not occupied by worship, one is conflicted by a spiritual illness.[56] One of the few places in which melancholia is literally mentioned by Al-Ġazālī is in the book *The Alchemy of Happiness*. He describes it rather succinctly as a disease that doctors diagnose "when someone loses all pleasure and interest in worldly affairs and withdraws from others."[57]

From his background as a Sufi, Al-Ġazālī focuses mainly on spiritual illnesses, the causes of which he locates back to what he considers to be the most fundamental level of an individual: the soul (*nafs*). In his description of spiritual illnesses, he is mostly concerned with a kind of harmful behavior that stems from a restless soul that easily gives in to its urges. Culprits for the body are excesses in the form of too much sleep and food while harmful elements for the soul are formed by extreme emotions and undesirable thoughts. These thoughts can be ideas or memories that come into people's minds and confront them with unpleasant events from the past, for example. Al-Ġazālī describes them as thoughts that come from the devil and incline the soul toward evil (*waswās*). They can be compared to obsessive thoughts that can further weaken a "weak heart" and plunge it into a negative spiral.[58]

Ideally, every soul has a certain balance that maintains a peace of mind. To explain how this balance is maintained, Al-Ġazālī symbolizes this with the following four characteristics: wisdom, justice, courage, and moderation. These respectively ensure that good is distinguished from bad, that anger and lust are controlled, and that the intellect (*ʿaql*) determines final choices. In the end, moderation balances the previous three so that extreme emotions do not predominate. However, when the former three emotions do dominate, man falls prey to his emotions, the most dangerous of which are desire and anger, and corrupts the soul. Ultimately, this leads to "madness" (majnūn).[59] Furthermore, Al-Ġazālī also discusses other factors that cause melancholia, one trigger being extreme fear or tension (anxiety) that leads to frustration and restlessness. This emotion develops in the qalb and the nafs and causes fear of old age, death, God, and poverty among other things. They are considered the result of a troubled qalb that does not fully trust in God.[60]

For Al-Ġazālī, spiritual balance and discipline are key factors in maintaining mental well-being. In addition, a spiritual illness does not have to necessarily indicate a mental illness, but merely a possibility. This is especially apparent from what he describes as the evil whisperings of the devil (waswās). This can be explained in more psychological terms and can be described as cognitive disturbances in the thinking process. While overflowing with symbolic language, what Al-Ġazālī is describing indicates a natural and close relationship of a healthy spirit and mind with ethical behavior and moral conduct. Therefore, he believes that ethical conduct and physical and mental illness are related and that there is an ethical component to mental and spiritual balance, and likewise healing and restoring of health by means of ethical measures and leading a(n Islamically) virtuous life.[61]

In discussing causes for diseases, Al-Ġazālī points out that different degrees of understanding of the complex layers of human beings provide different outlooks on diseases. He argues there are first- and second-degree causes to diseases that get conflated. In the case of melancholia, the doctor's explanation of an excess of black bile in the body as a cause of melancholia is a limitation of the physician's knowledge approaching the problem only from the outside.[62] According to Al-Ġazālī, God has put this person in a condition that makes him turn away from their worldly life and turns them to their Creator. The black bile is therefore alone a second-degree cause and God's means to carry out this plan. From his Sufi point of view, melancholia could be regarded as a positive event and probably as a sign of God to His servant that he should turn to Him more.

This last remark and, in fact, Al-Ġazālī 's whole attitude toward illness, plays into the discussion of the modern medical anthropological terms "disease" and "illness." Whereas "disease" refers to the malfunctioning of physical and/or psychological processes, the term "illness" refers to the perception of the disease by the patient himself.[63] The former is viewed from what is today called a biomedical perspective, while the latter comprises the total experience of symptoms as felt by the patient, their family, and surroundings. A sense of purpose and meaning is interwoven with the term "illness." People with disabilities and mental health problems cope with physical and/or mental ailments as a part of everyday life. Consequently, one struggles to understand why something happened and what the purpose of the suffering is. Faith and religion take an indispensable part in this psychological aspect of the disease. Giving meaning to these matters is a strong element within the Islamic tradition and one where the paradigm of Islamic psychology could be of benefit to Muslims.

Treatments

From the perspective of Al-Ġazālī, a person can only control himself by maintaining balance and stability, both physically and spiritually. Thus, one should take care of one's soul and protect it as one cares for and protects their body. There is a mutual influence of these two and when the body gets sick, weakening of the soul inevitably follows and vice versa. Happiness (sa'āda) according to Al-Ġazālī is inextricably linked to knowledge of God and one must work to get oneself into a state of rest (an-nafs al muṭma'inna).[64]

The designated person to help someone to this end would be a šayk. In Sufism, a šayk is a spiritual guide who is authorized to teach Sufi students self-discipline and guide them on their path to becoming a Sufi. In this case, the šayk takes on a different part and is supposed to guide one toward a healthy nafs. Important characteristics for the šayk are intelligence, insight, compassion, and right advice. There is not one standard method of guidance, but this depends on the šayk himself. Although a šayk does not necessarily have to be a physician, they can act as a counsellor, offering a form of therapy.

This type of contact between a šayk and their patient can be seen as a form of psychotherapy with one-on-one guidance that revolves around shifting thoughts in the direction of the higher purpose in life (as defined by the šayk), thus trying to bring about changes in one's emotional state. For this reason, guidance from a šayk can also be labeled as spiritual-cognitive therapy. Its overall aim is to channel the mindset toward the divine and positive in order to nourish the soul to cure. In this case, the šayk takes on the role of psychotherapist and heals one from their spirituality illness. Other favored methods of Al Ġazālī are meditation and *ḏikr* (remembrance of God), both of which are intended to distract the heart and to steer toward God-consciousness.[65]

Al-Ġazālī limits himself mainly to descriptions of spiritual illnesses. His focus lies primarily on the *nafs* and he describes that it can get sick just like the body if it is not taken care of well, and how certain character traits and positive behavior help maintain the delicate balance of the soul. Controlling one's emotions and desires is a recurring theme in Sufism and reflects their complete trust in God (*tawakkul*) and a form of self-discipline for maintaining control over the soul.[66]

Concluding remarks

This chapter explores the meaning of Islamic psychology through studying the theories of the scholars Ibn Sīnā and Al-Ġazālī, with the objective of establishing greater insight into the religious viewpoint of human nature and its practical implications with regard to mental health and illness. The main aspect is the multidimensional view of humans, being the psycho-medical, psycho-philosophical, and psycho-spiritual dimensions, respectively addressing the body (*jism*), soul (*nafs*), and spirit (*rūḥ*). With Ibn Sīnā offering a detailed structure of the soul by placing a great deal of emphasis on inner senses and bodily as well as cognitive processes, Al-Ġazālī's spiritual approach focuses on a constant dynamic between four concepts: the *qalb*, *rūḥ*, *nafs*, and *'aql*. These concepts are a part of his religious psychology and play a crucial part in finding an inner sense of peace and balance—the ultimate goal in life. The nature and interaction of these dimensions play a key role in one's overall health, and by giving weight to all three, this perspective offers a holistic view of man. While parallels with psychoanalytic, cognitive, and behavioral schools were referenced, the religiously informed metaphysical element, which is recognized in Islamic psychology and seems neglected in the biomedical paradigm, is of the utmost importance. Another important aspect is the pragmatism and diversity in their approaches, which is apparent in their outlook on melancholia. The legacy of these Muslim scholars and their contemporaries is worth re-examining for further insights.

As mental health conditions are increasing worldwide, people with mental health conditions often experience severe human rights violations, discrimination, and stigma. Moreover, depression is one of the leading causes of disability worldwide, with suicide being the second leading cause of death among 15- to 29-year-olds. Increased investment is required on many fronts—one of which is for mental health awareness to increase understanding and reduce stigma. The outline of Islamic psychology as presented in this chapter is limited in the sense that it only serves as an introduction to the topic. Unfortunately, Islamic psychology is still in its infancy. While there is growing interest in the subject and despite the substantial progress that has been made over the past few decades, it is still lacking in an agreed upon definition and coherent framework. However, further delving into this topic is worth the effort. A better understanding of Islamic psychology could lead to new approaches in treatment that more closely align with the Muslim worldview. For Muslim communities in the West, it can be difficult to seek help when facing psychological problems. More research on Islamic psychology could lower the barriers for Muslims to seek help and bridge the existing gap between Muslim patients and healthcare professionals.

Notes

1. Kaplick, P.M. and Skinner, R. (2017). "The Evolving Islam and Psychology Movement." *European Psychologist*, 22(3), 198–204.
2. Ibidem.
3. Reber, J.S. (2006). "Secular Psychology: What's the Problem?" *Journal of Psychology and Theology*, 34(3), 193–204.
4. Eysenck, M.W. (2009). *Fundamentals of Psychology*. Hove: Psychology Press, 11.
5. Hoffer, C. (1994). *Islamitische genezers en hun patiënten*. Het Spinhuis: Amsterdam.
6. Dein, S., Alexander, M., and Napier, A.D. (2008). "Jinn, Psychiatry and Contested Notions of Misfortune among East London Bangladeshis." *Transcultural Psychiatry*, 45(1), 31–55.
7. Keshavarzi, H. and Ali, B. (2018). "Islamic Perspectives on Psychological and Spiritual Well-Being and Treatment." In Moffic, H.S. et al. *Islamophobia and Psychiatry: Recognition, Prevention, and Treatment*. New York: Springer, 41–53.
8. Kaplick and Skinner, "The Evolving Islam and Psychology Movement."
9. Ibidem, 199.
10. Ibidem.
11. Versteegh, K. (2008). "Wetenschap in de islamitische samenleving." In Driessen, H. (ed.) *In het huis van de islam*. Nijmegen and Amsterdam: Uitgeverij SUN; Iqbal, M. (2002). *Islam and Science*. Farnham: Ashgate Publishing, 278–287.
12. Kaplick and Skinner, "The Evolving Islam and Psychology Movement."

13. Awaad, R. et al. (2019). "Mental Health in the Islamic Golden Era: The Historical Roots of Modern Psychiatry." In Moffic, H.S. et al. (eds.), *Islamophobia and Psychiatry: Recognition, Prevention, and Treatment.* New York: Springer, 3–17.

14. This is part of the narrative of the "Islamization of knowledge" movement. For more on this movement, see Al-Attas, S.M.N. (1978). *Islam and Secularism.* Kuala Lumpur: ABIM; Al-Faruqi, I.R. (1982). "Islamization of Knowledge: Problems, Principles and Prospective." In *Proceedings & Selected Papers of the Second Conference on Islamization of Knowledge.* Herndon: International Institute of Islamic Thought and Civilization.

15. McGinnis, J. (2010). *Avicenna.* Oxford and New York: Oxford University Press

16. Zahabi, S.A. (2019). "Avicenna's Approach to Health: A Reciprocal Interaction Between Medicine and Islamic Philosophy." *Journal of Religion and Health,* 58(5), 1698–1712.

17. Bakhtiar, L. (1999). "Introduction." In Avicenna, *The Canon of Medicine (al-Qanun fi'l-tibb).* Chicago: Great Books of the Islamic World, xl–xlv.

18. Hoffer, *Islamitische genezers en hun patiënten.*

19. Rahman, F. (1952). *Avicenna's Psychology.* London: Oxford University Press.

20. Ibidem.

21. Ibidem.

22. Massington: Massington, L. , Radtke, B., Chittick, W.C., Jong, F. d., Lewisohn, L., Zarcone, T., Ernst, C., Aubin, F., & Hunwick, (. (2012). Taşawwuf. In P. Bearman (ed.), *Encyclopaedia of Islam New Edition Online (EI-2 English).* Brill. Accessed March 8, 2016. https://doi.org/10.1163/1573-3912_islam_COM_1188

23. Armstrong, K. (2001). *Islam: Geschiedenis van een wereldgodsdienst.* Amsterdam: De Bezige Bij; Chittick, W.C. (2001). *Sufism: A Short Introduction.* Oxford: Oneworld Publications; Stoddart, W. (1976). *Sufism: The Mystical Doctrines and Methods of Islam.* Wellingborough: The Aquarian Press.

24. Fazal-ul-Karim, M. (2000). *Ihyā' 'ulūm-ud-dīn (The Revival of Religious Learnings), Book III.* Lahore: Ashraf Printing Press; Skellie, W.J. (1977). *The Religious Psychology of Al-Ghazzali: A Translation of His Book of the Ihya on the Explanation of the Wonders of the Heart with Introduction and Notes.* Ann Arbor: The Hartford Seminary Foundation.

25. Al-Ghazali, M. (1933). *Ihyā' 'ulūm ad-dīn, Vol. III.* Cairo: Al-Matbu'a al-Uthmaniyya al-Misriyya.

26. Ibidem. Skellie, *The Religious Psychology of Al-Ghazzali.*

27. Abdel Haleem, M.A.S. (2016). *The Qur'an: English Translation and Parallel Arabic Text.* New York: Oxford University Press, 38:71–72.

28. Ibidem, 17:85.

29. Skellie, *The Religious Psychology of Al-Ghazzali.*

30. Ibidem.

31. Ibidem.

32. See the article by Tanzia Mobarak (2022) "Variation" in Approaches to Human Psyche: Exploring Al-Ghazālī's Influence on Freudian Psychoanalysis, *Comparative Literature: East & West,* 6:1, 64–79.

33. Al-Attas, M.N. (1990). *The Nature of Man and the Psychology of the Human Soul: A Brief Outline and a Framework for an Islamic Psychology and Epistemology.* Kuala Lumpur: International Institute of Islamic Thought and Civilization.

34. Haque, A. (1998). "Psychology and Religion: Their Relationship and Integration from Islamic Perspective." *The American Journal of Islamic Social Sciences,* 15(4), 97–116.

35. Abu-Raiya, H. (2012). "Towards a Systematic Qur'anic Theory of Personality." *Mental Health, Religion & Culture,* 15(3), 217–233.

36. Marmura, M.E. (2005). *The Metaphysics of the Healing: A Parallel English-Arabic Text*. Provo: Brigham Young University Press.
37. Skellie, *The Religious Psychology of Al-Ghazzali*.
38. Haque, A. et al. (2016). "Integrating Islamic Traditions in Modern Psychology: Research Trends in Last Ten Years." *Journal of Muslim Mental Health*, 10(1), 75–100.
39. Dols, M. (1987). "Insanity and its Treatment in Islamic Society." *Medical History*, 31(1), 1–14.
40. Ibidem.
41. Moussaoui, D., Agoub, M., and Khoubila, A. (2012). "How Should Melancholia be Incorporated in ICD-11?" *World Psychiatry*, 11(1), 69.
42. DSM-V, or "Diagnostic and Statistical Manual of Mental Disorders," is a medical manual published by the American Psychiatric Association that serves as the international standard in psychiatric diagnosis.
43. Dols, M. (1992). *Majnun: The Madman in Medieval Islamic Society*. Oxford: Clarendon Press.
44. See the World Health Organization's webpage on Mental Health at http://www.who.int/health-topics/mental-health.
45. Dols, *Majnun*, 80.
46. Avicenna (1999). *The Canon of Medicine (al-Qanun fi'l-tibb)*. Chicago: Great Books of the Islamic World.
47. Ibidem, 146.
48. Ibidem; Dols, *Majnun*.
49. Ibidem.
50. Dols, *Majnun*, 81.
51. Avicenna, *The Canon of Medicine*.
52. Dols, *Majnun*, 133.
53. Avicenna, *The Canon of Medicine*.
54. Wensinck: Wensinck, A.J., & Sadan, J. (2012). Khamr. In P. Bearman (ed.), Encyclopaedia of Islam New Edition Online (EI-2 English). Brill. Accessed July 8, 2016. https://doi.org/10.1163/1573-3912_islam_COM_0490.
55. Avicenna, *The Canon of Medicine*; Dols, *Majnun*.
56. Fazal-ul-Karim, *Ihyā' 'ulūm-ud-dīn*.
57. Al-Ghazzali, M. (1991). *The Alchemy of Happiness* (C. Field, translator). New York: M.E. Sharpe, 20–21.
58. Fazal-ul-Karim, *Ihyā' 'ulūm-ud-dīn*.
59. Al-Ghazali, M. and Winter, T.J. (ed.) (1995). *Al-Ghazali on Disciplining the Soul*. Cambridge: Islamic Texts Society, 5–6 and 19–23.
60. Abdallah, C.H. et al. (2012). "Generalized Anxiety Disorder (GAD) from Islamic and Western Perspectives." *World Journal of Islamic History and Civilization*, 2(1), 44–52.
61. Bayrakdar, M. (1985). "The Spiritual Medicine of Early Muslims." *Islamic Quarterly*, 29(1), 1–26.
62. Al-Ghazzali, *The Alchemy of Happiness*.
63. Kleinman, A. (1988). *The Illness Narratives: Suffering, Healing, and the Human Condition*. New York: Basic Books.
64. Al-Ghazzali, *The Alchemy of Happiness*, 27.
65. Al-Ghazali and Winter, *Al-Ghazali on Disciplining the Soul*.
66. Hoffman, V. J. (1995). "Islamic Perspectives on the Human Body: Legal, Social and Spiritual Considerations." In Cahill, L.S. and Farley, M.A. (eds.), *Embodiment, Morality, and Medicine*. Dordrecht: Kluwer Academic, 37–55; Fazal-ul-Karim, *Ihyā' 'ulūm-ud-dīn*.

References

Abdallah, C.H. et al. (2012). "Generalized Anxiety Disorder (GAD) from Islamic and Western Perspectives." *World Journal of Islamic History and Civilization*, 2(1), 44–52.

Abdel Haleem, M.A.S. (2016). *The Qur'an: English Translation and Parallel Arabic Text*. New York: Oxford University Press.

Abu-Raiya, H. (2012). "Towards a Systematic Qur'anic Theory of Personality." *Mental Health, Religion & Culture*, 15(3), 217–233.

Al-Attas, M.N. (1990). *The Nature of Man and the Psychology of the Human Soul: A Brief Outline and a Framework for an Islamic Psychology and Epistemology*. Kuala Lumpur: International Institute of Islamic Thought and Civilization.

Al-Attas, S.M.N. (1978). *Islam and Secularism*. Kuala Lumpur: ABIM.

Al-Faruqi, I.R. (1982). "Islamization of Knowledge: Problems, Principles and Prospective." In *Proceedings & Selected Papers of the Second Conference on Islamization of Knowledge*. Herndon: International Institute of Islamic Thought and Civilization.

Al-Ghazali, M. (1933). *Ihyā' 'ulūm ad-dīn, Vol. III*. Cairo: Al-Matbu'a al-Uthmaniyya al-Misriyya.

Al-Ghazali, M. and Winter, T.J. (ed.) (1995). *Al-Ghazali on Disciplining the Soul*. Cambridge: Islamic Texts Society.

Al-Ghazzali, M. (1991). *The Alchemy of Happiness* (C. Field, translator). New York: M.E. Sharpe.

Armstrong, K. (2001). *Islam: Geschiedenis van een wereldgodsdienst*. Amsterdam: De Bezige Bij.

Avicenna (1999). *The Canon of Medicine (al-Qanun fi'l-tibb)*. Chicago: Great Books of the Islamic World.

Awaad R. et al. (2019). "Mental Health in the Islamic Golden Era: The Historical Roots of Modern Psychiatry." In Moffic, H.S. et al. (eds.), *Islamophobia and Psychiatry: Recognition, Prevention, and Treatment* (pp. 3–17). New York: Springer.

Bakhtiar, L. (1999). "Introduction." In Avicenna, *The Canon of Medicine (al-Qanun fi'l-tibb)*. Chicago: Great Books of the Islamic World, xl-xlv.

Bayrakdar, M. (1985). "The Spiritual Medicine of Early Muslims." *Islamic Quarterly*, 29(1), 1–26.

Chittick, W.C. (2001). *Sufism: A Short Introduction*. Oxford: Oneworld Publications.

Dein, S., Alexander, M., and Napier, A.D. (2008). "Jinn, Psychiatry and Contested Notions of Misfortune among East London Bangladeshis." *Transcultural Psychiatry*, 45(1), 31–55.

Dols, M. (1987). "Insanity and its Treatment in Islamic Society." *Medical History*, 31(1), 1–14.

Dols, M. (1992). *Majnun: The Madman in Medieval Islamic Society*. Oxford: Clarendon Press.

Eysenck, M.W. (2009). *Fundamentals of Psychology*. Hove: Psychology Press.

Fazal-ul-Karim, M. (2000). *Ihyā' 'ulūm-ud-dīn (The Revival of Religious Learnings), Book III*. Lahore: Ashraf Printing Press.

Haque, A. (1998). "Psychology and Religion: Their Relationship and Integration from Islamic Perspective." *The American Journal of Islamic Social Sciences*, 15(4), 97–116.

Haque, A., et al. (2016). "Integrating Islamic Traditions in Modern Psychology: Research Trends in Last Ten Years." *Journal of Muslim Mental Health*, 10(1), 75–100.

Hoffer, C. (1994). *Islamitische genezers en hun patiënten*. Het Spinhuis: Amsterdam.

Hoffman, V.J. (1995). "Islamic Perspectives on the Human Body: Legal, Social and Spiritual Considerations." In Cahill, L.S. and Farley, M.A. (eds.), *Embodiment, Morality, and Medicine* (pp. 37–55). Dordrecht: Kluwer Academic.

Iqbal, M. (2002). *Islam and Science*. Farnham: Ashgate Publishing.

Kaplick, P.M. and Skinner, R. (2017). "The Evolving Islam and Psychology Movement." *European Psychologist*, 22(3), 198–204.

Keshavarzi, H. and Ali, B. (2018). "Islamic Perspectives on Psychological and Spiritual Well-Being and Treatment." In Moffic, H.S. et al. (eds.), *Islamophobia and Psychiatry: Recognition, Prevention, and Treatment* (pp. 41–53). New York: Springer.

Kleinman, A. (1988). *The Illness Narratives: Suffering, Healing, and the Human Condition.* New York: Basic Books.

Marmura, M.E. (2005). *The Metaphysics of the Healing: A Parallel English-Arabic Text.* Provo: Brigham Young University Press.

Massington: Massington, L. , Radtke, B., Chittick, W.C., Jong, F. d., Lewisohn, L., Zarcone, T., Ernst, C., Aubin, F., & Hunwick, (. (2012). Taṣawwuf. In P. Bearman (ed.), *Encyclopaedia of Islam New Edition Online (EI-2 English).* Brill. Accessed March 8, 2016. https://doi.org/10.1163/1573-3912_islam_COM_1188. McGinnis, J. (2010). *Avicenna.* Oxford and New York: Oxford University Press.

Mobarak, Tanzia. (2022) "Variation" in Approaches to Human Psyche: Exploring Al-Ghazālī's Influence on Freudian Psychoanalysis." *Comparative Literature: East & West*, 6(1), 64-79.

Moussaoui, D., Agoub, M., and Khoubila, A. (2012). "How Should Melancholia be Incorporated in ICD-11?" *World Psychiatry*, 11(1), 69–72.

Rahman, F. (1952). *Avicenna's Psychology.* London: Oxford University Press.

Reber, J.S. (2006). "Secular Psychology: What's the Problem?" *Journal of Psychology and Theology*, 34(3), 193–204.

Skellie, W.J. (1977). *The Religious Psychology of Al-Ghazzali: A Translation of His Book of the Ihya on the Explanation of the Wonders of the Heart with Introduction and Notes.* Ann Arbor: The Hartford Seminary Foundation.

Stoddart, W. (1976). *Sufism: The Mystical Doctrines and Methods of Islam.* Wellingborough: The Aquarian Press.

Versteegh, K. (2008). "Wetenschap in de islamitische samenleving." (Science in Islamic society) In Driessen, H. (ed.), *In het huis van de islam.* Nijmegen and Amsterdam: Uitgeverij SUN, 278-287.

Wensinck: Wensinck, A.J., & Sadan, J. (2012). Khamr. In P. Bearman (ed.), Encyclopaedia of Islam New Edition Online (EI-2 English). Brill. Accessed July 8, 2016. https://doi.org/10.1163/1573-3912_islam_COM_0490.

Zahabi, S.A. (2019). "Avicenna's Approach to Health: A Reciprocal Interaction between Medicine and Islamic Philosophy." *Journal of Religion and Health*, 58(5), 1698–1712.

CHAPTER 2

A Sociological Understanding of Intralingual Translations of the Concept of Disability on Twitter in Egypt[1]

Heba Fawzy El-Masry

Abstract

This chapter shows that disability is labeled in Egypt by different Arabic words and phrases that function as intralingual translations of the same concept within the same culture. A sociological approach to studying these intralingual translations reflects the power of cultural heritage, which portrays disability in a negative light, and its influence on the widespread perception of disability in Egypt. The chapter tests Bourdieu's theory of translation in intralingual translation and in web analysis. It explores the influence of popular culture on the widespread perception of disability by analyzing discourse about disability on Twitter. It assesses efforts to combat the association of disability with negative meaning components within the domain of language use. Although the same terms are now used in Arabic to label the same concept related to disability, the different perceptions about them translate into different usages of the same words by the state on the one hand and by common people who are influenced by *doxa* (a society's taken-for-granted, unquestioned truths) in the Egyptian society on the other hand. The roots of *doxa* about disability lie in the Egyptian cultural legacy, which is reflected in proverbs, some religious beliefs, and even films, and that can be investigated in light of a sociology of translation that adapts Pierre Bourdieu's conceptual tools into a theory that helps in understanding the influence of social patterns on the *habitus* (the set of skills and social resources that govern how people engage with the world) of the ordinary people as reflected on Twitter.

Keywords: Disability, intralingual translation, sociology of translation, cultural heritage, Egypt

Introduction

Disability is labeled in Egypt by different Arabic words and phrases that function as intralingual translations of the same concept within the same culture. A sociological approach to studying these intralingual translations reflects the power of cultural heritage, which portrays disability in a negative light, and its influence on the widespread perception of disability in Egypt. The study tests a Bourdieusian theory of translation in intralingual translation and in web analysis; it explores the influence of popular culture on the widespread perception of disability by analyzing discourse about disability on Twitter and assesses efforts to combat the association of disability with negative meaning components within the domain of language use.

Assigning meaning to the concept of disability

Translation is a cultural act that involves transferring meaning from one cultural and linguistic system to another. It also involves transferring meaning between different groups that function within the same cultural and linguistic system. Roman Jakobson classifies translation into three types:

1. Intralingual translation, which he defines as "the interpretation of verbal signs by means of other signs of the same language."[2]
2. Interlingual translation, which he defines as "an interpretation of verbal signs by means of some other language."[3]
3. Intersemiotic translation, which he defines as "an interpretation of verbal signs by means of signs of non-verbal sign-systems."[4]

Central to the present study is intralingual translation that involves assigning meaning to one concept within the same linguistic system or "verbal code."[5] Jakobson explains that people's experience of things or concepts involves the "non-linguistic acquaintance" of these things or concepts, which is complemented with the use of some verbal code in order to assign meaning to them.[6] However, the same verbal sign in the same code may have different meaning components that reflect varying perceptions of such concept. Such is the case with the terms that label إعاقة i'āqa ("disability") in Arabic.

The use of the term إعاقة i'āqa to label disability is modern. Mohammed Ghaly observes that its derivatives had a different significance in early Islamic literature, explaining that "'ā'iq," for example, meant "that [thing] driving away from what is good."[7] Arabs used many other terms to refer to people with disabilities in the past. According to Ghaly, Islamic sources, especially those of Islamic jurisprudence and theology, include several terms and expressions that refer to people with disabilities as a group, such as أصحاب العاهات *aṣḥāb al-'āhāt* ("people with defects"), أهل البلاء *ahl al-balā'* ("people of affliction"), أهل العافية *ahl al-'āfiyya* ("people of wellness"), and أصحاب الأعذار *aṣḥāb al-a'dhār* ("people with excuses"), whose disabilities have been recognized as excuses from specific religious obligations.[8]

It seems that terms that labeled disability were sometimes used "in a context that could indicate contempt" in classical times when not used in the context of jurisprudence and theology; therefore, the Prophet considered "using precise and non-offensive terminology."[9]

According to *al-Mu'gam al-Wasīt*, the verb عاق *'āq* means "to hinder or to prevent someone from reaching or doing something."[10] Ghaly observes that the "most common Arabic equivalents used now for disability are *i'āqa* [...]*'awaq* and *ta'wīq*" and that the "passive participles of these verbal nouns, a person with disability, are respectively *mu'āq, mu'āq*, and *mu'awwaq*."[11] The nouns إعاقة *i'āqa* and معاق *mu'āq* are the terms that were chosen by the translators of the United Nations when rendering the terms "disabled" and "disability" into Arabic: the UN Declaration on the Rights of Disabled Persons is officially translated as الإعلان الخاص بحقوق المعوقين, *al-I'lān al-Khās bi Ḥuqūq al-Mu'awaqīn*, and the UN Convention on the Rights of Persons with Disabilities is officially translated as اتفاقية حقوق لأشخاص ذوي الإعاقة, *Ittifaqiyyat Ḥuqūq al-Ashkhās Dhawī al-I'āqa*.[12] The definitions of persons with disabilities in the two documents involve the meaning of dealing with hindrances that are imposed by some form of impairment: the declaration defines the disabled person as "any person unable to ensure by himself or herself, wholly or partly, the necessities of a normal individual and/or social life, as a result of deficiency, either congenital or not, in his or her physical or mental capabilities," while the convention states that persons with disabilities "include those who have long-term physical, mental, intellectual or sensory impairments which in interaction with various barriers may hinder their full and effective participation in society on an equal basis with others" (4).[13] The term is also used in the 2014 Constitution of Egypt and is used in this sense by the Egyptian government.[14] In light of the rights of persons with disabilities that are cited in the UN documents, the linguistic definition gains the meaning component of "equality in terms of rights."

In light of these definitions of the term معاق *mu'āq* in modern Arabic usage and in the UN documents, a componential analysis of the Arabic term when used on the governmental level reveals that it has the following meaning components:

1. physical inability to move normally or mental disability.
2. rights to equality and non-discrimination in work, education, leisure, and so forth.

The hindrances that the persons with disabilities happen to deal with do not mean that disability is a source of embarrassment. However, the terms معاق *mu'āq* and اعاقة *i'āqa* have a derogatory meaning and are frequently used as an insult in daily interactions in Egyptian society. The roots of such derogatory usage lie in the wrong perception that many Egyptians have about disability; such perception is influenced by the popular culture that adds derogatory meaning components to the terms labeling disability.

Although the same terms are now used in Arabic to label the same concept related to disability, the different perceptions about them translate into different usages of the same words by the state on the one hand and by common people who are influenced by *doxa* in the Egyptian society on the other.[15] The roots of *doxa* about disability lie in the Egyptian cultural legacy, which is reflected in proverbs, some religious beliefs, and even films, and that can be investigated in light of a sociology of translation that adapts Pierre Bourdieu's conceptual tools into a theory that helps in understanding the influence of social patterns on the *habitus* of the ordinary people as reflected on Twitter.

Theorizing Twitter

Twitter is a type of social media network where "'ordinary' people in ordinary social networks (as opposed to professional journalists) can create user-generated news."[16] It is a form of microblogging, which makes it easy for ordinary people to interact, share "digital media," and distribute information or news.[17] It allows people to follow those they find of interest and to read the content they produce; thereby, it leads to interaction with strangers unlike a social network such as Facebook where people usually interact with users they already know offline.[18] Content production on Twitter depends on the individual (usually regular) contributions of each user and is therefore based on "self-presentation" or "self-production."[19]

Dhiraj Murthy explains that social media took a "demotic turn" that made ordinary users more visible as these sites granted the ordinary users the ability to "break news", produce media content, or voice their opinions publicly.[20]

Murthy elaborates that social media is "event-driven"; thereby, it gives ordinary people the chance to produce content along with traditional media outlets.[21] In fact, some traditional media outlets depend on Twitter-based content such as newspapers, which allocate a column or segment to popular tweets about a particular event.[22]

Twitter offers such a wealth of data that it has become the focus of many studies that contribute to a new field that Ben Zimmer calls Twitterology. Instead of questionnaires and other time-consuming methods of data collection, Twitter has the advantage of immediacy, as it constantly provides a "limitless array of language in action."[23] However, Noam Chomsky says that Twitter "is not a medium of serious interchange," implying that it is too superficial to be a source of data for social scientists.[24] This charge of superficiality recalls the traditional views about the types of discourse that should or should not fall within the scope of rhetoric in Arabic. As a course of study, rhetoric in Arabic has been based on analyzing the Quran, poetry, and prose; everyday discourse has been regarded inferior and, thereby, unworthy of being studied.[25] This viewpoint is challenged by ʿEmād Abdul-Laṭīf, who criticizes the paradox of valuing and studying a classical language that is not used in everyday life while disrespecting the colloquial language on the theoretical level although it is practically used most of the time.[26] Abdul-Laṭīf adopts a new approach to Arabic rhetoric: he states that discourse that can persuade, affect, or entertain an audience falls within the scope of Arabic rhetoric; thereby, he extends the limits of this course of study to include everyday verbal and semiotic interchange.[27] Since tweets often perform one or more of these functions, they are serious enough to be studied.

Central to this study is the fact that social media is an outlet for Egyptians to write freely using Egyptian Colloquial Arabic (ECA).[28] Zoë Kosoff observes that "Egypt is a polyglossic environment" where different levels of spoken and written Arabic are used in accordance with the user's "socioeconomic background."[29] al-Saīd Badawy identifies five levels of Arabic in Egypt:

1. Fuṣḥa al-turāth ("Fuṣḥa of heritage"), which is Classical Arabic (CA).[30]
2. Fuṣḥa al-'aṣr, which is Modern Standard Arabic (MSA).[31]
3. 'āmiyyat al-mothaqafīn or Cultured ECA, which Kosoff regard as "equivalent to Educated ECA."[32]
4. 'āmiyyat al-motanawerīn or Literate ECA.[33]
5. 'āmiyyat al-omiyyīn or Illiterate ECA.[34]

Kosoff explains that "CA and MSA are highly structured" and are "acquired only through formal education" while "ECA is grammatically less structured" than the two "and is acquired as a first language."[35] CA and MSA are considered superior levels of Arabic in Egypt and are often used in the newspapers, news bulletins on TV, education, official and legal documents, and literature. ECA is used in everyday situations, and is the language predominantly used on Twitter since the use of MSA is often restricted to governmental accounts and news accounts, while ECA is used by celebrities, intellectuals, and ordinary people when they tweet.

Regarding MSA and ECA, both share many of the words that label disability. However, the colloquial use gives the terms the derogatory meaning components. In other words, the colloquial translation of the concept is derogatory. Therefore, studying the colloquial use of the same words in the case of disability and the context in which these words are used on Twitter can provide insights into society as a whole.

A sociological approach to intralingual translation

This study uses the four conceptual tools of field, capital, *habitus*, and *doxa* to explore the influence of discourse about disability in Egypt on the use of the term among ordinary people. Bourdieu's work had its impact on sociological studies in translation that gained momentum with the sociological turn that translation studies took in the 1990s.[36] The conceptual tools Bourdieu used in understanding social reality have been adapted into translation theories that have been tested in the realm of translating different literary genres.[37] This study employs this sociology in understanding intralingual translations of the concept of disability in Egypt.

Field

Bourdieu defines field as "a network of objective relations [...] between positions [...] each position [...] [being] objectively defined by its objective relationship with other positions" or by the distribution of capital among the different social agents who operate in the field.[38] The field is a smaller locus than the social space that consists of various fields, and the social spaces of individuals vary according to the fields they operate in.[39]

According to Rodney Benson and Erik Neveu, Max Weber and Émile Durkheim describe modernity as "a process of differentiation," which results in forming "semiautonomous and increasingly specialized spheres of action."[40] The field that this study focuses on is Twitter, which can be differentiated from other fields in accordance with the types of capital distributed within it and its relative degree of autonomy.[41] Benson remarks that fields are not entirely autonomous; they affect one another and are affected by "the dominant system of hierarchization" to varying degrees.[42]

In order to understand the relation between Twitter and other fields, it has to be located against them by using "the method of social 'mapping'."[43] Following the technique described by Benson, I locate Twitter in the field of cultural production where "writers, artists, musicians, and scientists engage in symbolic production" and that is part of the field of power, or what Benson describes as "field at the dominant pole of the all-encompassing field of social classes."[44] The field of Twitter overlaps with the field of society's popular culture, which is the closest to the cultural pole, and the field of state or government, which is closest to the economic and political pole. Twitter is a battleground where the forces that represent the two dominant poles vie over capital distributed in it in order to produce—and symbolically impose—their knowledge of social reality (Fig. 2.1).

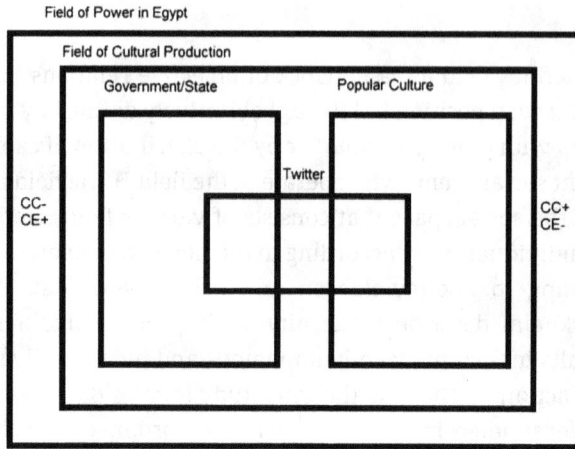

Figure 2.1: The structural location of Twitter[45]

Twitter is therefore semi-autonomous; it is influenced by the field of government and the field of popular culture as agents who operate in both fields also operate on Twitter and contribute to it, playing a role in its very existence.

Capital

Bourdieu defines capital as "accumulated labour (in its materialized form or its 'incorporated,' embodied form) which, when appropriated on a private, i.e., exclusive, basis by agents or groups of agents, enables them to appropriate social energy in the form of reified or living labour."[46] He refers to three types of capital that are distributed in the field: economic capital, cultural capital, and social capital.

Bourdieu defines economic capital as one that is "immediately and directly convertible into money and may be institutionalized in the form of property rights."[47] On Twitter, economic capital can be gained through tweeting about merchandise and offering to sell them. In this case, the tweets transform into monetary capital.

Bourdieu identifies three states of cultural capital: the embodied state that he describes as the "form of long-lasting dispositions of the mind and body," the objectified state that materializes into cultural goods, and the institutionalized state that includes academic qualifications and degrees.[48] On Twitter, the form of cultural capital one gets is recognition, which can take several forms, including verification marks granted by Twitter to figures of influence, or through retweets and favorites, which usually reflect endorsement or approval or at least involve interaction. The more retweets and favorites, the more interaction (which can sometimes be negative but is part of the game of struggles in which agents of conflicting positions on Twitter may engage in an attempt to acquire recognition and change or delineate the borders of cultural sub-fields they discuss on Twitter). Borrowing Carolin Gerlitz and Anne Helmond's term "the like economy," I will call this type of recognition "the retweet/favorite economy." Gerlitz and Helmond argue that "the hits and links" on Facebook "function as central measurements for user engagement."[49] Similarly, the retweet or favorite can become a measurement unit on Twitter. Thus, the retweet or favorite button becomes a "social [button]" or a "social bookmarking [item]."[50]

Social capital is "the aggregate of the actual or potential resources which are linked to possession of a durable network of more or less institutionalized relationships of mutual acquaintance and recognition," or is "membership in a group," which gives its members "the backing of the collectively owned capital."[51] The strength of an agent's social capital resides in the network of connections the field player can "effectively mobilize and on the volume of the capital (economic, cultural or symbolic) possessed [...] by each of those to whom he is connected."[52] On Twitter, social capital may be derived from the prestige that one's followers have on this platform, which can help one's message to reach a larger number of tweeps through prestigious tweeps (such as social or Internet celebrities).[53] The number of followers can also be a measurement of social capital. In Egypt—where Twitter played a major role in mobilizing people to participate in the two revolutions of 2011 and 2013—Article 19 of the media law considers public and private accounts of more than 5,000 followers as media outlets.[54]

This economy of recognition that measures the types of capital distributed in the field through verification marks, retweets/favorites, and number of followers refutes Johan Lindell's claim that the social theory "fails to capture [...] capitals of agents in the field."[55]

Habitus

Bourdieu defines *habitus* as the system of "durable, transposable dispositions, structured structures predisposed to function as structuring structure."[56] Bourdieu argues that *habitus* produces a history that is shaped in
accordance with the objective structures of the fields in which the agent
operates; therefore, he calls *habitus* "the past present" because objective
structures reproduce themselves in a new form through the *habitus* of
the agents who operate in the same field.[57]

However, Bourdieu's view of *habitus* is not one-dimensional. He
explains that the reproduction of the objective structures is a process
of approbation in which the *habitus* of the agent takes the norms out
of stagnation and reproduces them after revising and changing them
in a non-mechanistic fashion that guarantees their continuity.[58] Thus,
Bourdieu views the relation between the field's objective structures and
the dispositions of the agents who operate in it as a dialectic one. Such a
view illustrates the fact that the *habitus* of individuals can effect change
in the field.

Johan Lindell argues that the social theory fails to "capture individual
habituses […] of agents" in the field of social media websites.[59] However,
following even personal accounts for a long time can reveal the dispositions of the tweep to the extent of predicting the tweep's views regarding
issues he or she often discusses. The archive of tweets can serve as a history of dispositions that are structured by the society and that simultaneously structure and sometimes change social norms.

Doxa

In Bourdieu's sociology, *doxa* is a conceptual tool that refers to "the set
of assumed beliefs that motivate the agency of producers of culture and
their struggle over capital."[60] It is the synchronized or harmonious relationship between the dispositions of the agent and the objective structure
of the field.[61] However, it is not fixed; what can be doxic at one moment in
time can be rejected at another.[62]

According to Bourdieu, doxic practices are ones that are harmonious with the generally accepted beliefs and assumptions in the field;
therefore, doxic practices are taken for granted because *doxa* often goes
unquestioned.[63] Once *doxa* is questioned, it becomes subject to orthodox

or heterodox discourse. Bourdieu describes orthodoxy as the discourse of authority that serves to keep the power relations in the field unchanged, and he describes heterodoxy as the discourse that questions *doxa* and attempts to break it.[64]

It is common on Twitter to classify it into subfields according to the background, country, language, culture, or ethnicity of the different circles or groups of tweeps that are active on this platform. As Twitter overlaps with the fields of government and popular culture in a certain country, the agents who operate in the latter two fields mirror their discourses. When discussing disability on the level of language usage in Egypt, there seems to be three circles that operate on Egyptian Twitter: the governmental (represented by the state's official accounts), the ordinary people who reflect the dominant cultural perception of disability, and the ordinary people who defy the derogatory perception of disability but do not adopt the governmental terminology and who represent the minority that defies the orthodox discourse.

To understand the orthodox discourse in relation to disability in Arabic-speaking Egyptian Twitter circles, the next section studies doxic discourse about disability in the Egyptian society and culture.

Doxic discourse about disability in the Egyptian culture

An investigation of discourse about disability in the Egyptian society reveals the difference in its perception between the government and non-governmental circles in Egypt. The governmental perception is reflected in governmental documents, where the persons with disabilities are viewed as members of society who happen to suffer from a disability and who have the right to equality and non-discrimination.[65] Therefore, the terms اعاقة *i'āqa* ("disability") and معاق *mu'āq* ("a person with disability") are often used in governmental documents as terms that label a condition that involves no derogation. However, the perception of disability in modern Egyptian society and popular culture is different as it regard persons with disabilities as inferior to other members of the Egyptian society. To contextualize the derogatory use of terms that label disability in the Egyptian popular culture, I explore the image of persons with disabilities in proverbs, Sufism, and films.

Proverbs

Egyptian proverbs document negative beliefs about disability during the past two centuries. According to Ibrāhīm Aḥmad Sha'lān, collecting Egyptian proverbs started in the eighteenth century, many of which clearly reveal the derogatory perception of persons with disabilities ever since.[66] Examples include the following proverbs:

أعمى ويسرق من مفتح

A'ma w yesra' men mefataḥ.
A blind man tries to steal a sighted man!

This proverb is used to express amazement at attempting the impossible.[67] It involves mocking the blind and regarding them as inferior.[68]

الأعوران طلع السما يفسدها

al-A'war en tala' al-sama yefsedha.
If the one-eyed man goes to paradise, he will ruin it.

The proverb is an exaggeration that describes one-eyed people as evil, cunning, and corrupt, and it reflects the tendency in Egyptian popular culture to describe persons with physical disabilities in general as evil and corrupt (Taymūr Pasha 35).[69]

جابوا العمية ترد الرمية.

Gabo al-'amia trod al-ramia.
They brought a blind woman to collect falling objects.

The proverb is used to describe a situation where a task is assigned to someone who cannot do it, and it involves mocking persons with disabilities and highlighting the idea of their inefficiency in the work field.[70]

عامية وعارجة وكيعانها خارجة.

'Amiyya wa 'arga w kī'anha kharga.
She is blind, lame, and too thin that her elbow bones look deformed.

The proverb is used to describe an unattractive or even ugly woman, and it uses words that describe disability as insults.

عورة ودخلتها من العصر [71]

'Ūra wa dukhletha min al-'asr.
She is one-eyed, yet she is getting married this afternoon.

This proverb reflects a belief in the Egyptian society that plain girls are luckier than pretty ones in love and marriage. However, the proverb discriminates against persons with disabilities as it uses the term that labels a disability as a description of ugliness.

مكسحة وتقول للسايغ: تقل الخلخال

Mekasaḥa w te'ūl lel sayegh: ta'el al-kholkhāl.
A woman with leg paralysis asks the jeweller to make a heavy anklet for her.

This proverb refers to somebody who takes pride in something that should not be a source of pride or somebody who asks for something useless.[72] The proverb involves mocking people with leg paralysis and even referring to their disabled body parts as something they should not adorn or attract the eyes to.

اللي جوزها يقول لها يا عورة، الجيران يلعبوا بيها الكورة

Illy guzha ye'ūl laha ya 'ura, al-gīran yel'abu biha al-kura.
If a husband calls his wife one-eyed, her neighbors will kick her around like a football.

The proverb stresses the importance of the husband's respect for his wife, and claims that if a husband insults his wife, so will her neighbors. Therefore, the term that refers to disability here is used as an insult.

زي كلب الدخاخني أعور وكييف

Zai kalb al-dakhakhni a'war wa kaiyyīf.
He is like the tobacconist's dog that is one-eyed yet addicted to tobacco.

The proverb refers to a lowly "deformed" person that desires what is meant to be for people of a higher status.[73] The adjective that describes disability here is thus used as an insult because it suggests inferiority and ugliness.

These and many other proverbs reflect the fact that the perception of persons with disabilities in popular culture (which influences most ordinary Egyptians' dispositions) is negative. The proverbs use the terms that label persons with disabilities or adjectives that describe their physical conditions as insults.

Religious beliefs (Sufism)

Just like they give themselves continuity and strength through proverbs that are part of everyday discourse, the negative perceptions of persons with physical or mental disabilities in Egypt also regenerate themselves through some religious beliefs that perpetuate the idea that persons with disabilities are inferior to others and that God favors them with His blessings as a form of compensation.

The tendency to think of persons with mental and physical disabilities as particularly divinely blessed or closer to God than other members of society has its roots in Sufism.[74] Khalīl notes that the Sufi philosophy revolves around understanding man's physical and metaphysical status.[75] He states that Sufism regard persons with disabilities as "phenomena" whose "obvious mental or physical incompleteness" may reflect "a divine wisdom."[76] He also states that Sufism assumes that persons with disabilities "may be complete" in a way that "people who do not belong to the Sufi community" cannot perceive, and that persons with disabilities may have "a spiritual function" that they perform in the community.[77] On the basis of the mystic assumption that God compensates disabled people for their mental or physical disabilities by making them perform spiritual functions that non-Sufis cannot perceive, Sufi *awlia'* or religious masters grant persons with disabilities honorary titles.[78] Table 2.1 contains examples of the titles that Sufi masters give to persons with mental disabilities.

Table 2.1: Titles given by Sufi masters to persons with mental disabilities[79]

The term literally means "attracted," but generally means "insane" when used in daily life in Egypt. However, a *magdhūb* in Sufism is someone who has been employed by some metaphysical power to perform a spiritual function (Khalīl 298).	مجذوب *magdhūb* ("attracted")
If Sufi religious masters or *awliā'* state that a person with disability is a spiritual person, they grant him or her any of these titles (Khalīl 298).	درويش *darwīsh* ("dervish")
	بتاع ربنا *betā' rabanna* ("a man of God")
	بركة *baraka* ("a blessing")
	من أهل الله *men ahl Allah* ("one of the people of God")
	طيب *ṭayyib* ("kind")
	فيه شيء لله *fih shei' li Allah* ("there is something divine about him")
	بينه وبين ربنا عمار *beinu w bein rabena 'amār* ("he is on good terms with God")

The following is an example of titles that Sufis give to people with physical disability. This title is given to blind people: كريم العينين *karīm al-'ainain* ("a person with dignified eyes").[80]

Although the Sufi philosophy tends to respect persons with physical and mental disabilities, this respect is rooted in an assumption of compensation for inferiority. The claim that the mentally and physically disabled perform an unknown spiritual function and the honorary titles, though not negative, cement the roots of *differentiation* between persons with disabilities and other members of the society as mysticism partly contributes to the popular culture in Egypt.

The Egyptian cinema

During its long history, which spans more than a hundred years, Egyptian cinema has been a mirror of Egyptian culture in general. However, film makers tended to be more sophisticated in their treatment of some social issues than ordinary people; such tendency was reflected in the representation of persons with disabilities at the early stages of Egyptian cinema. During its beginnings, the majority of film makers (producers, directors, actors, and so on) in Egypt belonged to aristocracy: they were well-educated, and they descended from wealthy families, and profit was not necessarily the primary goal behind film productions. The aristocratic beginnings of Egyptian cinema had a strong impact on it for a long time, and there were many films that presented persons with disabilities in a positive light. This is evident in films like الخرساء *al-Kharsā'* ("The Dumb"), which portrays the plight of a deaf and dumb girl who gets raped; وحيدة *Waḥīda* ("Lonely"), which portrays the story of a deaf girl who escapes Cairo to avoid the negative treatment of those around her and decides to live alone in Alexandria; الشموع السوداء *al-Shomū' al-Sawdā'* ("The Black Candles"), which revolves around the love story of a blind man and his nurse; الوديعة *al-Wadī'a* ("Meek"), which describes the difficulties facing a man in love with a woman with leg-paralysis; ديك البرابر *Dīk al-Barāber* ("The Only Son"), which revolves around exploiting the mentally disabled son of a wealthy man; and توت توت *Tūt Tūt* ("Choo-Choo"), which revolves around the sexual exploitation of a woman with mental disability. These and other films represent people with disabilities and shed light on their problems without turning them into a laughingstock.

However, a gradual change started in the 1980s as new producers became key agents in the field. Profits became of primary importance, attracting the audience became more important than moral messages, and mocking persons with disabilities became a form of comedy in films like أمير الظلام *Amīr al-Dhalām* ("Prince of the Dark") and صباحو كدب *Ṣabaḥo Kidb* ("Good Morning, Liars!"), which mock disability and portray the physically disabled as gullible.

Euphemism

A euphemism is "an indirect word or phrase that people often use to refer to [something] embarrassing or unpleasant, sometimes to make it seem more acceptable than it really is."[81] Because of the negative meaning components that have become attached to terms that label disability in Arabic when generally used in Egyptian society, euphemism has become used to avoid offending persons with disabilities. These euphemistic words or expressions are often used in the press, and they include expressions such as متحدو الاعاقة *mutaḥado al-i'āqa* ("challengers of disability"), which can be seen in the report of Yasmīn Yahia that is entitled *Bel-Ṣuwar, Takrīm Abtāl Miṣr le Mutaḥado al-I'āqa bi Ḥoḍūr Wazīr al-Riyyāḍa* ("Minister of Sports Honours the Egyptian Heroes Challenging Disability—In Pictures") and ذووا الاحتياجات الخاصة *Dhawū al-Iḥ tiyyagāt al-Khasa* ("people with special needs"), which can be seen in the report of Fatḥiyya al-Dīb, which is entitled *Wālidat Ṭālib min Dhawī al-Iḥtiyyagāt al-Khāsa bel-Sharqiyya Tonashed Wazīr al-Ta'līm Be'awdato le Faṣlo* ("Mother of a Student with Special Needs Pleads with the Minister of Education to Make Her Son Return to His Class").[82]

Having examined the social context and its influence on the perception of disability and on doxic discourse relating to disability in popular culture and hence in everyday life in Egyptian society, the next section analyses the use of Arabic words that label disability on Egyptian Twitter using a Bourdieusian theory of translation analysis.

Analysis

As a social platform, Twitter mirrors Egyptian society on the governmental and non-governmental levels in relation to the use of the terms that label disability, and it reflects the doxic discourse about disability in society. The admins of official accounts of governmental institutions on Twitter act as spokespersons; when they tweet or respond to others' tweets, they act on behalf of the institutions through "the delegation by virtue of which an individual [...] is mandated to speak and act on behalf of a group" (Bourdieu cited in Lindell 4).[83] As representatives of the governmental institutions, admins of official accounts of these institutions on Twitter use the terms that label disability in conformity with the 2014 Constitution of Egypt. An example is a tweet posted by the official account of the Egyptian Ministry of Communications and Information Technology (@MCIT_News), which announces "the beginning of the sixth round of Tamkīn Competition [...] for persons with disabilities" (Fig. 2.2).[84]

وزارة الاتصالات وتكنولوجيا المعلومات- مصر @MCIT_News · Nov 28

تعلن وزارة الاتصالات وتكنولوجيا المعلومات عن إطلاق الدورة السادسة من مسابقة تمكين لتطوير البرمجيات وتطبيقات الهواتف المحمولة للأشخاص ذوي الإعاقة للعام المالي 2018/2019. للتسجيل، يرجى الضغط هنا bit.ly/2QkOMZ8

#ذوي_الإعاقة #ICT #CairoICT2018 #MCIT #PwDs

Translate Tweet

♡ 1   ↻ 1   ♡ 3   ✉

Figure 2.2: Tweet by the Egyptian Ministry of Communications and Information Technology[85]

Similarly, the official account of Ministry of Social Solidarity (@MOSS_Egypt) posts a tweet that reports the minister's assertion that "the ministry continues to support persons with disabilities and old people who cannot work" (Fig. 2.3).

وزارة التضامن الاجتماعي @MOSS_Egypt · Nov 22

#وزارة_التضامن_الاجتماعي| عادة والي: الدعم كان يعزز الاعتمادية الآن هو دعم مرتبط بإعادة التسجيل والعمل واستمرار الدعم فقط لمن لديهم الإعاقات والمسنين الغير قادرين على العمل

#3سنوات_تكافل_وكرامة

#تكافل_وكرامة

Translate Tweet

♡ 4   ↻   ♡ 7   ✉

Figure 2.3: Tweet by the Egyptian Ministry of Social Solidarity[86]

In both cases, the governmental accounts use MSA; they use the expressions ذوو الاعاقة *dhawu al-iʾāqa* and من لديهم الاعاقة *man ladayhim al- iʾāqa*, which both mean "persons with disabilities" in the sense that the UN documents and the 2014 Constitution of Egypt do, and such use does not imply inferiority.

However, inferiority seems to be an essential meaning component of Arabic terms in ECA, which label disability on the non-governmental level when used in everyday life situations in Egypt. This is evident in the use of such terms by individual accounts on Twitter in the contexts of football, politics, or personal relations.

According to Abdul-Laṭīf, the language of some football fans is characterized by profanity.[87] Vulgarity is common among football fans in Egypt, but it is noteworthy that words that label disability in general and leg paralysis in particular are often used as insults of players. Sports events are a gold mine for debates. Since Twitter is event-driven, some tweeps comment on sports to persuade their audience (usually followers, or whoever happens to read their tweets if retweeted) of their viewpoint or to simply express their viewpoint, which may affect the audience who might agree with him or her, and they often use insults to describe underperforming players. After Egypt's disqualification from the World Cup 2018, Twitter was replete with criticism and insults of the players, which—in many cases—included the use of terms such as معاقينmu'aqīn ("disabled") and مكسحينmekasaḥīn ("people with leg paralysis") as insults in tweets that mostly performed persuasive functions. An example is the following tweet:[88] "What were you expecting from Salah? This national team of people with leg paralysis who cannot even pass the ball failed to make an organised attack or to create any chance that he could make use of [...]." The tweep attempts to persuade the audience (followers who happen to read the tweet) that Salah did his best and that his teammates were not helpful. The insulting use of مكسحين to refer to Salah's teammates in this tweet equates a form of physical disability with uselessness and implies that persons with disabilities are inferior to other members of society.

منتظرين من صلاح إيه ... إلّا مافيه لعبة واحدة منظمة ولا ربع فرصة يقدر يتعامل معاها من منتخب
مكسحين مش عارفين يتغلوا الكورة .. مش فاهم اللعبة دي كل يوم كانت بتدرب على إيه من أيام ماتش الكونغو
الزبالة .. وخطة كوبر في ماتش لازم يفوز كانت إيه

Translate Tweet

♡ 4   ⟲ 17   ♡ 17   ✉

Figure 2.4: Tweet describing Egypt's national football team as "people with leg paralysis"

As units of recognition on the platform of Twitter, the number of times the tweet has been retweeted and favorited shows that such insulting use of the term that labels disability in ECA is part of the doxic discourse about physical disability among individuals and in popular culture in

Egypt (Fig. 2.4). At the same time, none of the tweeps who reply to the tweet expresses any objection to such derogatory use of the term.

The following tweet also performs a persuasive function as the tweep argues that players other than Salah were useless, saying that Salah "played alongside a bunch of [physically] disabled players."

في ظل اداء منتخابنا العقيم الذي لم يفعل اي شئ يستحق عليها الفوز ، هل أحد لاحظ ربنا كافئ فقط من ؟

نعم هو محمد صلاح الذي تحامل علي نفسه في إصابته و إستغلاله و كل شئ لإسعاد الجماهير و اللاعب الوحيد

المجتهد في ظل كومة معاقين يلعبون بجانبه ..

⊕ Translate Tweet

♡ 8   ⇄ 61   ♡ 375   ✉

Figure 2.5: Tweet describing Egypt's national football team as playing alongside "a bunch of [physically] disabled players"

Like the previous tweet, this one is also recognized by getting retweeted more than sixty times and favorited more than 350 times (Fig. 2.5), and none of the eight tweeps who reply to this tweet object to the use of the term as an insult.

The term مكسحين *mekasaḥīn* is used to insult the players selected for the national team in the next tweet in which the tweep attempts to convince his audience of his viewpoint through using sarcasm, saying: "A bunch of people with leg paralysis have been selected for the national team, but Croatian Maḥmūditsh 'Alā'itsh has not been selected."

انضمام شلة مكسحين للمنتخب و عدم انضمام محموديتش علاءيتش الكرواتى الجنسية 🙂

pic.twitter.com/FnBTQBKgza اجيري#

⊕ Translate Tweet

♡ 1   ⇄ 1   ♡ 9   ✉

Figure 2.6: Tweet using "people with leg paralysis" in a sarcastic manner

The tweet uses the term to mock the selection of players of the national team and uses the term that labels disability in ECA to suggest that these players are useless, and his use of the term in this insulting manner goes without questioning and without objection in the reply he receives. On the contrary, his tweet gets recognition through retweets, favorites, and a reply (Fig. 2.6).

Another tweep employs sarcasm to express anger, using two words that refer to persons with disabilities to insult the players of his own team, writing: "Zamalek substitutes paralysed [players] with physically disabled ones" (Fig. 2.7).

الزمالك بيطلع مشاليل و ينزل معاقين مكانهم.

Translate Tweet

8   7

Figure 2.7: Tweet describing "paralysed" football players being substituted by "ones [...] with physical disabilities"

The tweep uses the terms مشاليل *mashalīl* ("paralysed") and معاقين *mu'aqīn* ("disabled") in a derogatory manner. The recognition reflected in the retweets and favorites suggests that such derogatory use of the term in ECA is an accepted practice in Egyptian society on the non-governmental level, and the derogatory use of the term translates the perception of persons with disabilities as inferior in the Egyptian popular culture.

The next tweep also expresses frustration at team players by being sarcastic and using the term مكسحين *mekasaḥīn*: "Our top goal scorer is a defender because our forwards are [people] with leg paralysis" (Fig. 2.8).

هدافنا مدافع عشان مهاجمينا مكسحين

Translate Tweet

2   1   4

Figure 2.8: Tweet claiming that the forward football players are "[people] with leg paralysis"

The tweet gets retweeted once and favorited four times, and none of the tweeps who reply oppose the derogatory use of the term that labels a form of physical disability in ECA.

A fifth tweep uses the term معاقين *mu'aqīn* ("disabled") in a sarcastic manner as an insult when commenting on the performance of two players in ECA, writing: "Maybe these two players are spies and are pretending to be [physically] disabled."

يكونش العيال دي جواسيس وعاملين معاقين؟!

◉ Translate Tweet

♡ 4   ⟲ 12   ♡ 48   ✉

Figure 2.9: Tweet claiming two football players are spies "pretending to be [phys-
ically] disabled"

The tweet gets recognition in the form of twelve retweets, forty-eight
favorites, and four replies, which include no opposition to the derogatory
use of the term that labels disability (Fig. 2.9), and this economy of recognition suggests that this derogatory use is doxic.

The practice of using words that label disability as insults is also
found in the context of politics. Like tweets on sports, tweets on politics
are usually event-driven, and they often seek to persuade or affect the
audience. An example is the next tweet in which the tweep sarcastically
praises the Muslim Brotherhood reign because "persons with mental disabilities hold the state's high offices" for the first time.

من أهم ما يمز حكم الأخوان وحكومتهم أنها أول حكومة تهتم بالمعاقين . فللمرة الأولى يتولى معاقين زهنيا
مناصب رفيعة بالدولة !!!!!

◉ Translate Tweet

♡   ⟲ 2   ♡   ✉

Figure 2.10: Tweet claiming that the state's high offices are held by "persons with
mental disabilities"

The tweet gets retweeted twice (Fig. 2.10). In the next tweet, a tweep criticizes a governor's aides: "I am not going to criticise the governor alone. The whole system is not working. We need people who can do more than talk and who can think and put their plans into action. However, the governor is not a magician, and all his aides have leg paralysis."

معنديش استعداد اهاجم المحافظ لوحده الشيلة علي بعضها بايظه احنا محتاجين عقول تفكر وتعرف تنفذ مش
ترعي وبس المحافظ مش ساحر وموظفينه كلهم مكسحين

  🌐 Translate Tweet

  💬 2   🔁 12   ♡ 4   ✉

Figure 2.11: Tweet describing the governor's aides as "all [having] leg paralysis"

The tweet that gets retweeted twelve times and favorited four times (Fig. 2.11) receives no opposition to the derogatory use of the term مكسحين *mekasaḥīn* in the replies, and this economy of recognition suggests that the use of the term in an offensive manner in ECA is a doxic practice in the field.

    The use of words that label disabilities as insults extends to the realm of expressing emotions or commenting on social relations, which is experience driven. Tweets that relate to this realm are usually posted to entertain or to affect the audience by striking a chord, thereby prompting recognition or interaction with them. An example is the next tweet in which the tweep sarcastically says: "Why do we want those who do not want us [?] Are we mentally disabled [?]"

ليه الى بنعوزه مابيعوزناش والى مابيعوزناش احنا بنعوزه معاقين ذهنيا ولا اي 😅 😂 😂 😂 😂 😂

  🌐 Translate Tweet

  💬 9   🔁 1   ♡ 33   ✉

Figure 2.12: Tweet using "mentally disabled" in a sarcastic manner

The tweep uses معاقين ذهنيا *mu'aqīn dhehniyyan* ("mentally disabled") to mock herself for having unreciprocated feelings for someone. The use of smiley faces suggests that the offensive use of the expression that refers to persons with disabilities in ECA aims at giving the tweet a humorous effect, and the recognition economy reflected in the number of retweets and favorites of the tweets shows that such use is doxic (Fig. 2.12). Furthermore, none of the replies opposes such offensive use of this expression.

The following tweep wonders why some men do not take the first step, saying: "Why cannot they take the first step? do they have leg paralysis?"

هما مبيعرفوش ياخدوا ال first step ليه هما مكسحين ؟

Translate Tweet

○   ↿↾ 2   ♡ 12   ✉

Figure 2.13: Tweet asking if men who do not "take the first step" have "leg paralysis"

Although the sarcastic tweet is offensive as it uses مكسحين *mekasaḥīn* ("people with leg paralysis") to mock men who do not take the initiative, it gets recognition through getting retweeted twice and favorited twelve times, and it receives no replies that may oppose such derogatory use of the word that labels persons with disabilities in ECA (Fig. 2.13).

Another tweep criticizes people in her life, saying: "I am sad that I am wasting my youth among foolish, stupid, mentally disabled people."

انا زعلانه ع شبابي اللي بيضيع وسط ناس حمقي متخلفين معاقين ذهنيا .

Translate Tweet

○   ↿↾ 4   ♡ 11   ✉

Figure 2.14: Tweet expressing sadness over being among "foolish, stupid, mentally disabled people"

Though offensive, the tweet is retweeted four times and favorited eleven times (Fig. 2.14), and the economy of recognition suggests that the offensive use of the term that refers to mental disability in ECA is a doxic practice in the field.

A fourth tweep writes: "I feel that God proves to me every day that my friends are loony, stupid, disabled, and retarded."

بحس إن ربنا كل يوم بيبتلي إن صحابي معاتيه، أغبية، معاقين، متخلفين كده يعني

🌐 Translate Tweet

💬 1   🔁   ♡ 1   ✉

Figure 2.15: Tweet describing friends as "loony, stupid, disabled, and retarded"

The tweet gets favorited once (Fig. 2.15), and the only reply to the tweet does not oppose the offensive use of the word that refers to persons with disabilities.

These, and the hundreds of tweets that a simple Twitter search for Arabic words that label disabilities generates, reveal that the negative meaning components of inferiority and uselessness are primary in ECA terms thar label disability when used by individuals, and that the practice of using these words as insults is doxic in popular culture in Egypt and in Egyptian society on the non-governmental level. Such practice is an intralingual translation of the negative perception of disability in the popular culture in Egypt, which is different from the governmental intralingual translation in MSA that reflects the governmental perception of persons with disabilities as explained in the 2014 Constitution of Egypt.

Some individuals attempt to avoid offending persons with disabilities with words that have offensive meaning components in Egyptian popular culture; therefore, they use euphemistic expressions in ECA. An example is the following tweet in which the tweep asks the audience for recommendation: "I need you to recommend an electric wheelchair for a disability challenger" (Fig. 2.16).

عايز توصية لنوع كرسي متحرك كهرباني لحالة من متحدي الإعاقة - رينج السعر لحد 12000
ياريت حد يفيدني لو عنده معلومات بالموديل أو مكان موثوق

🌐 Translate Tweet

💬 9   🔁 49   ♡ 13   ✉

Figure 2.16: Tweet describing a person with disabilities as "a disability challenger"

Another example is the following tweep who offers help: "If there are any elderly or sick people or persons with special needs who need to be driven to their polling stations, I can drive them from their houses and back if they live in Maṣr al-Gadīda" (Fig. 2.17).

لو فيه ناس من كبار السن أو المرضى أو ذوو الإحتياجات الخاصه محتاجين حد يوصلهم إلى لجنتهم الإنتخابيه أنا مستعد بنفسي أخدهم من أمام منازلهم و أرجعهم لها في نطاق مصر الجديده

Translate Tweet

Figure 2.17: Tweet describing persons with disabilities as "persons with special needs"

The use of euphemistic expressions in ECA is a third form of intralingual translation of the concept of disability that attempts to avoid conjuring the negative meaning components inherent in the doxic use of the Arabic words that label disabilities in everyday interactions in Egyptian society.

The use of euphemistic expressions seems to be the solution to avoid conjuring negative meaning components when using terms that label disabilities in everyday situations in Egypt. I contacted three persons with disabilities on Twitter and two of them preferred the use of euphemistic expressions. Marina Ayman (@marinaayman9) says that the expression ذوو الاعاقة *dhawu al-i'āqa* ("persons with disabilities") is offensive in two ways: first, it suggests that she cannot lead her life normally like others and she believes that this suggestion is not true; second, she feels offended when she hears the term (due to its negative legacy in Egyptian popular culture). Ahmed Yossef (@ahmedyossef21) also finds the use of ذوو الاعاقة *dhawu al-i'āqa* offensive and suggests the use of the expression ذوو الهمم *dhawu al-himam* ("people with determination"). Mohammad abu Ṭālib (@iAbutalebz) has no problem with the use of ذوو الاعاقة *dhawu al-i'āqa*, which is used by the UN and the Egyptian government because a euphemistic expression such as ذوو الاحتياجات الخاصة *dhawu al-iḥtiyyagāt al-khāṣa* ("people with special needs") is inaccurate since it may also refer to elderly people.

The opinions of the three tweeps I contacted reveal that the popular culture has a stronger influence than the government in issues related to the perception of persons with disabilities. Thus, the popular culture grants the doxic intralingual translation of the concept of disability in ECA more dominance and influence, making it stronger than the intralingual translation of the same concept in MSA that is used by the government.

In fact, the energy of the agents moved by the force of the cultural pole is so strong that it "deforms the space around it" and forces "all the other space to organise itself around it."[89] Therefore, it forces individuals to use euphemisms (a third form of intralingual translation of disability) if they wish to avoid offending persons with disabilities in the field of Egyptian Twitter. It also seems that it has started to force the government to change its practice as it has started using as euphemistic expression the term القادرون باختلاف *al-qaderūn bekhtelāf* ("the differently able"), as evident in the following tweet by the account of Misr El-Kheir, which is a state-run charity organization (@MisrElKheir) (Fig. 2.18).[90]

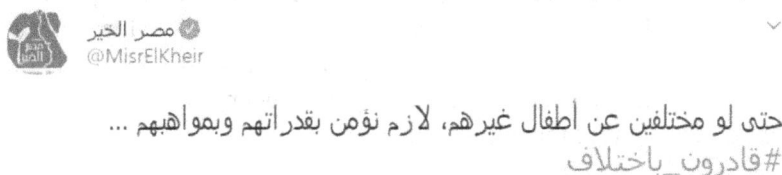

مصر الخير
@MisrElKheir

حتى لو مختلفين عن أطفال غيرهم، لازم نؤمن بقدراتهم وبمواهبهم ...
#قادرون_باختلاف

Translate Tweet

231 views   0:02 / 1:00

10:00 PM · Oct 1, 2018 · TweetDeck

3 Retweets   **10** Likes

Figure 2.18: Tweet by Misr El-Kheir

As the government fails to symbolically impose its terminology, it changes it. The change is due to what Benson calls "the harmony of circuits of production and reception."[91] Benson observes that the Bourdieusian field theory "challenges the dichotomy of 'passive' versus 'active' audiences."[92] Benson explains that the objective structures of the field and the subjective experiences of the individual agents who operate in it are intertwined because the objective structures are incorporated into the *habitus* of the agents during their life trajectories as the agents move "within and through a series of fields."[93] In the case of Twitter, the predominant derogatory meaning of words that label disability in ECA maintains the power of the force of the popular culture, but it has also started to force the agent of the political and economic pole to adjust its terminology in order to be in harmony with the objective structures instead of resisting them. In other words, the objective structures that constitute the *habitus* of the audience forces the government to adjust its message. The ordinary tweeps are active both as content producers that preserve the power of the cultural heritage and as content receivers since the government has started to change its terminology to avoid conjuring up the derogatory meaning of Arabic words directly labeling disability inherent in their minds due to the influence of culture.

Conclusion

The study contributes to the field of translation by testing Bourdieu's sociology in the context of intralingual translations of the concept of disability. Despite the existence of bots, Twitter continues to be a field that mirrors the *doxa* and the relation between the pole of politics/economy and the pole of culture in the field of cultural production whose agents also operate in the field of Twitter.

The sociological approach to the analysis of intralingual translations of the concept of disability as evident in the content produced by Egyptian tweeps on Twitter reveals that the doxic discourse about disability, which associates disability with negative meaning components, is influenced by popular cultural legacy. Such legacy continues to influence the *habitus* of individuals in Egyptian society and to give itself strength in the Egyptian popular culture by being produced in new forms and by appearing in new platforms such as Twitter. It also reveals that such cultural legacy, which is deeply rooted in Egyptian society, is still stronger than the government. Therefore, it seems that using euphemistic expressions to refer to disability is the best choice.

Notes

1. Twitter has since transitioned to X.
2. Jakobson, Roman (2000). "On Linguistic Aspects of Translation." In Venuti, Lawrence (ed.), *Translation Studies Reader*. London: Routledge, 114.
3. Ibidem.
4. Ibidem.
5. Ibidem, 113.
6. Ibidem.
7. Ghaly, Mohammed (2008). *Islam and Disability: Perspectives in Islamic Theology and Jurisprudence* (PhD thesis, Leiden University), 40–41.
8. Ibidem, 41–42. Ghaly also lists some examples of sole terms used in classical Arabic and Islamic literature to refer to specific types of mental and physical disabilities, which include "'*araj* ('lameness') [...] *Al-fālij* ('hemiplegia') [...] *Nāqiṣ al-khalq*," which "literally means one whose creation is incomplete," *muq'ad*, which refers to "one afflicted with an illness in body so that he/she cannot walk," and *aksaḥ*, which means lame, and so forth.
9. Ibidem, 37. Ghaly states that some of the *Companions of the Prophet* used terms that referred to persons with disability in a derogatory manner, and that the Prophet attempted "to restate the term." Ghaly states that the companions "called a person with mental insanity '*majnūn* ('insane')" and that the Prophet "is reported to have said, 'This [man] is *muṣāb*, ('sick or ill'). *Junūn* ('insanity') comes [only] as a result of constant disobedience of God—The Almighty."
10. al-Tabarani (2004). *al-Mu'gam al-Wasīṭ*. Cairo: Maktabet al-Shurūq al-Dawliyya, 659.
11. Ghaly, *Islam and Disability*, 40.
12. Compare United Nations General Assembly (UNGA) (1975, December 9). *al-I'lān al-Khās bi Ḥuqūq al-Mu'Awaqīn* [Declaration on the Rights of Disabled Persons]. Minneapolis: Human Rights Library University of Minnesota. UNGA (1975, December 9); *Declaration on the Rights of Disabled Persons*. Office of the United Nations High Commissioner for Human Rights (OHCHR); also compare UNGA (2006, December 13). *Convention on the Rights of Persons with Disabilities and Optional Protocol*. New York: UNGA; UNGA (2006, December 13). *Ittifaqiyyat Ḥuqūq al-Ashkhās Dhawī al-I'Āqa wa al-Protocol al-Ikhtiyyari* [Convention on the Rights of Persons with Disabilities and Optional Protocol] New York: UNGA.
13. United Nations, *Convention on the Rights of Persons with Disabilities and Optional Protocol*, 4. United Nations, *Declaration on the Rights of Disabled Persons*, 1.
14. Constitution of the Arab Republic of Egypt (2014), https://adsdatabase.ohchr.org/IssueLibrary/EGYPT_Constitution_EN.pdf.
15. By state, I mean the governmental bureaucratic fields, the state-run educational institutions (schools and universities), and state-run traditional media that use the governmental terminology in relation to disability (especially TV).
16. Murthy, Dhiraj (2012). "Towards a Sociological Understanding of Social Media: Theorizing Twitter." *Sociology*, 46(6), 1060. For those unfamiliar with Twitter, Dhiraj Murthy explains it as follows: "Upon logging in, a user is presented with their profile page. On Twitter, this page is known as a timeline. Its purpose is to act as a live feed which displays tweets both by the user as well as anyone the user is following." Twitter allows its users to post 280 characters per tweet.
17. Ibidem, 1061. Murthy defines microblogging as "an internet-based service in which (1) users have a public profile in which they broadcast short public messages or updates [...] (2) messages

become aggregated together across users, and (3) users can decide whose messages they wish to receive, but not necessarily who can receive their messages."

18. Ibidem, 1060–1061.

19. Ibidem, 1062.

20. Ibidem, 1063–1064.

21. Ibidem, 1064.

22. For instance, al-Taḥrīr newspaper had a column called تويت وجبنة Tweet wa Gebna (Tweet and Cheese), which used to appear on the first and final pages in 2011. I obtained this information through a conversation with Mohammed Atef (@Atef), who worked as a journalist for al-Tahrīr newspaper then and is now director of digital marketing at @AlainBRK.

23. Zimmer, B. (2011, October 29). "Twitterology: A New Science?" The New York Times, Section SR, 9.

24. Ibidem. Noam Chomsky is quoted by Ben Zimmer.

25. 'Abdul-Laṭīf, 'Emād (2019). "Balāghat Gomhūr Korat al-Qadam: Ta'ṣṭs Nadhary wa Namūdhag Ṭaṭbīqy." al-'Umda, 6, 11–30, 12.

26. 'Abdul-Laṭīf, 'Emād (2005). "Balāghat al-Mokhāṭab: al-Balāgha al-'Arabiyya men Intāg al-Khetāb al-Solṭawy ela Moqawamatoh." In Kamel, Salwa Abdel-Aziz (ed.), Power and the Role of the Intellectual. Cairo: Cairo University, 7–36.

27. 'Abdul-Laṭīf, "Balāghat Gomhūr Korat al-Qadam," 12.

28. Kosoff, Zoë (2014). "Code-Switching in Egyptian Arabic: A Sociolinguistic Analysis of Twitter." Al-'Arabiyya, 47, 83–99.

29. Ibidem, 83.

30. Badawy, al-Saīd (1973). Mostawayāt al-'Arabiyya al-Mo'āṣera [Levels of Modern Arabic]. Cairo: Dār al-Ma'āref, 110.

31. Ibidem.

32. Ibidem, resp. 113 and 84.

33. Ibidem, 114.

34. Ibidem, 115.

35. Kosoff, "Code-Switching in Egyptian Arabic," 84.

36. Hanna, Sameh (2016). Bourdieu in Translation Studies: The Socio-Cultural Dynamics of Shakespeare Translation in Egypt. London: Routledge, 2.

37. E.g., Gouanvic, Jean Marc (2005). "A Bourdieusian Theory of Translation, or the Coincidence of Practical Instances: Field, 'Habitus', Capital, and 'Illusio.'" The Translator, 11(2), 147–166; Hanna, Bourdieu in Translation Studies; El-Masry, Heba Fawzy (2018). A Comparative Study of Arthur John Arberry and Desmond O'Grady's Translations of the Seven Mu'allaqāt (PhD thesis, Warwick University). In "A Bourdieusian Theory of Translation," Jean-Marc Gouanvic develops a translation theory on the basis of four conceptual tools of Bourdieu's sociology (field, habitus, capital, and illusio), and he employs it in the analysis of fiction translation. In Bourdieu in Translation Studies: The Socio-Cultural Dynamics of Shakespeare in Translation in Egypt, Sameh Hanna uses Bourdieu's sociology in exploring the modes of producing and consuming drama translation in Egypt in light of the socio-cultural contexts of the translations. In A Comparative Study of Arthur John Arberry and Desmond O'Grady's Translation of the Seven Mu'allaqāt, Heba Fawzy El-Masry employs a Bourdieusian theory of translation in the analysis of the English translations of classical poetry.

38. Bourdieu, Pierre (1995). The Rules of Art: Genesis and Structure of the Literary Field (Susan Emanuel, trans.). Stanford: Stanford University Press, 231.

39. Hanna, *Bourdieu in Translation Studies*, 21.
40. Benson, Rodney, and Neveu, Erik (2005). "Introduction: Field Theory as a Work in Progress." In Benson, Rodney, and Neveu, Erik (eds.), *Bourdieu and the Journalistic Field*. Cambridge: Polity Press, 2–3.
41. Benson, Rodney (1999). "Field Theory in Comparative Context: A New Paradigm for Media Studies." *Theory and Society*, 28(3), 464.
42. Ibidem, 464–465.
43. Ibidem, 465.
44. Ibidem, resp. 465–466 and 456.
45. Ibidem, 466. All figures created by author.
46. Bourdieu, Pierre (1996). "The Forms of Capital." In Richardson, J.G. (ed.), *Handbook of Theory and Research for the Sociology of Education*. New York: Greenwood Press, 241.
47. Ibidem, 243.
48. Ibidem.
49. Gerlitz, Carolin, and Anne Helmond (2013). "The Like Economy: Social Buttons and the Data-Intensive Web." *New Media and Society*, 15(8), 1349.
50. Ibidem, 1351.
51. Bourdieu, "The Forms of Capital," 248–249.
52. Ibidem, 249.
53. A tweep is a Twitter user.
54. Supreme Council for Media Regulation (2018). *Qanūn Tandhīm al-Saḥāfa Wa al-I'Lām Wa al-Maglis al-a'la* [Law, Media, and Higher Council Organising Law]. Supreme Council of Media Regulation. Article 19.
55. Lindell, Johan (2017). "Bringing Field Theory to Social Media, and Vice Versa: Network-Crawling an Economy of Recognition on Facebook." *Social Media + Society*, 1(11), 3. There is another form of gain that does not fall into any of the three categories that Bourdieu discusses; this form is the emotional feeling of satisfaction that a tweep may experience from expressing one's thoughts or feelings even if this tweep receives no recognition in the realm of Twitter. Such emotional gain is immeasurable.
56. Bourdieu, Pierre (1990). *The Logic of Practice*. Cambridge: Polity, 53.
57. Ibidem, 54.
58. Ibidem, 57.
59. Lindell, "Bringing Field Theory to Social Media, and Vice Versa," 3.
60. Hanna, *Bourdieu in Translation Studies*, 159.
61. Bourdieu, *The Logic of Practice*. 68.
62. Hanna, *Bourdieu in Translation Studies*, 159.
63. Bourdieu, Pierre (1977). *Outline of a Theory of Practice*. Cambridge: Cambridge University Press, resp. 162 and 166.
64. Bourdieu, Pierre (1993). *Sociology in Question*. London: Sage, 73.
65. For example, in the constitution on p. 75.
66. Sha'lān, Ibrahīm Aḥmad (1992). *Mawsū'at al-Amthāl al-Sha'biyya al-Misriyya* [Encyclopedia of Popular Egyptian Proverbs]. Cairo: Dār al-Ma'ārif.
67. Taymūr Pasha, Aḥmad (2014). *Al-Amthāl al-'Āmiyya* [Popular Proverbs]. Cairo: Mo'asasat Hindawy lil Ta'līl wa al-Thaqafa, 35.
68. Khalīl, Abdul-Ḥakīm (2017). *al-Thaqāfa al-Sha'biyya wa Dhawu al-Iḥtiyyagāt al-Khāṣa* [Popular Culture and People with Special Needs]. Cairo: GEBO, 206–207.

69. Taymūr Pasha, *Al-Amthāl al-'Āmiyya*, 35.

70. Ibidem, 149.

71. Sha'lān, *Mawsū'at al-Amthāl al-Sha'biyya al-Misriyya*, 117.

72. Taymūr Pasha, *Al-Amthāl al-'Āmiyya*, 430.

73. Ibidem, 245.

74. Khalīl, *al-Thaqāfa al-Sha'biyya wa Dhawu al-Iḥtiyyagāt al-Khāṣa*, 297.

75. Ibidem.

76. Ibidem, 289.

77. Ibidem.

78. Ibidem.

79. All tables created by author.

80. Ibidem, 297.

81. Oxford University Press (2007). "Euphomism." In *Oxford Advanced Learners Dictionary* (7th ed.), 521.

82. Yahia, Yasmīn (2016). Bel-Ṣuwar, Takrīm Abṭāl Miṣr le Mutaḥado al-I'Āqa bi Ḥoḍūr Wazīr al-Riyyāḍa [Minister of Sports Honours the Egyptian Heroes Challenging Disability—in Pictures]. *al-Youm al-Sabe'*; al-Dīb, Fatḥiyya (2018, November 20). Wālidat Ṭālib min Dhawī al-Iḥtiyyagāt al-Khāsa bel-Sharqiyya Tonashed Wazīr al-Ta'Līm be'Awdato le Faṣlo. *al-Youm al-Sabe'*.

83. Lindell, "Bringing Field Theory to Social Media, and Vice Versa," 4.

84. I am providing screenshots of tweets for the purpose of documentation since tweets can be deleted, accounts can be deactivated, and the number of retweets/favorites (on which I depend as an economy of recognition that reflects *doxa* at a particular point in time) can change.

85. Ministry of Communications and Information Technology [@MCIT_News]. (2018, November 28). Tu'Len wezarat al-itisalāt wa tuknologia al-Ma'Lūmāt 'an itlāq al-dawra al-sadisa men mosabaqat Tamkīn letatwīr al-barmagiyyāt wa tatbīqāt al-Hawātif al-Mamūla lel-askhās [Tweet]. Twitter.

86. Ministry of Social Solidarity [@MOSS_Egypt]. (2018, November 22). #Wezarat_altaḍamun_ aligtemā'I Ghāda Wāli: al-da'm kān yu'azez al-i'timadiyya al-ān huwa da'm murṭabit be i'ādit al-tasgīl wal 'amal wa istemrār al-da'm faqaṭ [Tweet]. Twitter.

87. 'Abdul-Laṭīf, "Balāghat Gomhūr Korat al-Qadam," 15.

88. The names of the tweeps and the documentation of the tweets have been removed upon the request of the editor. If any reader needs documentation information for the purpose of verification, please contact the author.

89. Benson and Neveu, "Introduction," 469.

90. Misr El-Kheir [@MisrElKheir]. (2018, October 2018). *Ḥatta law mokhtalefīn 'an aṭfāl gheirhom, lāzem no'men beqodrathom wa mawahebhom #qāderūn_bekhtelāf*. Twitter. During December 2018, the celebration of the day of people with disabilities, which is organized every year by the Egyptian government, was titled احتفالية القادرون باختلاف *Iḥtifaliyyat al-Qaderūn be Ikhtelāf* ("Celebration of the Differently Abled") for the first time. Hassan, Samah (2018, December 24). al-Nas al-Kāmel le Kalemat al-Ra'īs al-Sisi fi Iḥtifaliyyat 'Qaderūn bekhtelaf. *el-Watan*.

91. Benson, "Field Theory in Comparative Context," 463.

92. Ibidem.

93. Ibidem, 467.

References

al-Dīb, Fatḥiyya (2018, November 20). Wālidat Ṭālib min Dhawī al-Iḥtiyyagāt al-Khāsa bel-Sharqiyya Tonashed Wazīr al-Ta'Līm be'Awdato le Faṣlo. *al-Youm al-Sabe'*. https://www.youm7.com/story/2018/11/20/4036966/والدة-طالب-من-ذوي-الاحتياجات-الخاصة-بالشرقية-تناشد-وزير-التعليم-بعودته . Accessed March 17, 2019.

al-Tabarani (2004). *al-Mu'gam al-Wasīṭ*. Cairo: Maktabet al-Shurūq al-Dawliyya.

'Abdul-Laṭīf, 'Emād (2005). "Balāghat al-Mokhāṭab: al-Balāgha al-'Arabiyya men Intāg al-Khetāb al-Solṭawy ela Moqawamatoh." In Kamel, Salwa Abdel-Aziz (ed.), *Power and the Role of the Intellectual* (pp. 7–36). Cairo: Cairo University. https://www.academia.edu/6397185/

'Abdul-Laṭīf, 'Emād (2019). "Balāghat Gomhūr Korat al-Qadam: Ta'ṣṭs Nadhary wa Namūdhag Ṭaṭbīqy." *al-'Umda*, 6, 11–30. https://www.academia.edu/38199593/

Badawy, al-Saīd (1973). *Mostawayāt al-'Arabiyya al-Mo'āṣera* [Levels of Modern Arabic]. Cairo: Dār al-Ma'āref.

Benson, Rodney (1999). "Field Theory in Comparative Context: A New Paradigm for Media Studies," *Theory and Society*, 28(3), 463–498. https://www.researchgate.net/publication/226389050_Field_theory_in_comparative_context_A_new_paradigm_for_media_studies

Benson, Rodney and Neveu, Erik (2005). "Introduction: Field Theory as a Work in Progress." In Benson, Rodney and Neveu, Erik (eds.), *Bourdieu and the Journalistic Field* (pp. 1–25). Cambridge: Polity Press.

Bourdieu, Pierre (1977). *Outline of a Theory of Practice*. Cambridge: Cambridge University Press.

Bourdieu, Pierre (1990). *The Logic of Practice*. Cambridge: Polity.

Bourdieu, Pierre (1993). *Sociology in Question*. London: Sage.

Bourdieu, Pierre (1995). *The Rules of Art: Genesis and Structure of the Literary Field* (Susan Emanuel, trans.). Stanford: Stanford University Press.

Bourdieu, Pierre (1996). "The Forms of Capital." In Richardson, J.G. (ed.), *Handbook of Theory and Research for the Sociology of Education* (pp. 241–258). New York: Greenwood Press.

Constitution of the Arab Republic of Egypt (2014).

El-Masry, Heba Fawzy (2018). *A Comparative Study of Arthur John Arberry and Desmond O'Grady's Translations of the Seven* Mu'allaqāt (PhD thesis, Warwick University).

Gerlitz, Carolin and Anne Helmond (2013). "The Like Economy: Social Buttons and the Data-Intensive Web." *New Media and Society*, 15(8), 1348–1365.

Ghaly, Mohammed (2008). *Islam and Disability: Perspectives in Islamic Theology and Jurisprudence* (PhD thesis, Leiden University). https://openaccess.leidenuniv.nl/handle/1887/12617

Gouanvic, Jean Marc (2005). "A Bourdieusian Theory of Translation, or the Coincidence of Practical Instances: Field, 'Habitus', Capital, and 'Illusio.'" *The Translator*, 11(2), 147–166. https://www.tandfonline.com/doi/abs/10.1080/13556509.2005.10799196

Hanna, Sameh (2016). *Bourdieu in Translation Studies: The Socio-Cultural Dynamics of Shakespeare Translation in Egypt*. London: Routledge.

Hassan, Samah (2018, December 24). al-Nas al-Kāmel le Kalemat al-Ra'īs al-Sisi fi Iḥtifaliyyat 'Qaderūn bekhtelaf. *el-Watan*. https://www.elwatannews.com/news/details/3889224

Jakobson, Roman (2000). "On Linguistic Aspects of Translation." In Venuti, Lawrence (ed.), *Translation Studies Reader* (pp. 113–118). London: Routledge.

Khalīl, Abdul-Ḥakīm (2017). *al-Thaqāfa al-Sha'biyya wa Dhawu al-Iḥtiyyagāt al-Khāṣa* [Popular Culture and People with Special Needs]. Cairo: GEBO.

Kosoff, Zoë (2014). "Code-Switching in Egyptian Arabic: A Sociolinguistic Analysis of Twitter."
    Al-'Arabiyya, 47, 83–99. https://www.jstor.org/stable/24635374

Lindell, Johan (2017). "Bringing Field Theory to Social Media, and Vice Versa: Network-Crawling
    an Economy of Recognition on Facebook." *Social Media + Society*, 1(11), 1–11. https://doi.
    org/10.1177/2056305117735752

Ministry of Communications and Information Technology [@MCIT_News] (2018, November
    28). *Tu'Len wezarat al-itisalāt wa tuknologia al-Ma'Lūmāt 'an itlāq al-dawra al-sadisa men
    mosabaqat Tamkīn letatwīr al-barmagiyyāt wa tatbīqāt al-Hawātif al-Mamūla lel-askhās* [Tweet].
    Twitter.

Ministry of Social Solidarity [@MOSS_Egypt] (2018, November 22). *#Wezarat_altaḍamun_aligtemā'I
    Ghāda Wāli: al-da'm kān yu'azez al-i'timadiyya al-ān huwa da'm murṭabit be i'ādit al-tasgīl wal
    'amal wa istemrār al-da'm faqaṭ* [Tweet]. Twitter.

Misr El-Kheir [@MisrElKheir] (2018, October 2018). *Ḥatta law mokhtalefīn 'an atfāl gheirhom, lāzem
    no'men beqodrathom wa mawahebhom #qāderūn_bekhtelāf.* [Tweet]. Twitter.

Murthy, Dhiraj (2012). "Towards a Sociological Understanding of Social Media: Theorizing Twitter."
    Sociology, 46(6), 1059–1073.

Oxford University Press (2007). "Euphemism." In *Oxford Advanced Learners Dictionary* (7th ed.), 521.

Sha'lān, Ibrahīm Aḥmad (1992). *Mawsū'at al-Amthāl al-Sha'biyya al-Misriyya* [Encyclopaedia of
    Popular Egyptian Proverbs]. Cairo: Dār al-Ma'ārif.

Supreme Council for Media Regulation (2018). *Qanūn Tandhīm al-Saḥāfa Wa al-I'Lām Wa al-Maglis
    al-a'la* [Law, Media, and Higher Council Organizing Law]. Supreme Council of Media Regulation.
    http://scm.gov.eg/قانون-المجلس /

Taymūr Pasha, Aḥmad (2014). *Al-Amthāl al-'Āmiyya* [Popular Proverbs]. Cairo: Mo'asasat Hindawy
    lil Ta'līl wa al-Thaqafa.

United Nations General Assembly (UNGA) (1975, December 9). *al-I'lān al-Khās bi Ḥuqūq
    al-Mu'Awaqīn* [Declaration on the Rights of Disabled Persons]. Minneapolis: Human Rights
    Library University of Minnesota. http://hrlibrary.umn.edu/arab/b073.html

United Nations General Assembly (UNGA) (1975, December 9). *Declaration on the Rights of Disabled
    Persons*. Office of the United Nations High Commissioner for Human Rights (OHCHR). https://
    www.ohchr.org/en/professionalinterest/pages/rightsofdisabledpersons.aspx

United Nations General Assembly (UNGA) (2006, December 13). *Convention on the Rights of Persons
    with Disabilities and Optional Protocol*. New York: UNGA. http://www.un.org/disabilities/
    documents/convention/convoptprot-e.pdf

United Nations General Assembly (UNGA) (2006, December 13). *Ittifaqiyyat Ḥuqūq al-Ashkhās Dhawī
    al-I'Āqa wa al-Protocol al-Ikhtiyyari* [Convention on the Rights of Persons with Disabilities and
    Optional Protocol]. New York: UNGA. http://www.un.org/disabilities/documents/convention/
    convoptprot-a.pdf

Yahia, Yasmīn (2016). Bel-Ṣuwar,Takrīm Abtāl Miṣr le Mutaḥado al-I'Āqa bi Ḥoḍūr
    Wazīr al-Riyyāḍa [Minister of Sports Honours the Egyptian Heroes Challenging Disability—in
    Pictures]. *al-Youm al-Sabe'*. https://www.youm7.com/story/2016/8/2/2826440/ الصور-تكريم-أبطال-مصر-
    لتحدى-الإعاقة-الذهنية-بحضور-وزير-الرياضة. Accessed March 17, 2019.

Zimmer, B. (2011, October 29). "Twitterology: A New Science?" *The New York Times*. Accessed July 20,
    2019. https://www.nytimes.com/2011/10/30/opinion/sunday/twitterology-a-new-science.html

CHAPTER 3

Into Arabic: UNCRPD'S Rights Discourse and the Politics of Interpretation

Riham Debian

Abstract

This chapter deals with the discourse shift in the inclusion politics as manifested in the articulation of the United Nations Convention of Rights of Persons with Disabilities (UNCRPD) and its cultural transposition and translation through languages and across the North/ South divide. It particularly tackles the question of globalization of culture and internationalization of discourse and their implication for the politics of interpretation and translation of the rights discourse of Persons with Disabilities (PwD), its ramification with respect to both the shift from the politics of recognition to acknowledgment and the framing of persons with disabilities—as subjects with rights against the long-entrenched objectifying framework of charity. The chapter reads the UNCRPD and its Arabic translation to examine the politics of naming, its effect on the framing of person with disabilities (as object of charity versus subjects with rights), and its ramification with respect to the developing social policies/practices of inclusion. It seeks to conceptually engage with the Recognition/ Acknowledgment paradigm to investigate the type of inclusion represented in the Source Text and its transposition in the Target Text. To this end, the chapter opens a repertoire between Political Philosophy, Critical Discourse Analysis, and Translation Studies to structure its framework from the theoretical literature on the politics of recognition. The chapter utilizes Fairclough's three-dimensional model as a tool of analysis to examine the discursive event embedded in the production and dissemination of UNCRP, its implication with respect to both the politics of interpretation in the Source and Target Texts, and the discursive and socio-cultural practices across the civilizational divide.

Keywords: UNCRPD, politics of interpretation, inclusion, recognition, Critical Discourse Analysis, translation

Introduction

> Inclusion is not a strategy to help people fit into the systems and structures which exist in our societies; it is about transforming those systems and structures to make it better for everyone.[1]

> Within the framework of the globalisation of culture and the internationalisation of discourses, societies interact through translation, and thus it can be claimed that "we all live in 'translated' worlds" [...] never before has there been as much translation as there is today. Language and translation inevitably are tools for legitimizing the *status quo* or for subverting it.[2]

This chapter deals with the discoursal shift in inclusion politics in the articulation of the United Nations Convention of Rights of Persons with Disabilities (UNCRPD) and its cultural transposition and translation through language and across the North/South divide.[3] It particularly tackles the question of globalization of culture and internationalization of discourse and their implication for the politics of interpretation and translation of the rights discourse of Persons with Disabilities (PwDs), its ramification with respect to both the shift from the politics of recognition to acknowledgment and the framing of persons with disabilities—as subjects with rights against the long entrenched objectifying framework of charity.[4] The chapter reads the UNCRPD and its Arabic translation to examine the politics of naming, its effect on the framing of person with disabilities (as object of charity versus subjects with rights), and its ramification with respect to the developing social policies/practices of inclusion. It seeks to conceptually engage with the Recognition/Acknowledgment paradigm to investigate the type of inclusion represented in the Source Text and its transposition in the Target Text. It aims to distinguish between the two modes of inclusion discourse in the Arabic setting (top-bottom versus bottom-top approaches) and highlights the modus operandi for the move away from the add-to-the-list gesture politics of inclusion and toward the systemic restructuring and accommodation—along transformative and emancipatory lines and within broader issues of sustainable development, social policy, human rights, democratization, and strengthening civil society.

To this end, the chapter opens a repertoire between Political Philosophy, Critical Discourse Analysis, and Translation Studies to structure its framework from the theoretical literature on the politics of recognition, Critical Discourse Analysis' engagement with language as a tool for decoding social practices and process with their embeddedness in power and ideology, and the Cultural Turn in Translation Studies.[5] It utilizes Fairclough's three-dimensional model as a tool of analysis to examine the discursive event embedded in the production and dissemination of UNCRP, its implication with respect to both the politics of interpretation in the Source and Target Texts, and the discursive and socio-cultural practices across the civilizational divide.[6]

Language is/as a social practice: Recognition and disabilities dismantlement

In his seminal take on the interface between language and society, Fairclough opens his call for a critical study of language with a quoted query on the shackles of recognition and dismantlement: "How do we recognize the shackles that tradition places on us? For if we recognize them, we would be able to break them."[7] This opening query forms the philosophical base for his theory of language as a social practice and action embedded in the social process of interaction, whose methodological critical study showcases the imbrications between language and social and institutional practices, and their interface with broader socio-political structures and socio-cultural change. To this end, Fairclough pursues the integration of "discourse analysis with social analysis of socio-cultural change" through a di-fold argument for: first, "the role of discourse [...] in modern and contemporary (late modern) society [... that] has taken on a major role in socio-cultural production and change"[8] and, second, the centrality of textual analysis to a scientific understanding of discourse that transcends the "limited explanatory goals of the descriptive approach, for it necessarily requires reference outside the immediate situation to the social institution and the social formation in that ideologies are by definition representations generated by social forces at these levels."[9] The outcome is the three-dimensional modal for Critical Discourse Analysis (CDA) that links the micro-linguistic event to the macro-socio-cultural structure. This is done simultaneously through tying "textual analysis [...] with social analysis of organisational routines for producing and consuming texts [...] within the processes of production and consumption" and relating text to discourse and socio-cultural practice.[10] The end is "the 'real world' of social relations in institutional practices [...] represented linguistically" and codified textually and intertextually.[11]

In Fairclough's scheme, text is not (as it is traditionally understood) "a piece of written language—a primarily linguistic cultural artifact."[12] Rather, texts are "social spaces in which two fundamental social processes simultaneously occur: cognition and representation of the world, and social interaction."[13] Critical Discourse Analysis hence entails attuned attention to this multifunctionality of language in the text through focus on the interplay between the textual and intertextual and their relation to their context of production and reception. The end is an innovative discoursal analytical practice that enables shackles recognition and ultimate dismantlement through a view of discourse as "the use of language as a form of social practice and discourse analysis [as the] analysis of how texts work within socio-cultural practice."[14] The projected outcome is engagement in the activation of "innovative and unconventional language practice [... in pursuit of] involvement in alternative language practice" befitting the knowledge-based economy of late capitalist societies.[15] To this end, Fairclough constructs his three-dimensional model hinged on three basic tenets, a three-dimensional concept of discourse, and three stages for conducting Critical Discourse Analysis. The model is constructed around an internal relation between language and society through the socially constructive function of language with the latter as both the constructor of social phenomena, process, and practices. Discourse in this scheme has three formations. First is the text, which is the product of social interactive processes and practices decoded through its repertoire with the intertext. Second is the discursive producing practice, which at once gives rise to the text and enables the activation of controlled social practice in line with the "order of discourse" (available repertoires of genres, discourses, and narratives) and in tune with the "technologization of discourse." Technologization of discourse is defined as "calculated intervention to shift discursive practices as part of the engineering of social change."[16]

The third dimension is the social practice, which constitutes both the object and subject of the discursive through a discourse practice tailored to effect structural transformation of the public sphere of politics in accordance with the social function of the media of dissemination and the "functioning of discourse in institutions and institutional change" (Fig. 3.1).[17] In pursuit of critical analysis and disentanglement of the three overlapping dimensions, Fairclough proposes three stages to conducting Critical Discourse Analysis (Fig. 3.2).

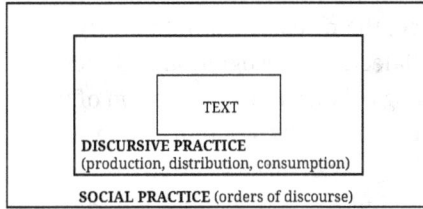

Figure 3.1: Fairclough's three-dimensional concept of discourse

The first stage, description, engages with the linguistic description of the language of the text, properties of the text, the texture of the text (as opposed to commentary on its content), and the order of its constructed discourse. The second stage involves interpretation of the text within its context through reconstruction of "the dialectical process resulting from the interface of the variable interpretative resources people bring to the text, and properties of the text"—that is, the relationship between the productive and interpretative discursive process of the text in its repertoire with the intertext with the end of producing meaning for the description.[18] The third stage engages with the explanation of the relationship between processes of production and interpretation and the social conditioning to decode its implication for the social practice—"how discursive processes are socially shaped [and] their social effect."[19] The aim is recognition of the Ideological Discursive Formations (IDFs) regulating social processes through the technologization of discourse that effects the engineering of socio-cultural change and practice.

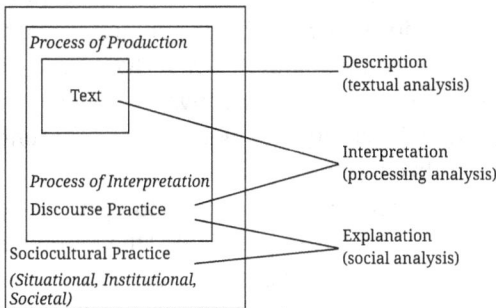

Figure 3.2: Fairclough's three stages for CDA

UNCPD: Recognition dialectics and the technologization of tolerance discourse

Within UN language, the discourse of human rights is embedded in the problematic dual dialectics of recognition and social inclusion on the one hand, and the ideological discursive formation of tolerance as an ideological category on the other.[20] Recognition, the mainstay of liberal politics, premises the equal dignity of all citizens on the recognition of the unique identity of each individual group. As such, it predicates the politics of universality of human dignity on the politics of difference between groups hinging the acknowledgment and status on something that is not universally shared and giving rise to inherent contradiction regarding the politics of inclusion, especially with respect to the normative measurement of difference and the liberal political suspicion of collective goals. As Taylor states: "inclusion is *logically* separable from the claim of equal worth."[21] This contradiction was transposed onto the debates on multiculturalism and the formulas of liberalist multiculturalism.[22] The latter formulated the "form of the politics of equal respect [...] in a liberalism of rights that is inhospitable to difference."[23] The result is what Žižek formulates in terms of "condescending tolerance [...] tolerance as a temporary compromise."[24] The latter promulgates an essentialist conception of the socio-symbolic identity pillared on the inerrant model of liberal citizenship with its dichotomization of rights/participation, private/public, and inclusion/exclusion and dictates of hegemonic ideologies of citizenship, the tenets of which are obligation, participation, and community with "space only for the able-bodied subject engaged in market participation."[25] The implications for the conception of difference (othering) and social inclusion are tantamount; first, the ideological discursive formulation of tolerance as "a political end" and "post-political ersatz."[26] Difference is condescendingly tolerated *despite* what has been constructed as debilitating difference with the imperative of socially engineering the formation of pluralistic society through inclusion. Second, inclusion is thus reformulated through the binarism of integration/segregation and against the mounting pressure of the regulating thrust of "liberal multiculturalism's basic ideological operation": "the 'culturalization of politics' [where] political differences, differences conditioned by political inequality, economic exploitation, etc., are naturalized/neutralized into 'cultural' differences, different 'ways of life' [...] that cannot be overcome, but merely 'tolerated'."[27]

The regulating thrust of multiculturalism was given impetus by the 1990 outburst in theorization of recognition as a surrogate politics to distributive rights giving rise to politics of difference, identity-politics, and two formulations of inclusion in synergy with justice.[28] The first formulation, inter-subjective inclusion, postulates the centrality of recognition to dialogic identity formation and social wellbeing with the logic for social struggle centered on the demand for recognition.[29] According to both Taylor and Honneth, this demand for recognition becomes the vital human need and the prerequisite for social justice and peace—effected through love, respect, and esteem, against and in reaction to prior misrecognition.[30] The second formulation, institutional recognition, reconceptualizes the concept away from Taylor and Honneth's focus on the level of the individual psyche to position recognition within the realm of institutional politics and redistributive claims.[31] Eschewing what she terms as "psychologization" of recognition discourse, Fraser argues for "recognition as an issue of justice" with status and parity denied to individuals "as a consequence of institutionalized patterns of cultural values [...with] misrecognition [...] a form of institutionalized subordination—and thus, a serious violation of justice."[32] For Fraser, the dissociation of struggle for recognition from the struggle for distribution speaks of "the widespread decoupling of cultural politics from social politics, of the politics of difference from the politics of equality" bringing forth "recognition without ethics."[33] The latter fetishizes cultural mis-/recognition to evade the examination of the structure of capitalism propelling the disparity of participation in social life. Fraser's postulation is parity of participation realized through coupling of recognition and redistribution as a perspective on and dimension of justice with distribution as the objective condition preluding the intersubjective condition of participatory parity, for the realization of which it is necessary that "institutionalized patterns of cultural value express equal respect for all participants and ensure equal opportunity for achieving social esteem."[34] Echoing Žižek, Fraser's focus on the institutional guardianship of participatory parity seek to redress the shortcoming of the psychologization of recognition and the condescending formulation of tolerance through positing inclusion on account of—not despite of—difference with the human variation model as a scheme for conception and inclusion of social difference.

Social movements' struggle for recognition and enfranchisement gave impetus to institutional inclusion in public policies, which pressed the need for technologization of discourse with respect to minorities' representation in language, their construction in discourse, and the interpretation of categories of rights, politics of participation, and social citizenship in both political and social practices. For Persons with Disabilities, the technologization of discourse has been problematic on a number of accounts. First, on the representation level, Persons with Disabilities were not constructed as a social group. Earlier discussion of disabilities was pervaded by the medical model. The medical model treated disability on the individualized scale "as an individual physical or mental characteristic with significant personal and social consequences."[35] It constructed the disabled identity in accordance with the limitation of its functionality, labeling it as an impairment and dysfunction that had to be remedied through medical correction and material compensation. The latter constitutes the medial model preposition of justice, which recognizes the social impediment to inclusion, seeks rectification through cash subsidies or in Fraser's scheme redistribution, yet falls short of identifying recognition/misrecognition as a plane for justice and inclusion. The effect is the perpetuation of the stereotypical structuring of dependent disabled identities and their construction as object of charity. The World Health Organization's manual of 1980 is a testament of the medical model's identity representation of disabilities which is linguistically articulated around the conceptual category of handicap, with the world 'handicap' being used persuasively (188 occurrences in the course of 207 pages).

The manual has been critiqued for its ineptitude to "state clearly enough the role of social and physical environment in the process of handicap and [...] [its encouragement of] 'the medicalization of disablement.'"[36] Second, on the discursive level, the social model came as a reaction to the medicalization of disablement and its deterministic objectifying stance with respect to identity representation of disabled bodies. Its development in the seventies was in the context of the disability movement in the UK, which sought to rethink and rearticulate disabilities' identities around a surrogate model of identity presentation and construction. The social model's basic focus was the economic, environmental, and cultural impediment underpinning and reproducing disabilities. Its prepositions were di-fold: first, a radical interpretation of disability structured through uncoupling of disability from handicapping limitation; second, an alternative view of justice centered on recognition of personhood within difference and redistribution of resources (outside the objectifying charity) within the rights framework. Their discursive-triggered activism developed along two conceptions of difference: minority group and human variation model. The latter, less problematic than the former, discursively reformulated inclusion and justice along social restructuring and engineering administered through recognition of the enabling difference to set the claim for restructuring the environmental, cultural, and economic barriers and hence enable the disabled bodies to functionally perform their roles as social citizen. The outcome is activism-triggered discursive practice that brought forth technologization of disabilities' rights discourse codified in the language of UNCRPD.

The latter's contexts of production and reception showcase the interface between social and textual practice and reflect and inflect the discursive practice of identity construction and representation of Persons with Disabilities. The new articulated discourse of the UNCRPD positions subjects' position within the broader context/discourses of sustainable development, multiculturalism, democratization, minority rights, and strengthening of civil society and has propelled a cross-cultural discursive practice in the translational context of internationalization of discourse and globalization of culture. Ultimately, the UNCRPD discursively enacts structural re-engineering of disabilities' difference, recognition, and social citizenship through transforming measures of enfranchisement for (and by) Persons with Disabilities to construct a structural inclusion pillared on recognition of presence on account of human variation and along structural adjustment to make the system work for everyone.

UNCRPD: Description of the discursive event and transformative inclusion

Adopted on December 13, 2006 at the United Nations Headquarters in New York, the CRDP and its Optional Protocol was opened for signature on March 30, 2007. The convention garnered eighty-two signatories with one ratification and forty-four for its optional protocol— "the highest number [...] in history to a UN Convention on its opening day."[37] The Convention entered into force on May 3, 2008. To date (October 2018), the convention has 161 signatories and 177 ratifications: the protocol 92 signature and 92 ratifications (Fig. 3.3 and Fig. 3.4).

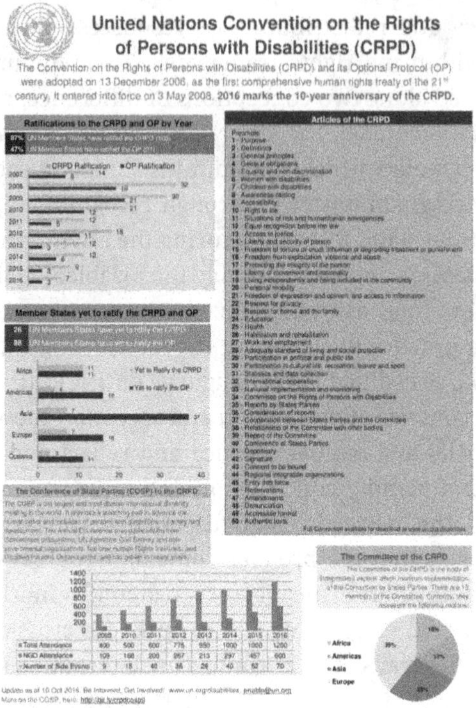

Figure 3.3: Statistics on the United Nations Convention on the Rights of Persons with Disabilities and its Optional Protocol

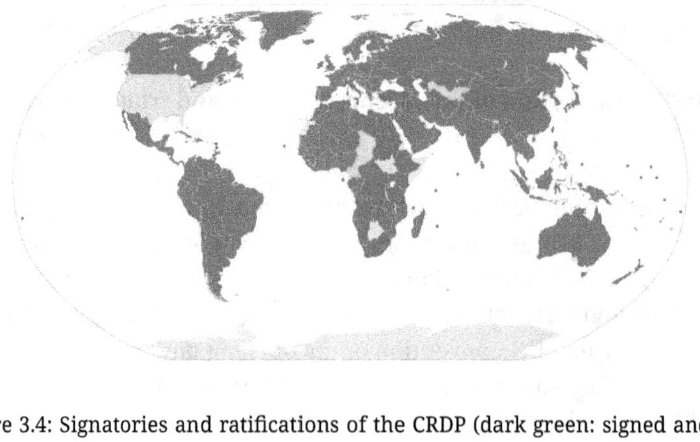

Figure 3.4: Signatories and ratifications of the CRDP (dark green: signed and ratified; light green: signed but not ratified; grey: not signed)

The convention was the output of the attitude changing activism of the people with disabilities in the US (1980s and 1990s) culminating in institutional inclusion in the American with Disabilities Act and ADA amendment in 2008. Unlike UK disabilities' movement in the seventies, the American disabilities' movement codified the shift in the conception of people with disability from being viewed "as 'objects' of charity, medical treatment and social protection toward viewing persons with disabilities as 'subjects' with rights, who are capable of claiming those rights and making decisions for their lives based on their free and informed consent as well as being active members of society."[38] This attitudinal shift was encapsulated in their novel oxymoronic self-identification as "persons with disabilities," which unlike its predecessor "handicap" redressed the linguistic omission of personhood to position disability in the discourse of enabling difference entitled to enfranchisement through redistributive inclusion.[39] This self-labeling was the category of representation in the CRPD, whose negotiation was conducted during eight sessions of an Ad Hoc Committee of the General Assembly from 2002 to 2006—making it the fastest negotiated human rights treaty. As such, the convention became "the first comprehensive human rights treaty of the [twenty-first] century [...] open for signature by regional integration organisations."[40] It became a human rights instrument with an explicit and social development dimension. Emanating from socio-cultural practices of Persons with Disabilities (bottom-up), the convention adopts "a broad categorization of persons with disabilities." It reaffirms the human rights and fundamental freedoms of persons with disabilities, and clarifies and qualifies the categories of rights, areas of enabling adaptations, and measures for rights protection. More importantly, the convention stipulates a politics of vigilant interpretation and monitoring through Article 40, the Conference of State Parties (COSP) and the Committee of Rights of Persons with Disabilities (CRPD).[41]

CRPD: Measures of subject ascription and the politics of interpretation

Article 40 stipulates the organization of an annual conference of the States Parties to review and monitor the implementation of the convention. Since 2008, eight conference sessions were held. Following the ratification of the convention, a Committee on the Rights of Persons with

Disabilities was established (initially twelve and currently eighteen members)—CRPD. The CRPD is a UN body, which meets twice a year to review reports and petition from the state parties (member states and those who signed the protocol). As a measure for subject ascription and inclusion, the CRPD constitutes a monitoring body to disabilities' rights violation, whose interpretation is conducted by persons with disabilities hence a guarantee against the potential of recognition reduction into a gesture politics of inclusion. Indeed, both the COSP and CRDP present an implementation framework to recognition of presence that is premised on acknowledgment of prior disenfranchisement and present entitlement to enfranchisement and rights through identification of the power legacy of marginalization and taking effective recourses to redress and enfranchise. That is to say, it is an acknowledgment that professes acceptance on account of difference. The words "recognize" and "acknowledge" are the prominent words articulating the recognition paradigm the text constructs.

Description and text analysis

The text is divided into three parts: first is the "Permeable." Articulated in twenty-three items, it represents the logic of present convention, which centers on acknowledgment and recognition of the personhood of Persons with Disabilities, and their entitlement to universal rights, whose prior violation warrants present redress. It presents the purpose and justification of the convention through reinstating disabilities' rights within human right. The second section, made of fifty articles, provides for articulation of disabilities' rights with definitions to the environmental, social, economic, and cultural barriers propelling disabilities. The third section, entitled "Optional Protocol," is articulated in eighteen articles tackling the mechanism of monitoring the convention by the state parties.

The semantic argumentation structure of the convention is structured along the since/therefore argumentative logic. It does so with the permeable which contains premises indicators that are linguistically relaying the since dictate through gerund phases. The inclusion discourse is linguistically marked through the prominence of premise indicators "recognizing" (twelve out of twenty-three), which acknowledge the disabled rights within human rights and multiculturalism and through dictates of sustainability and development—acceptance and inclusion on account of difference to individual persons with disability. This preliminary structuring of the inclusion politics is fostered in the conclusion indicator to the preamble: "Convinced that." Item (y) speaks of the injustices and the necessity of redressing previous injustices to enable full participation and utility across world's divides: developing and developed countries.

Table 3.1 represents the argumentation structure of since-gerund phrases with the frequency of occurrence of each linguistic item.

Table 3.1: Argumentation structure of since-gerund phrases

Realizing Convinced that	Concerned that/about	Recalling Considering	Reaffirming Emphasizing Highlighting	Recognizing
1 1	1 1	2	1 1 1	12

The "therefore" premises come through the second and third section in the articles and protocols. The therefore premise is linguistically indexed via the verb phrase of "Have agreed." The second section "Articles" specifies the parameters of inclusion through detailed identification of the impediments to their full enfranchisement and detailed exposition of the measures to guarantee their full recognition. The word "recognition" and its verb "recognize" take prominence in the two sections with five occurrences of "recognition" in the Articles and twenty-two occurrences for the verb "recognized" in the "Protocols." The conclusion indicator "In witness thereof" seals the politics of recognition and inclusion discourse through linguistic binding of translation to authenticity— a legalese jargon indexing the legally binding nature of the translation. Article 50 stipulates the authenticity of the text and its authentic translation across languages: "Authentic texts: The Arabic, Chinese, English, French, Russian and Spanish texts of the present Convention shall be equally authentic." Article 50 and the "Protocol" binds the Convention to institutional inclusion through stipulating the authenticity of translated text and the obligation of state parties to monitor and supervise the implementation of the

Inclusion discourse and Recognition politics of the rights of persons with disabilities.[42]

Authentic text into Arabic: The cultural translation of inclusion and recognition politics

Description: Text analysis

The Arabic translation of the convention follows the literal translation typology. A standard translation choice for authoritative documents, literal translation, favors minimalist translation intervention. Literal translation is characterized by its linguistic faithfulness and textual fidelity with minimal translational intervention. The Source Languages' "grammatical constructions are converted to their nearest [Target Language] equivalents," "the lexical items are [like word-for word] translated out of context" and no omission, addition, or modulation is permitted.[43] Qualified as a "pre-translation process" by Newmark, literal translation is a mainstay translational method for technical and legal text type due to its preservation of the Source Text form and assumed authentic/faithful transposition of the content—not the communicative message, as recommended by Newmark.[44] In the UN, literal translation is the principle for translating UN documents by virtue of its minimalist intervention scheme. The main goal is to preserve the fidelity and authenticity of the documents and its legally binding authority. Despite the contemporary more liberal approach, UN instructions for translation remain bound to the principle of literalness and fidelity as a primary translational concern.[45]

Against the focus on fidelity and faithfulness, the Arabic translation of CRPD exhibits modulation with respect to the content of the ST. The modulation specifically occurs on the lexical and syntactical structuring of the discourses of recognition/acknowledgment and inclusion. The lexical modulations warrant examination especially due to their deviation from equivalence and faithfulness and tacit implication with respect to inclusion discourse transposition and the TT discoursal domestication. The prominent premise indicators in ST—"recognize" and "recognizing"—are modulated in the TT from تعترف in items (ت،ف،ن،م،ط،ح،ب،و) of the permeable into (ى)(ل)تقر ،(ه)تدرك—the literal semantics of statement and cognition. The words "Ensure" and "Ensuring" are throughout translated into كفالة،يكفل in items 2, 3, 4, 6, 7, and 9. The Arabic equivalent of ensure is يضمن. Article 3 of the general principle of the convention states its obligation to effect "Full and effective participation and inclusion in society."[46] This phrase is translated into: كفالة مشاركة و اشراك الاشخاص ذوى الاعاقة بصورة كاملة و فعالة.[47] Article 4 of the general principles exhibit similar lexical modulation with "to ensure" translated into بكفالة: "State parties undertake to ensure and promote the full realization of human rights."[48] The Arabic translation is تتعهد الدول الأطراف بكفالة وتعزيز إعمال كافة حقوق.[49] Item 3 of Article 5 exhibits similar modulation on the syntactical level through the reshuffling of the since premise into a parenthetic phrase: "In order to promote equality and eliminate discrimination, State Parties shall take all appropriate measures."[50] The Arabic translation is تتخذ الدول الأطراف، سعيا لتعزيز المساواة والقضاء على التمييز، جميع الخطوات المناسبة لكفالة توافر الترتيبات التيسيرية المعقولة للأشخاص ذوي الإعاقة.[51]

Cultural domestication and religious signification: الكفالة and charity discourse

These modulations resort to omission of "inclusion" and addition of كفالة (strategies that do not sit well with literal translation and UN prescribed practice). These modulations pinpoint the cultural signification and domestication of the inclusion discourse and recognition politics in the TT. The lexis الكفالة belongs to the religious domain and is used in Islamic exegetical tradition to denote a patronizing relation between the caretaker and his adopted child—adoption is illegitimate in Islam. As such, the invocation of the religious domain, along with its instrumentalization with respect to the state, constructs the state as a patron (instead of a legal guardian and arbiter) vis-à-vis Persons with Disabilities structuring the latter's object position to the state and society. It also constitutes a deviation from both the lexical framing of legal discourse and UN documentary writing style, whose language is characterized by its "bureaucratic jargon and usage [...] vague, general or ambiguous words [...] calculated ambiguity [...] deliberate imprecision and generalities" specifically due to its exercise of diplomacy and delicate balance of interest among the negotiating parties.[52]

Ultimately, this framing domesticates the inclusion of Persons with Disabilities within the conceptual Islamic paradigm of التكافل الاجتماعي—lexically translated as social solidarity, social interdependence, and symbiosis. The Islamic concept of التكافل الاجتماعي premises social harmony and peace on the provision of sustenance to the needy by the rich, which not only structures a hierarchal relation between the benefit-provider and the beneficiaries, but also transposes the discussion of justice and inclusion on the individual spiritual terrain as a matter of spiritual elevation. This formulation, though resonating with the psychologization of recognition of Intersubjective inclusion, does not clearly articulate the institutional measures for inclusion or position provision in the realm of personhood and citizenry rights. As such, it posits the danger of reduction into a token politics of inclusion and a condescending formula of tolerance—acceptance and provision despite disability not on account of the potential ability of disability—especially given the semantic domain of collation. The words كفالة ,يكفل collocate with the poor, orphan, marginalized, and outcast, with the latter as objects of charity by the more fortunate individuals. These dimensions of the Islamic concept language posit condescending notions of rights decoupled from conception of empowerment and enfranchisement.

Against this religiously centered domestication, strides have been taken toward inclusion and enfranchisement. In Egypt, especially in the aftermath of June 30 revolution and under a political leadership attuned to the internationalization of discourse and globalization of culture, concrete measures have been taken to enfranchise Persons with Disabilities on the institutional political level, the market-centric social practice, and the educational practice. The latter (a site of both institutional and intersubjective inclusion) needs continual reconceptualization, especially in the absence of media socially attuned to translating the political leadership's take on the rights of Persons with Disabilities.

Into Arabic in Egypt: Interpretation and institutional inclusion (discursive practice)

In February 2018, President Abdel Fatah Al-Sisi issued law no. 10, 2018 on the Rights of Persons with Disabilities. The law constitutes the legislative formulation of the interpretative framework adopted by Egypt upon its ratification of the convention. The law recognizes "persons with disabilities on an equal basis with others before the law[;] with regard to the concept of legal capacity dealt with in paragraph 2 of the said article, is that persons with disabilities enjoy the capacity to acquire rights and assume legal responsibility ('ahliyyat al-wujub) but not the capacity to perform ('ahliyyat al-'ada'), under Egyptian law."[53]

This formulation was followed by a plethora of implementation measures designed to enfranchise the Persons with Disabilities through furthering the capacity to perform. In July 2018, President el-Sisi announced the establishment of a technical center for services for disabled persons—the first of its kind in Africa designed to enable people with hearing or speech related disability to use technology to communicate through mobile phones. In the Seventh International Conference on Information Technology Convergence and Services for People with Disabilities (ICT4PwDs), President Al-Sisi patronized a technologically facilitating initiative—online websites of governmental institutions to cater to the diverse needs of persons with disabilities. Under the Presidential direction, the Ministry of Housing undertakes the allocation of 5 percent of the national project on public housing to Persons with Disabilities and initiatives are taken to enhance "accessibility of accommodation" (Article 2) in four governorates—Qena, Ismailia, Alexandria, and Cairo. The Egypt Information and Communication Technology Trust Fund (ICT-TF) of the Ministry of Communications and Information Technology (MCIT) and the United Nations Development Programme (UNDP) offers training and educational programmes for Persons with Disabilities in about 112 slum areas in Cairo. Many service projects have been established in Governorates in Upper Egypt in cooperation with NGOS, to advocate for rights and equal opportunities of Persons with Disabilities and enhance their talents to enable them to operate and manage small projects for hand crafts. The Federation of Egyptian Industries' initiative of "Equal for a better living" aims at providing 1,000 employment opportunities in the private sector for persons with disabilities.

In drafting the 2014 constitution, specifically in response to Persons with Disabilities' activism for inclusion, the Egyptian constitution committee included a Person with Disability among the members of the committee for constitution drafting. The 2015 parliamentary elections were conducted through proportional lists running in all constituencies, which gave Persons with Disabilities a onetime quota resulting in the inclusion of nine candidates: eight elected and one presidentially appointed.[54] On December 26, 2017, the Egyptian Parliament issued its approval on a draft law for the establishment of the National Council for People with Disabilities, which is structured as an independent body with technical, financial, and administrative independence. [55] The council administrative structure includes seventeen Persons with Disabilities in addition to public figures with expertise in disabilities' rights. These institutional measures and legislative strides for inclusion propelled parallel inclusion scheme in the social practices, which have been led by the Egyptian private economic sector—the harbinger of technological innovation and technologization of discourse in contemporary cultural economy.

Social practice and the politics of labeling: Market participation and technologization of disability discourse

Within the dictate of business social responsibility and in tune with its innovative emergence and practice, Careem, a three-year-old hyper growth startup in the Middle East in app-based car booking space, started its awareness-raising campaign on disabilities' rights on December 14, 2018. The launch of its campaign along with its yet newest feature, "Careem Assist"—designed to assist people with motor disability, index the market participation in both the social and discursive practice of

Figures 3.5: Careem's Campaign

disability inclusion. In addition to providing for ramps and disability-specific services, Careem's campaign engages in the politics of new labeling and naming as the panacea for re-signification of disability. The campaign repackages the term used in the Arabic translation ذوى الاعاقة into ذوى الارادة. (Fig. 3.5). This repackaging not only reformulates the identity representation along the challenge paradigm, but it is also reflexive of the context-dependent overture of the company's CEOs and origin in Dubai. The official Emirate label of the Persons with Disabilities is اصحاب الهمم, people with stamina. Though not the preferred label by the internationalized discourse on disability, this re-naming and repackaging speak of a thriving practice and attempted interventions with the globalized human rights culture. These interventions are in need of planning and calculation to affect the projected outcome of inclusion along the dual planes of recognition and redistribution. The yet incomplete formulation of inclusion on the cultural scheme is evident in the lack of standardized labeling with respect to the Persons with Disabilities identity-referencing and representation and its implication with respect to potential lapses in the interpretation of their rights. Figure 3.6 showcases the unfinished process of consolidation in the KSA context and the linguistic disjunction and cultural dissonance between the institutional discourse and the not-yet socially debated disabilities' rights. A Saudi awareness campaign on disabilities' rights to recognition reads as follows: "don't call a handicapped a 'handicap' but name him/her as a person of special needs. Campaign on the handicapped rights." In KSA, they are labeled ذوى الاحتياجات الخاصة.

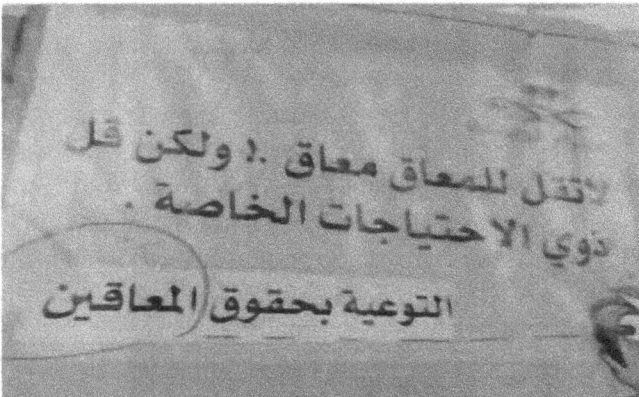

Figure 3.6: Saudi Campaign for Persons with Disabilities' rights

Intersubjective and institutional: cultural translation and justice

The lack of a standardized idiom to reference Persons with Disabilities pinpoints the problematic of cultural translation and accommodation of global categories to local settings. It more specifically pinpoints a lacuna with respect to the culture of self-identification and referencing (the outcome of disabilities' activism in Western context) and its implication for the potential objectification of Persons with Disabilities in other contexts. In the context of the internationalization and globalization of culture, we all find ourselves in "translated worlds."[56] The state parties partaking in the authentication of the Convention and its translation into social practices have instituted institutional recognition and a top-bottom scheme toward inclusion. These preliminary steps remain in need of translation through social debate and reconceptualization of Disabilities in plural and Persons with disabilities in diverse plural by those who enjoy the enabling burdens of disabilities. Or else, the institutional measure and schemes would be reduced to token politics of modernization and internationalization and with no subject-position ascription to and Intersubjective inclusion of the persons with disabilities—especially in the absence of standardized media discourse and media framing of the nuances of institutional inclusion discourse on the rights of Persons with Disabilities.

Conclusion

The chapter opened a repertoire between Critical Discourse Analysis, political philosophy, and translation theory to examine the interface between the textual and social practice of the UNCRPD, its Arabic translation, and the Arab-specific culturalized take on inclusion discourse within the context of globalization of culture and internationalization of discourse. The chapter's findings are: first, the UNCRPD is structured through an activism-based discursive practice on inclusion and recognition that involves the dual aspects of intersubjective and institutional inclusion with both the psychological and redistribution dimensions of recognition to the effect of construction of Persons with Disabilities as subjects with rights through the human variation model entitlement to enfranchisement through access. Second, the Arabic translation purports a culturalization of the Persons with Disabilities' rights to inclusion and recognition through domestication of the inclusion discourse within the religious paradigm of the Islamic exegetical thesis of التكافل الاجتماعي ("social solidarity, interdependence, and symbiosis"). This culturalization constitutes a double-edged weapon due to its potential objectification stance with respect to the personhood and citizenry rights of Persons with Disabilities—best reflected in the lack of a standardized Arabic term for labeling and identity-representation of Persons with Disabilities. Third, the internationalization and globalization of human rights discourse and culture is propelling moves toward technologization of discourse in the Arab region and Arabic language, especially considering Arabic language assumption of the stature of diplomatic language. Arabic language was included among the official languages of the United Nations in 1973. The technologization of discourse on disabilities' rights has been initiated by the private sector in the Egyptian context and the NGOs in other Arabic countries. Yet, more concerted efforts are needed in standardization of labeling vocabulary and representation categories of inclusion and social justice.

The chapter ultimately argues for the importance of culture and translation as a ground for meaning dissemination and signification, and the frame through which society and political reality becomes signified to trigger social process and practices through language. This argument for the re-signification impact of culture in political reality is structured in line with the new formulation of culture in social scientific debates, which according to Buden "has become this political stage itself, the very condition of the possibility of society and of our perception of what is today political reality."[57] Accordingly, cultural translation becomes the founding step for political change through reframing reality and framing a plan of actions toward inclusion—a plan embedded in a language game in continual need of interpretation and intersubjective signification. On a final note, in the Egyptian higher-education context, in response to the presidential directive and dual-dimension formulation of inclusion,[58] the Supreme Council of Egyptian Universities issued an integration decision (Fig. 3.7). In the integration decision, the Persons with Disabilities are mainstreamed into one category with one measure to their inclusion in an assessment scheme—a framing that resulted in a panic attack and breakdown to a student with a mental disability. The system is yet in need of transformation to enable its working for everyone.

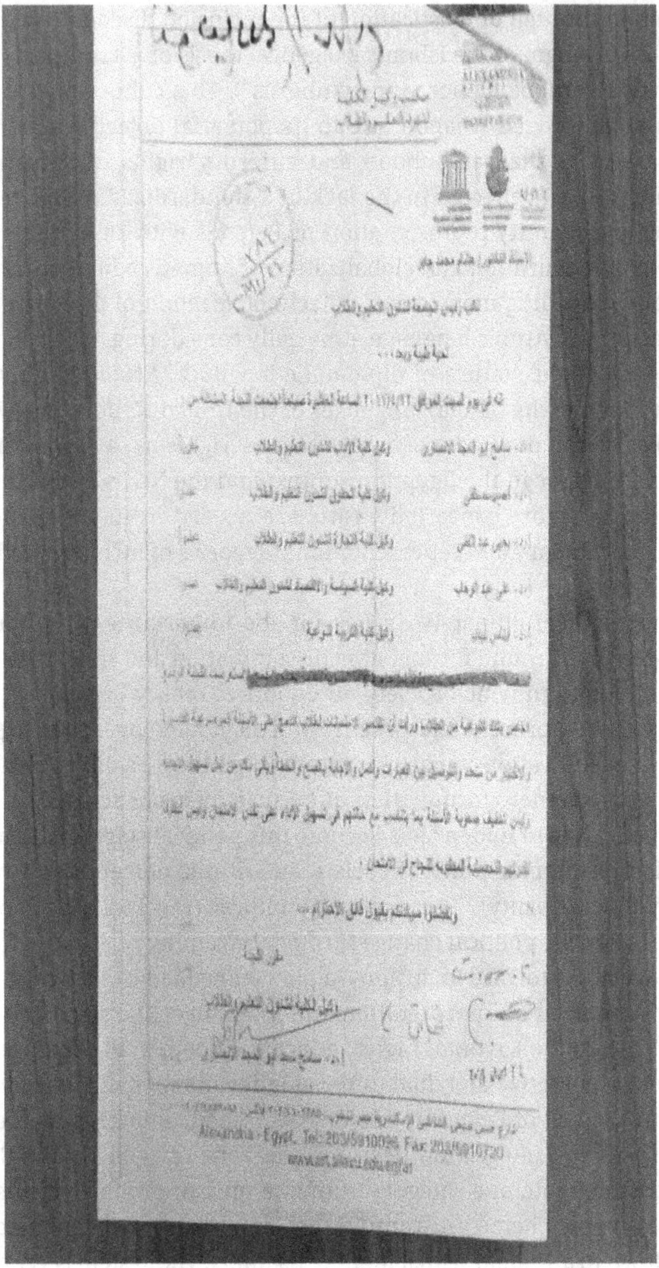

Figure 3.7: The Supreme Council Integration Decision with its MCQ assessment procedures for students with disabilities

Notes

1. Richler, Diana (2018, April 15). *Inclusion Without Limits: What Has to Change?* [Keynote]. Pushing the Boundaries: Disability, Inclusion and the Jewish Community, Toronto.
2. Castro, O. (2013). "Introduction: Gender, Language, and Translation at the Crossroads of Disciplines." *Gender and Language*, 7(1), 6.
3. United Nations General Assembly (UNGA) (2006, December 13). *Convention on the Rights of Persons with Disabilities and Optional Protocol.* New York: UNGA.
4. Maldenov, T. (2013). "The UN Conventions on Rights of Persons with Disabilities and its Interpretation." *ALTER. European Journal of Disability Research*, 7(1), 68–82.
5. Žižek, S. (2008). "Tolerance as an Ideological Category." *Critical Inquiry*, 34(4), 660–682; Fraser, N. (2001). "Recognition Without Ethics?" *Theory, Culture & Society*, 18(2–3), 21–42; Honneth, A. (1995). *The Struggle for Recognition: The Moral Grammar of Social Conflicts.* Cambridge, MA: MIT Press; Taylor, C. (1994). *Multiculturalism: Examining the Politics of Recognition* (Amy Gutmann, ed.). Princeton: Princeton University Press.
6. Fairclough, N. (1995). *Critical Discourse Analysis: The Critical Study of Language.* London: Longman Inc.
7. Fairclough, N. (1989). *Language and Power.* New York: Longman Inc, 1.
8. Fairclough, *Critical Discourse Analysis*, 2.
9. Ibidem, 45.
10. Ibidem, 9.
11. Ibidem, vii.
12. Ibidem, 17–18
13. Ibidem, 20.
14. Ibidem.
15. Ibidem, 3.
16. Ibidem.
17. Ibidem, 49.
18. Ibidem, 9.
19. Ibidem, 1.
20. Resp. Taylor, *Multiculturalism*, and Žižek, "Tolerance as an Ideological Category."
21. Taylor, *Multiculturalism*, 68. Italicisation in the original.
22. Resp. Taylor, *Multiculturalism*, 69, and Žižek, "Tolerance as an Ideological Category."
23. Ibidem, 60.
24. Žižek, "Tolerance as an Ideological Category," 664.
25. Parker, S. (2004). "Searching for the Absent Citizen: Enabling and (Dis)abling Discourses of Social Citizenship." *Australian Journal of Human Rights*, 12(2), 1.
26. Žižek, "Tolerance as an Ideological Category," 660.
27. Ibidem, 669.
28. E.g., Young, I.M. (1990). *Justice and the Politics of Difference.* Princeton: Princeton University Press. The origin of the term "identity politics" is sometimes traced to the 1960s Civil Rights Movement, but it was articulated by women of color in their 1977 Combahee River Collective Statement. The term refers to collective group identities like race, ethnicity, sex, religion, caste, sexual orientation, and physical disability as the basis for political analysis and action. Its main

objective is to empower individuals to articulate their discrimination and invisibility through consciousness raising and action.

29. Taylor, C. (1994). *Multiculturalism*; Honneth, A. (2001). "Recognition or Redistribution?" *Theory, Culture & Society*, 18(2–3), 43–55; Honneth, A. (1995); *The Struggle for Recognition*.
30. Ibidem.
31. Fraser, "Recognition without Ethics?"
32. Ibidem, 26
33. Ibidem, 21.
34. Ibidem, 29.
35. Putnam, D., et al. (2019). *Disability and Justice* (Edward N. Zalta, ed.). Stanford: The Stanford Encyclopedia of Philosophy.
36. World Health Organization (WHO) (1980). *International Classification of Impairments, Disabilities, and Handicaps: A Manual of Classification Relating to the Consequences of Disease, Published in Accordance with Resolution WHA29.35 of the Twenty-ninth World Health Assembly, May 1976*. WHO.
37. *Convention on the Rights of Persons with Disabilities (CRPD)*. United Nations, Department of Economic and Social Affairs.
38. Ibidem.
39. Up until 2004, persons with disabilities were patronizingly treated as an object of charity—not subjects with rights. A disability is broadly defined as a condition or function judged to be significantly impaired relative to the usual standard of an individual or group. The term is used to refer to individual functioning, including physical impairment, sensory impairment, cognitive impairment, intellectual impairment mental illness, and various types of chronic disease. Conventional definitions of "disabled" and "disability" stem from social service programs and benefits programs such as Social Security. These definitions, dating back many years, uniformly used the term "disabled" or "disability" to mean "unable" to work, to handle gainful employment, and so forth. If you look up definitions of "disabled" you will find these kinds of definitions. "Disability" and "Disabled" are terms that are undergoing change due to the disability rights movement both in the US and the UK. To a lesser extent this is occurring worldwide. To most people today the term "disabled" still means just that, and, more broadly, means "unable to perform" this or that physical or mental function. Even more broadly, a large group of physical or mental conditions are "disabilities," things people have also called "afflictions" or "impairments" or "injuries" or "diseases." Beginning in the 1970s, people labeled as "disabled" began seeking changes in society that would allow them to have a better life. Since the 1980s, this effort has generally been termed "disability rights" advocacy or "disability rights activism." The term is "disability rights," not "disabled rights" or "handicapped rights" simply because historically and politically that's the term that the activists themselves have come to call it. So, the correct term is "Disability Rights." "Calling a person disabled, not *the* disabled but *a* disabled person is almost always considered correct. This is the primary term used in the UK and amongst academics and activists in the United States. Many people still use 'handicapped' or 'crippled' or 'afflicted.'" None of these terms is looked upon with favor by anyone in the organized US or UK disability rights movement. "Handicapped" is truly detested in UK circles. Handicapped is offensive—it is a limiting term. "Challenged" is just sugarcoating, as is impaired or any other word that attempts to "dance around" the subject matter. The idea of being challenged emerged about ten years ago and is condescending. People with disabilities are not challenged—you are challenged to play chess and one of you wins. Disabilities you live

with—you struggle—you face them head on. There is only learning to accept and move onward. They are not dismissing the fact that they are disabled, but they are dismissing it as a negative experience. "I am autistic. I am an *aspie*. I am deaf. I am blind. I am disabled." There are some words, three especially, that have been rejected nearly universally: "retardation" and any derivative like "retard," "tard," "retarded"; "spastic" and "spaz"; "cripple" and "crip." Just like the N-word is used between peers, "spaz" and "crip" are used between close friends.

40. *Convention on the Rights of Persons with Disabilities (CRPD)*. UN DESA.

41. United Nations, *Convention on the Rights of Persons with Disabilities and Optional Protocol*.

42. Ibidem, 31.

43. Newmark, P. (1988). *A Textbook of Translation*. New York and London: Prentice Hall, 45.

44. Ibidem, 16. See also Sarcevic, S. (1997). *New Approaches to Legal Translation*. The Hague: Klawer Law International. Sarcevic argues that due to the main goal of legal translation, reproduction of "the content of the source text as accurately as possible," it has been agreed among both lawyers and linguists "that legal texts had to be translated literally. This dictum became the rule for legal translation even after legal translators won the right to produce texts in the spirit of the target language"—the general principle for legal translation remains fidelity to the source text.

45. In the UN manual for Arabic translation, the UN acknowledges "the room for the exercise of stylistic judgments," yet its final conclusion is that fidelity to the original text must be the primary concern.

46. United Nations, *Convention on the Rights of Persons with Disabilities and Optional Protocol*, 5.

47. UNGA (2006, December 13). *Ittifaqiyyat Ḥuqūq al-Ashkhās Dhawī al-I'Āqa wa al-Protocol al-Ikhtiyyari* [Convention on the Rights of Persons with Disabilities and Optional Protocol]. New York: UNGA.

48. United Nations, *Convention on the Rights of Persons with Disabilities and Optional Protocol*, 5.

49. United Nations, *Ittifaqiyyat Ḥuqūq al-Ashkhās Dhawī al-I'Āqa wa al-Protocol al-Ikhtiyyari*.

50. United Nations, *Convention on the Rights of Persons with Disabilities and Optional Protocol*, 7.

51. United Nations, *Ittifaqiyyat Ḥuqūq al-Ashkhās Dhawī al-I'Āqa wa al-Protocol al-Ikhtiyyari*.

52. Cao, D. and Zhao, X. (2008). "Translation at the United Nations as Specialized Translation." *The Journal of Specialized Translation*, 9, 39–54, 46–47.

53. United Nations Treaty Collection (2006), https://treaties.un.org

54. Soliman, A. (2018, October 31). "A New Legislation for the Egyptian Persons with Disabilities: Hopes and Fears." *Rethinking Disability*.

55. Ibidem. According to Soliman, the law was drafted and proposed by the MP Dr Heba Hagrass and came as a culmination for the accumulative efforts of the committee of "Social Solidarity, Family and PwD" in the Egyptian Parliament. Hagress qualifies the law as "comprehensive," reflecting a "human rights perspective rather than charity or philanthropic approach" with affirmative discrimination as the logic of its composition through quotas, exemptions, or facilitations. The legislative treats PwDs as "equal citizens who have rights and obligations and not a group or individuals deserving charity support."

56. Castro, "Introduction."

57. Buden, B. et al. (2009). "Cultural translation: An Introduction to the Problem, and Responses." *Translation Studies*, 2(2), 196.

58. In his speech at the first Arab forum for special education schools, President al-Sisi highlights two concepts in the state's inclusion discourse: first, the need for collective participation (from the governmental institutions, NGOs, and private sectors toward reconceptualization and reformulation of societal culture with respect to disabilities; second, inclusion as a

process to social re-education and reformulation of the acceptance of the other and cognition/ recognition of cultural diversification and plurality. This nuanced framing of inclusion—not yet translated into media discourse—pinpoints to the interactive relation between institutional and intersubjective inclusion, which remains in a process of translation predicated on the social practice of endorsing the institutional discourse. Thus arises the necessity of cultural translation of discourse into social process and practice to enable the perception of PwDs as individuals with special (different) needs.

References

Buden, B. et al. (2009). "Cultural Translation: An Introduction to the Problem, and Responses." *Translation Studies*, 2(2), 196–219.

Cao, D. and Zhao, X. (2008). "Translation at the United Nations as Specialized Translation." *The Journal of Specialized Translation*, 9, 39–54.

Castro, O. (2013). "Introduction: Gender, Language, and Translation at the Crossroads of Disciplines." *Gender and Language*, 7(1), 5–12. https://doi.org/10.1558/genl.v7i1.5

Convention on the Rights of Persons with Disabilities (CRPD). United Nations, Department of Economic and Social Affairs. https://social.desa.un.org/issues/disability/crpd/ convention-on-the-rights-of-persons-with-disabilities-crpd

Fairclough, N. (1989). *Language and Power*. New York: Longman Inc.

Fairclough, N. (1995). *Critical Discourse Analysis: The Critical Study of Language*. London: Longman Inc.

Fraser, N. (2001). "Recognition Without Ethics?" *Theory, Culture & Society*, 18(2–3), 21–42.

Honneth, A. (1995). *The Struggle for Recognition: The Moral Grammar of Social Conflicts*. Cambridge MA: MIT Press.

Honneth, A. (2001). "Recognition or Redistribution?" *Theory, Culture & Society*, 18(2–3), 43–55. https:// doi.org/10.1177/02632760122051779

Maldenov, T. (2013). "The UN Conventions on Rights of Persons with Disabilities and its Interpretation." *ALTER. European Journal of Disability Research*, 7(1), 68–82.

Newmark, P. (1988). *A Textbook of Translation*. New York and London: Prentice Hall.

Parker, S. (2004). "Searching for the Absent Citizen: Enabling and (Dis)abling Discourses of Social Citizenship." *Australian Journal of Human Rights*, 12(2), 1–25.

Putnam, D. et al. (2019). *Disability and Justice* (Edward N. Zalta, ed.). Stanford: The Stanford Encyclopedia of Philosophy.

Richler, Diana (2018, April 15). *Inclusion Without Limits: What Has to Change?* [Keynote]. Pushing the Boundaries: Disability, Inclusion and the Jewish Community, Toronto. https://www. jewishcanada.org/speakers-and-presenters/diane-richler

Sarcevic, S. (1997). *New Approaches to Legal Translation*. The Hague: Klawer Law International.

Soliman, A. (2018, October 31). "A New Legislation for the Egyptian Persons with Disabilities: Hopes and Fears." *Rethinking Disability*. https://rethinkingdisability. net/a-new-legislation-for-the-egyptian-persons-with-disabilities-hopes-and-fears/

Taylor, C. (1994). *Multiculturalism: Examining the Politics of Recognition* (Amy Gutmann, ed.). Princeton: Princeton University Press.

United Nations General Assembly (UNGA) (2006, December 13). *Convention on the Rights of Persons with Disabilities and Optional Protocol*. New York: UNGA. http://www.un.org/disabilities/documents/convention/convoptprot-e.pdf

United Nations General Assembly (UNGA) (2006, December 13). *Ittifaqiyyat Ḥuqūq al-Ashkhās Dhawī al-l'Āqa wa al-Protocol al-Ikhtiyyari* [Convention on the Rights of Persons with Disabilities and Optional Protocol]. New York: UNGA. http://www.un.org/disabilities/documents/convention/convoptprot-a.pdf

United Nations Treaty Collection (2006). https://treaties.un.org

World Health Organization (WHO) (0891). *International Classification of Impairments, Disabilities, and Handicaps: A Manual of Classification Relating to the Consequences of Disease, Published in Accordance with Resolution WHA29.35 of the Twenty-ninth World Health Assembly, May 1976*. WHO. https://iris.who.int/handle/10665/41003

Young, I.M. (1990). *Justice and the Politics of Difference*. Princeton: Princeton University Press. https://doi.org/10.2307/j.ctvcm4g4q

Žižek, S. (2008). "Tolerance as an Ideological Category." *Critical Inquiry*, 34(4), 660–682. https://doi.org/10.1086/592539

Exploring the Inclusivity of Disability Related Language in a Multilingual Research Context: A Case Study of the Algerian Context

Imene Zoulikha Kassous[1]

Abstract

Algeria signed the Convention on the Rights of Persons with Disabilities (CRPD) in 2007, ratified it in 2009, and started communicating with the Office of the United Nations High Commissioner for Human Rights (OHCHR) committee of the United Nations Human Rights Office during 2015. Many papers have been published recently in this area in three different languages: Arabic, French, and English. Indeed, Algeria is known for its multilingual context due to its historical encounters with Arabs and French in addition to the demands of globalization. Arabic, French, and English are used in academic, professional, and personal communications, such as research. In this respect, the purpose of this analysis is to demonstrate the inclusivity of the current language use in Algeria in relation to disability and the extent these papers maintain inclusive language that respects and accepts everyone regardless of their differences while promoting equitable opportunities. In this respect, some of the most recent studies that are available online have been analysed. The research papers were selected based on a restricted timeline (2015–2020) and the search was performed in all three languages on international and Algerian database platforms. Findings have demonstrated that there is an instability in the use of terminology, including awkward translations from other languages into Arabic as well as the use of problematic and offensive terms.

Keywords: Disability, inclusion, inclusive language, critical disability theory, Algeria

Introduction

Although the inauguration of the Convention on the Rights of Persons with Disabilities (henceforth CRPD) has provided a standardized language to describe and refer to persons with disabilities, debates concerning disability-related terminology have still not been settled. One of the main conversations revolves around the merit of person-first versus disability-first terminology. Other discussions seek to refute labels that eliminate disability, for example, people with special needs, or problematic representations, such as the trope of the "super-crip" that glorifies in an exaggerated manner the achievements of persons with disabilities.

In this chapter, my focus is on the terminology used in Algeria to refer to and discuss disability. Algeria is one of the countries that have agreed on the principles of the convention in order to facilitate the work/personal life of persons with disabilities and promote inclusivity within its society. What can be observed in Algerian official papers and television talks is the inconsistency in the use of terminology when talking about the rights of persons with disabilities. From a critical disability theory lens, this linguistic ambivalence shapes perceptions of disability, the process of conceptualizing disability, the position of people with disability, and the kind of terminology used in research.[2]

This chapter aims to analyse the terminology used to refer to people with disabilities in Algerian academic research (education and psychology driven research) such as disability, impairment, inclusion, and integration. The purpose of this analysis is to explore the current language use in Algeria in relation to disability and the extent to which these papers maintain inclusive language. In accordance with the CRPD treaty application in Algeria, much research has been conducted in order to address the problematic situation of children/students with disabilities in the Algerian context.[3] Algeria is a multilingual context due to previous conquests (Islam), French colonization, and the ascendancy of English in the era of cultural globalization. Research studies are conducted in a number of different languages, but particularly French, Arabic, and English.

In this respect, forty-eight recently conducted studies (French: 16, Arabic: 21, English: 11) that are available online have been analysed. I conducted the search for papers in different international and national (Algerian) databases. The research papers were selected based on a restricted timeline (2015–2020) where three languages were used. In relation to CRPD, Algeria submitted initial reports of state parties due in 2012 during 2015, which is why I decided to focus my analysis from 2015 onwards.[4] Concerning the theoretical framework, critical disability theory and labeling theory were used to analyse the linguistic choices made in the selected papers and how it may shape individuals' perceptions of or attitudes toward disability. For data analysis, the collected data were analysed thematically in which the papers were closely read, and codes were assigned.

Linguistic situation in Algeria

Algeria is recognized by its multilingual status in which it has two national languages (Arabic and Tamazight) in addition to French and English as first and second foreign languages respectively. Although Algeria is known for being a multilingual nation, the status of each language is different from the other one. A descriptor of the Algerian linguistic context is its adherence to code switching, mixing, and borrowing, which is a result of being a diglossic society.[5] In this perspective, Le Roux clarifies that "bilingualism and multilingualism are real socio-linguistic phenomena in Algeria."[6] Bentahila indicated that bilingualism is dominant in Morocco except in Saharan and Mountain regions where old people and children use the Tamazight language only.[7] A similar situation is noticed in the Algerian context. Indeed, proceeding with this feature, French and Modern Standard Arabic are used in the academic sectors in Maghreb.[8] These languages are not considered as the mother tongue of people living in Morocco (or in Algeria).[9] The following section will describe the status of Arabic, Tamazight, French, and English in the Algerian context.

Status of Arabic language in Algeria

The privileged status of Arabic language in Algerian society cannot be disregarded as it is associated with the most dominant religion in Algeria, that is, Islam. After independence, one of the most important shifts that occurred was Arabization policy, which started partly in elementary school where the first two years had been Arabized. Also, ten hours of teaching in Arabic was "introduced from the 3rd to 7th years."[10]

There are reasons behind the policy of Arabization, and it is mainly embedded within the need to erase the aftermaths of the colonial processes of de-culturalizing Algeria under the mask of "civilising mission."[11] Going back to August 1962, the Algerian personality was aimed at being reconstructed on the basics of Islamic principles and Arabic and this was a formal and official request driven by the Ulama.[12][13]

A debate between modernists and traditionalists at the party Congress of 1964 meant that President Ben Bella "was forced to emphasise the importance of Algeria's Islamic-Arabic heritage."[14] Modernists behind Ben Bella were opposed by Boumediene and Ulama who believed that keeping French was a sort of "depersonalisation of Algeria" and that Arabization should be implemented and defended as a way to re-es-tablish Algerian culture and independence.[15] Surprisingly, during the Boumdiene presidential period that started in 1965, industrialization and bilingualism were defended by "Technocrats."[16]

The approach that was endorsed by the Algerian government is sim-ilar to the assimilative policies that were implemented by the French col-onizers. This has been confirmed by Benrabah who claims that after its independence Algeria took an assimilation approach that is based on the belief that people should learn and speak the same language leading to the establishment of "the policy of Arabisation."[17] As a result of imposing Arabization, Tamazight was neglected and ignored by the government, which led to protests that resulted in issuing Tamazight as a national lan-guage just like Arabic. It has recently gained a similar status to Arabic (a national and official language) after the constitutional changes that took place in 2016.[18]

Status of Tamazight in Algeria

Tamazight is an official and national language in Algeria. It has a sim-ilar status as Arabic language in the Algerian context. There were sev-eral steps that Tamazight language went through in order to become a national and official language. To begin with, after independence, Arabization policy was characterized by turning down and refusing the Algerian mother tongues such as Tamazight and other foreign languages in which its basics and foundation were a "narrow monolingualism."[19] Also, Benrabah argued that French and first Algerian languages that are Algerian Arabic and Tamazight were the main reason behind Arabization seeing them as a target.[20] He further suggested that the fact that we are still using all these languages in Algeria represents the refusal and fail-ure of Arabization policy.[21] Rouabah argues that, similar to the previous colonial attitudes, "the same model of language superiority and cultural marginalisation was re-introduced by the Algerian governors."[22]

An important event that contributed to the current linguistic sit-uation in Algeria was The Berber Spring in 1980 which resulted in the end of socialism.[23] Tamazight people wanted their culture and language (Tamazight) to be acknowledged nationally and officially.[24] Furthermore, refusal and resistance were also depicted in Tamazight's language use, which was a passive reaction before The Berber Spring broke out.[25] After several events, Berber language became a national language but not an official one during President Bouteflika's government in April 2002.[26] In this respect, Tamazight became a national language that is being taught in schools, and according to the new constitutional amendments Tamazight is now an official and national language.[27][28] In this research, I will not be able to analyse articles written in Tamazight due to my inability of speaking or reading the language.

Status of French in Algeria

The French language is also part of the Algerian identity and is considered as the first foreign language that is spoken in almost all contexts in Algeria and sometimes more than the official language. Although there have been several attempts to eliminate the French language, these attempts have failed. As has been previously explained, one of the purposes of Arabization policy was to eradicate the use of French language in Algeria. Thus, Algerian users of French language were radically affected by the policy of Arabization. Benrabah argued that after several decisions that had been made by the Algerian government, oppositions were created between "Arabophones" and "Francophones," speakers of Arabic versus speakers of Tamazight, and "democrats" versus "fundamentalists."[29] As a result of these disagreements, a cultural civil war took place where, in the 1990s, several Algerian intellectuals who were speakers of French were killed in addition to "female French teachers were slaughtered sometimes in their very classrooms in front of their pupils."[30]

Even though there were several attempts to obliterate the French language, it is still widely used in Algeria. Benrabah notes that "the political and social stability of the country would require the pluralist perspective based on the multilingual profile of Algeria."[31] This explains the fact that it is true that Arabization has been promoted after independence, but Algeria cannot be a monolingual country due to its historical background and, as Benrabah suggests, Algeria needs to accept its "linguistic pluralism" in order to promote a society that is solid, unified, homogenized, and consistent.[32] French language is still taught at all educational levels and is used in administrative contexts all over Algeria.

Status of English language in Algeria

There is an ongoing competition between proponents of English and those of the French language in Algeria. As previously mentioned, the linguistic situation of Algeria is seen as "linguistic plurality (diversity)"[33] in which there are two daily spoken languages that are colloquial Arabic and Tamazight in addition to French, which acts as the first foreign language while English is the second foreign language that "is not socially used."[34]

Looking back at the inclusion of English, the Minister of Education decided to incorporate English alongside French[35] where children were given the choice between two foreign languages, French versus English.[36] In this respect, being a mandatory first foreign language was no longer solely attributed to French and it became possible to choose the latter as a second foreign language[37] and this is due to including English as a strong competitor. However, things did not work as pro-Arabization lobbies wanted, as French was frequently chosen by pupils in opposition to English whose number of supporters was quite insignificant.[38] This preference is mainly due to the fact that French is the language of instruction for most postgraduate scientific studies.[39]

Driven by political ulterior motives instead of educational ones, English language education was introduced into primary schools in 1993.[40] After being piloted in 1993, English language inclusion in primary schools was nationally established in 1995.[41] Incorporating English language at the primary school level was not successful.[42] Recently, on July 21, 2019, the Minister of Higher Education and Scientific Research declared using English and Arabic for the writing of headings on official and administrative documents. This has created a debate between Francophone proponents and Anglophone proponents similar to what happened during the 1990s.[43]

Disability terminology in Algeria and the Arabic speaking countries: Translation issues and CRPD

Translation is not an easy process as no two languages are alike. Al-Sohbani and Muthanna pinpoint the role of culture and the need of translators' awareness of both target and source languages' cultural beliefs and principles for effective translation.[44]

Table 4.1: Terminology used in the CRPD in English, French, and Arabic

English	French	Arabic
Impairment	*Incapacités*	عاهة
Integration	*Intégration*	إدماج
Inclusion	*Insertion scolaire*	إشراك، إدماج الإشراك، الإدماج
Person with disabilities	*Personnes handicapées*	أشخاص ذوي الإعاقة

As this study will refer to the Convention on the Rights of Persons with Disabilities (CRPD) when explaining the choices made by the selected authors in this study, I will introduce certain translation issues that I have identified in the CRPD. When reading CRPD in English and Arabic, one can see the confusion that may occur at the level of some of the most important concepts in disability, which are "impairment," "integration," and "inclusion" (see Table 4.1). These words are translated as follows: "integration" (إدماج), "inclusion" (إشراك، إدماج), "impairment" (عاهة). Although inclusive education has been translated to different concepts in the Arabic language such as *"Al-Taaleem Al-Jamaa, Al-Taaleem Al-Damej, Al-Damj Al-Kollie, Al-Damj Al-Tarbawi, and Al-Damj Al-Shoomooli,"*[45] in the CRPD inclusion has been translated into الإشراك، الإدماج (*Al-Idmaj, Al-Ichrak*), which may be confusing, as the words "inclusion" and "inclusive" intend to address the same matter. Khochen-Bagshaw suggests that *"Al-Idmaj"* can implicate that students should adapt themselves according to the educational system as opposite to what should be expected.[46]

Different alternatives may be used and suggested when translating a word, however, using عاهة (*'āha*) as a replacement for impairment raises several issues. عاهة (*'āha*) means deformity rather than impairment, which implies a very negative connotation and denotation. Using this concept does not only discriminate persons with disabilities but also portrays a negative conceptualization of what impairment means. In addition to the negative connotation, the original use of the word عاهة has nothing to do with impairment but it rather means blight or blighted people.[47] Originally, "[i]n classical Arabic, the term 'āha denotes a mark that spoils the presumed wholeness of a thing. In Ibn Manẓūr's seventh-thirteenth-century dictionary Lisān al-'arab, 'āha is defined by a single word—āfa, which itself means 'blight' or 'damage'."[48] It should be clarified that there is a difference between using "blighted people" and "disability" as the latter is narrowed in comparison to the earlier concept.[49] In clearer terms, Richardson has demonstrated that "people of blights were characterised by physical deviance defined as debility, super-ability, and physiognomic undesirability."[50]

As different words have been refused in English, including "dumb" and "handicap," arguments for non-use of the word عاهة ("deformity," "blight") should not be refuted. Ghaly explained that there are some terminologies that have been eliminated due to the negative connotations they hold, such as "'cripple' and 'gimp'."[51] Similarly, the word عاهة ("blight") should not be employed due to its negative connotation and its original vagueness since it basically includes different elements and does not refer to impairment as proposed. The translation that Ghaly used in order to refer to impairment was إعتلال (i'tilāl).[52] This can be considered as a better translation than the one used in CRPD since "i'tilal" does not hold the same negative connotation as in "عاهة". The use of أصحاب العاهات ("people with impairment") has been also refuted in the document "Say and Do Not Say in the Area of the Rights of Persons with Disabilities" by Muhannad El-Ezza.[53]

Furthermore, the combination of "people with disabilities" has not been acknowledged or welcomed by people with disabilities due to making able-bodiedness a reference to what defines dis/ability.[54] Furthermore, the word disability (إعاقة) is already connected to some unwanted perspectives in the Arab world, which may make some people reluctant to use it and opt for people with special needs (أشخاص ذوي الاحتياجات الخاصة) as an alternative. Overall, using some types of vocabulary such as "'āha" can hinder the level of the inclusivity of Arabic language in regard to the terms that should be used in the field of disability. Preferred Terminology by USAID is given in Table 4.2.

Table 4.2: United State Agency for International Development (2007). Language and definitions. Washington, p. 2

Inappropriate language	Appropriate language
Visually impaired, visual impairment, "the blind"	Low vision, blind, person who is blind
Wheelchair bound, confined to a wheelchair, wheelchair person	Wheelchair user, person who uses a wheelchair
Handicap parking, disabled parking	Accessible parking, disability parking
Dumb, mute	Person who cannot speak, has difficulty speaking, uses synthetic speech, is non-vocal, non-verbal
Stutterer, tongue-tied	Person who has a speech or communication disability
CP victim, spastic	Person with cerebral palsy
Epileptic	Person with epilepsy, person with seizure disorder
Fit, attack	Seizure, epileptic episode or event
Crazy, lunatic, insane, mentally ill, mental disorder	Person with a psychosocial disability, person with an emotional disability
Retard, mentally defective, moron, idiot, imbecile	Person with an intellectual disability
Down's person, mongoloid	Person with Down syndrome

Slow learner, retarded	Person with specific learning disability
Dwarf, midget	Person of small stature, person of short stature, little person
"The paraplegic," "the quadriplegic"	Person with paraplegia, person with spinal cord injury
Birth defect	Person with a congenital disability, disabled from birth
Post-polio, suffered from polio	Person with post-polio syndrome, person with a disability as a result of polio
Homebound	Stay-at-home, hard for the person to get out

Research aims

This research aims to analyse different research papers written in the Algerian context in three different languages: Arabic, French, and English. It aims at unveiling the terminology that is used in the Algerian research area and the extent it abides by the general tenets promoted by CRPD and USAID. It aims at exploring the type of terminologies used in these studies and their consistency in the three languages.

Theoretical framework

The theories used in this study are critical disability theory (CDT) and labeling theory (LT) in order to analyse the linguistic choices made in the selected papers. According to Feys (2015), critical disability studies address both the rights of people with disabilities and how to promote culture of diversity and inclusion. It seeks at fostering and ameliorating the lives and experiences of this group of people.[55] In CDT, valuing diversity is one of the most primordial aspects that builds a society that believes in neurodiversity and embraces differences.[56] Thus, this research will be using critical disability theory as a lens to analyse aspects of the language used to refer to individuals with disabilities in the Algerian context. On the other hand, labeling theory is employed as it allows me to look into the perspectives from where these labels have derived and been constructed. The way children/individuals with disabilities are labeled affects their daily lives, as certain labels may have negative connotations and purposes of exclusion and a setting of boundaries that prevents them from participating as community members. In this perspective, Becker argued that the way people are labeled affects how they self-perceive themselves and how society perceives them.[57] Bernburg (2009) ratified that labeling theory is not only considered to be suitable for "other theories of crime and deviance" but it can also assist in understanding and interpreting "individual deviant behaviour," since this theory accentuates "social exclusion," which makes it compatible and corresponding to other sociological theories.[58] Using these theories will help in situating the image of the terminology used to describe people with disabilities in the Algerian context from a critical perspective.

Methodology

The methodology adopted for this research is based on a thematic analysis of a group of selected papers. I will present in this section the methodology I used in order to search and review the papers analysed in this study.

First, the analysed papers in this study have been published from 2015 to 2020. The reason for this decision was that Algeria submitted the first monitoring reports after signing and/or ratifying the Convention on the Rights of Persons with Disabilities due in 2012 during 2015. The methodology of the articles was not among the selection criteria as all papers were analysed regardless of their approach: quantitative, qualitative, or mixed methods. Any paper that was published in a field related to social sciences, psychology, or education was included. Exclusion criteria include timeline and field of study (education, psychology, social sciences). I made my search for articles on different online databases including The Algerian Scientific Journal platform, *Dar Almandumah*, *Insaniyat*, The Journal of Studies in Language, Culture and Society (JSLCS), and

Google Scholar in order to gather articles that tackled aspects of inclusion in the Algerian context. The number of research papers that I found
using the previously explained criteria is forty-eight: French: 16, Arabic:
21, English: 11.

Also, the level of visibility of Algerian research articles in the Algerian
context is quite limited, which means that there are certain works that
may have been unintentionally excluded. Babori and Aknouche explain
that "the poor visibility of research findings coming out of institutional
repositories is a major challenge for Algerian scholarship."[59] They also
recommend, for instance, the need for:

- enabl[ing] Google Scholar indexing features
- develop[ing] a national open access policy for institutional policies requiring mandatory deposit
- allow[ing] full text downloading of the grey literature in the
  repositories.[60]

From another angle, Zoreli argued that in order to promote inclusion in
the Algerian society, research is highly recommended in this area.[61] He
gave an example of the research done at the postgraduate level in one
of the Algerian universities and he found that none of the postgraduate
students worked on an inclusion/disability related topic.[62] Hence, he con-
cluded that students, supervisors, and researchers are not interested in
or have no concerns regarding the issues of individuals with disabilities.[63]

Along the same lines, the areas of research articles that were chosen
were mainly education, social sciences, and psychology in which some
articles were excluded because they did not belong to the previously
mentioned research domains. My focus on education, social sciences,
and psychology is driven by my research background, and also due to
the high percentage of papers written in this field in the Algerian context.
The keywords mentioned in Table 4.3 were used to do the search.

Table 4.3: Searching keywords

English	French (Français)	Arabic (اللغة العربية)
Inclusive Education	*L'insertion scolaire/ éducation inclusive*	تعليم جامع
Special Needs	*Besoins spéciaux*	الاحتياجات الخاصة
Special Educational Needs	*Besoins éducatifs particuliers ou spécifiques*	الاحتياجات التعليمية الخاصة
Disorder	*Désordre/ Trouble*	فوضى
Ability	*Capacité*	القدرة
Disability	*Handicap*	الإعاقة
Integration	*Intégration*	الدمج
Integrated Education	*Intégration scolaire*	الدمج المدرسي
Disabled	*Handicapés*	ذوي الإعاقة
Special Education	*Education spécialisée/ Enseignement spécialisé*	تربية خاصة
Persons with disabilities	*Personnes handicapées*	الأشخاص ذوي الإعاقة

The analyses of this research are based on the overall acceptance of terms according to the principles of inclusive language that have been adopted in the Convention on Rights of Persons with Disabilities (CRPD) (English, Arabic, and French) and the United States Agency for International Development (USAID) that provides a list of acceptable and unacceptable words that are used to describe individuals with disabilities.[64] As has been clarified above, CRPD choice of terminology cannot be said to be inclusive in the Arabic language but since Algeria has signed this treaty, it may have certain influential effects. Therefore, throughout this chapter reference will be made to both CRPD and USAID.

The collected data were analysed thematically in which the articles were deeply read, codes were assigned, and finally themes were selected. According to Braun and Clarke, identification, analysis, and reporting the themes found within the gathered data are what define thematic analysis as a method to analyzing data.[65] Although the articles are written in three different languages, thematic analysis has been done in English, thereby giving an overall sense of the type of terminologies used in each language.

Data analysis

Three main themes were derived from these analyses, which are as follows: positivity versus negativity of words, disability models, person-first versus identity-first language, and inclusion versus integration.

Positivity versus negativity of words

Most authors used terms in an inconsistent manner. Looking at the positive items included within these articles, the benefits of integration/inclusion for some children such as pupils with hearing impairments were accentuated.[66]

The term "children with special needs" is being avoided by many activists and organizations since everyone has special needs regardless of their differences.[67] Nonetheless, some authors used this expression (see Appendix 4.1, section A). Gernsbacher, Raimond, Balinghasay, and Boston found out that "the euphemism special needs is no more effective than the non-euphemised term disability."[68] The use of "mental retardation" has been described as undesirable and displeasing since it gives a sense of discrimination and exclusion[69], however, Boutebal and Yahi and other authors employed this unwelcomed expression to refer to individuals with disabilities (see Appendix 4.1, sections E and O).[70]

Describing children with disabilities as being deviant from the norm or majoritarian principles was also conspicuous. For instance, Nasser Bey and Ben Abdel Al-Rahman explained that there is a need to cultivate culture of acceptance among students particularly "normal children" towards "unusual children" as part of implementing integration.[71] Children with disabilities were described as "non-normal" in comparison to the common majoritarian perspectives of normality. The phrase/ expression "normal children" was used by several authors (see Appendix 4.1, section E).

It was noticed that the phrase "the disabled" re-occurred in various articles written in French. The word *handicapés* ("the disabled"), which is considered unacceptable and to be avoided, was used by some researchers such as Brahmi.[72] Furthermore, through looking into the English language papers, the most common words that were used did not depict the picture of disability as undesirable in which reference was made to the development that occurred in regard to terminology used to refer to disability.[73] Indeed, the use of undesirable terminology was also mentioned by some research in which Bessai in reference to the French language Collins Robert dictionary (1993) explained "that the term disability that has replaced other words as invalid, abnormal, and inappropriate, is one of 'these social cuts masking the harsh realities.'"[74]

In the three languages, although understanding was demonstrated to some extent, using words and phrases such as "handicapped," "mentally disabled," "the disabled," and "mental retardation" (see Appendix 4.1, sections B, D, H, I, and L) questions the awareness of the researchers in regard to words that should be used to address people with disabilities. Also, there are cases when direct translation from French to English was used: Association d'Aide aux Inadaptes Mentaux de Bejaia was translated into Association for Mentally Maladjusted Children or The Association for Mentally Unsound Children (the "challenge" of Bejaia).[75] Although translation can be difficult and can change the meaning of sentences, the names of the association in both languages portray a negative association between labeling and disability. In a study conducted by Hamdouche and Daas, there is an issue in terms of terminology between the abstracts written in Arabic and English in which *Mou'awaqoun* ("disabled") and *Mou'aaqoun* ("disabled") is translated into people with disabilities and the disabled.[76] Also, the authors provided a definition of "the disabled" using different references. They initially refer to the definition provided by the International Labour Organization (1955), that being "the inability to have a permanent job due to an impairment."[77] They also referred to other definitions that refer to acquired/inherited disabilities in addition to another definition that refers to inability of performing one's job because of some incapabilities that can be due to accident, illness, or from birth.[78]

Furthermore, Saidi and Bouizem referred to the fact that the concept of people with special needs has been used in order to avoid the psychological effects associated with words such as "disabled," "paralysed," and "a person with impairment."[79] Looking at the terminologies that were used in these articles, in the three languages, fluctuations of awareness can be observed in which one article contained both internationally acceptable and inacceptable concepts.

Disability models

The continuous debate between the social and medical models cannot be avoided when it comes to disability related research. The social model has been developed as a counter-reaction to the medical one in order to eliminate the overemphasis on pathologizing and medicalizing persons with disabilities.[80]

Indeed, it was conspicuous in the articles that were analysed that the medical model is the most dominant one. The words that were used imply a medical perspective toward disability such as suffering and disease. For instance, in an article about children with hearing impairment, Majkoune, Hamdeche, and Zellal described it as an infection (إصابة) that impedes the individual's life.[81] The use of some words such as "suffering," "disease," "normal," "intellectual deficiency," "incapacity related to behaviour," "incapacity," "fragile," "disorder," and "mental disorder" depicted a medical model attitude.[82]

The verb "suffering" has been used several times in these papers to refer to the fact that their impairment does not allow them to perform their daily tasks as other neurotypical individuals, implying sense of normalization. It is suggested that using concepts such as suffering indicates that people with disabilities are regarded as "victims and patients," suggesting also the idea of normalization and medicalization.[83] Also, the use of the word "suffering" may be intimidating as well since people do not suffer from autism but from some medical or psychiatric issues. The term "suffer" (souffre, يعاني) was used in all three languages. Examples include:

- Their children suffer from hearing disability ("hearing impairment") (يعاني أبنائهم من إعاقة الصمم).[84]

- The individual who suffers from hearing loss (الشخص الذي يعاني من فقدان سمعي).[85]
- A child who suffers from autism spectrum disorder (طفل يعاني من اضطراب طيف التوحد).
- Children who suffer from disabilities (الأطفال الذين يعانون من الإعاقة).[86]
- Forty-four percent suffer from physical disability.[87]
- Might suffer from low self-esteem.[88]
- *Les personnes souffrant des maladies telles la dyslexie* ("People suffering from diseases such as dyslexia").[89]

In a similar vein, Brahmi referred to children with disabilities using the categorical structure of individuals who "suffer" from various "pathologies," such as "trisomy 21" (Down syndrome).[90]

Disability was also depicted as a problem: "those who have mental problems," "physical problem," "are forms of neurological or mental problems," "normal learners," "able learners," "normal students";[91] "an ordinary child," "an abnormal formation";[92] "normal children," "normal schools," "mild mental disability," "minor mental disability," "mental retardation."[93] The phrase أسوياء "the fits" which as a noun can also be translated to "the normal," was used by many authors in opposition to people with disabilities (see Appendix 4.1, section V). Also, the word سليمين ("sound") was used to refer to neurotypical individuals.

There was an ostensible use of terms that portray medical attitudes toward people with disabilities, nonetheless, some researchers highlighted different ways of perceiving disability. According to Belaid and Sarnou, "a disability should not refer to what people are, but rather it is a weakness or an impairment that prevents people from performing necessary tasks."[94] These attitudes may also be regarded as a descriptor of charity model since the latter views people with disabilities as victims and weak.[95] Although both authors tried to avoid attributing disability to individuals, they portrayed a medical view in their description of disability using the word "weakness." Another element that was noticed in many studies is the sample of students with disabilities researched are mostly part of special classes, schools, or centers. This indicates the institutionalization of disability and people with disabilities noticed in different models of disability, including medical, individual, and charity models of disability.[96]

Moreover, intellectual disability was referred to as "mental weakness" that has different degrees (from mild to severe).[97] In the same article, the author mentioned that due to an increase in "mental weakness," the number of specialized classes has increased.[98] There was also reference to the fact that there are proponents of the social model who do not agree on referring to disability as "a sickness."[99]

Person first versus identity first language

As a way to promote inclusivity within social, cultural, and linguistic structures, person-first language aims at eliminating disability-first led discourses and gives priority for individuals over their differences from humanitarian lenses.[100] Although person-first seems as a panacea that would help to ensure inclusion in today's societies, there are individuals within communities of people with disabilities who do not agree with these choices, such as the autism community, which is divided between proponents and opposers.[101] Prioritizing one's disability emphasizes differences that can lead to exclusion. Nonetheless, Brown argued against people-first language, as she believed that it is a false assumption to say that autism can be detached from the individual.[102] It actually represents their identity, which establishes their value as individuals.[103] Discussion over whether person-first language or identity-first language is more effective and inclusive was also explicitly/implicitly indicated in the analysed research papers.

The structure of the Arabic language requires certain word ordering and grammatical rules. When it comes to the dilemma of person-first versus identity-first language choices, different authors used different structures within the same paper, which made it confusing to situate the position of the researchers.

To begin with, terms such as متخلف، معاق، البكم، الصم ("deaf," "dumb," "handicapped/disabled," "backward") are not only identity-first but also unacceptable ways of addressing people with disabilities (see Appendix 4.1, section P).[104] Furthermore, other labels such as المعوق \ المعاق، ذهنيا معوقين 21، صبغي للثلاثي حامل طفل ("child carrying (with) chromosome 21," "mentally disabled," "the disabled") implies identity and person first but the way it is structured is not accepted according to CRPD[105] and USAID[106] as they prioritize disability and phrase it in a manner that seems to be offensive (Appendix 4.1, sections D and R).

From another angle, other researchers used person-first language such as children with disabilities or children with special needs (see Appendix 4.1, sections A and K). According to USAID these words are accepted except for using children with special needs as everyone has special needs and requirements regardless of their differences.[107] When analyzing these pieces of research, it was noticed that grammatical differences can make it difficult to understand what stands for person first or identity first in each language. In the French language, examples of person first language were *enfants autistes* ("autistic children"), *personne handicapée* ("disabled/handicapped person or persons with disabilities"), and so on (see Appendix 4.1, section K). There may be a confusion when translating these concepts into English due to some grammatical rules that make the words that are supposed to be person-first in French transformed into identity-first language in English. This may suggest there is a need for revising these terms and adding the auxiliary verb (*avoir* or "have"), which may amplify and provide a more comprehensive image such as *enfants ayant un handicap* ("children with a disability"). Furthermore, using CRPD guidance for terminology would suggest that *personne handicapée* can be translated into persons with disabilities. However, Giami, Korpes, and Lavigne translated *les personnes handicapées* to be translated as "handicapped persons."[108] For this reason, I use two translations of *personne handicapée*: "person with disabilities" and "disabled/handicapped person."

Other examples of person-first language were when referring to a specific disability or difference such as: "students with dyslexia," "learners with LD" (learning disabilities), "learners with reading impairment."[109] On the other hand, identity-first language was also used: "dyslexic" "autistic students."[110] The way language was chosen does not seem to have one particular angle as the same article contained both person-first and identity-first terminologies, which questions whether authors are aware of these differences. As previously illustrated, Belaid and Sarnou explain that disability should not be attributed to the individual, which may explain a tendency toward person-first language and a separated status between disability and people.[111] Nonetheless, they also describe people with disabilities as being weak and vulnerable who require assistance in which their difference is perceived as causing limitations.[112]

Inclusion versus integration

In the educational setting, a distinction between inclusive and integrative education has been made. According to CRPD General Comment Number 4, integration refers to a situation where children with disabilities are physically placed into a mainstream school, but they are required to acclimate himself/herself according to the setting.[113] On the other hand, inclusion refers to amending the whole curriculum and teaching pedagogies as well as the environment in order to make it inclusive and welcoming to everyone.[114] It indeed brings both neurotypical and disabled children together in the same classroom using an inclusive curriculum that meets everyone's needs.[115]

In the reviewed research papers, inconsistency and ambivalence were dominant. Bouzid and Mekhoukh have demonstrated the difference between integration and inclusion by referring to the English translation of each concept in which they translated *l'intégration* to "mainstreaming" and *l'inclusion* to "inclusive education."[116] Reference to this distinction was made in order to emphasize the shift that happened in scientific research in which the focus has been on moving from mainstreaming to inclusive education during the late 1980s and start of the 1990s.[117] It should be explained that in the French version of CRPD, inclusive education has been translated into *insertion scolaire*, which is different from *l'intégration scolaire*.

A similar observation was made in an article written in English in which Boutebal and Yahi used the term "integrative education" or "integration" to refer to both integration and inclusion with reference to their French equivalent ("integrative education," from *l'éducation inclusive*, *l'éducation integrative*).[118] On the other hand, Bessai used the term "inclusion" and "integration" as synonyms in which inclusive education was defined as "an educational system that takes into account individual needs in teaching and learning of all children in vulnerable situations; children with disabilities, street children, children belonging to ethnic minorities, children from nomads/refugees, families [...] etc.."[119] Nonetheless, he later referred to integration and the possibility of integrating children with disability in which he states "we must distinguish between two types or two ways of integration: integration with integrated support at school and integration with support from outside the school."[120] The use of terms does not provide a clear image about the author's understanding, conceptualization of or attitudes toward integration and inclusive education. From another angle, Bouraoui and Chabi explain that "inclusive education is not school integration."[121]

In a similar vein, in Arabic there are different terms that are currently used to refer to inclusion/integration. According to Khochen-Bagshaw, "Inclusive education has been translated as *Al-Taaleem Al-Jamaa, Al-Taaleem Al-Damej, Al-Damj Al-Kollie, Al-Damj Al-Tarbawi, and Al-Damj Al-Shoomooli.*"[122] She further explains that some concepts portray that students are the ones who should adapt to the system rather than the system adapting to them, such as *"Al-Idmaj and Al-Indemaj."*[123] From another angle, she suggests that *"Al-damj"* reflects a more inclusive stance, that is, this concept mirrors that students are "part of the system."[124] In the Algerian context, Serridj demonstrated this issue by making a distinction in Arabic between the different meanings of integration in Arabic and their equivalence in English.[125] However, this understanding may not be shared by all researchers and stakeholders in Algeria. Table 4.4 is adapted from Serridj using her translation of certain concepts.

Table 4.4: English translation of the different meanings of the word "integration"[126]

English Equivalence	Arabic
Integration	الدمج بمعنى التكامل
Mainstreaming	الدمج بمعنى توحيد المساق التعليمي
Inclusion	الدمج الشامل أو الاستيعاب

In Table 4.4 it can be noticed that the word "integration" (الدمج) is used in all concepts with different additional words that would describe the English equivalence. In the analysed set of articles, the term "integration" (الدمج) was used to describe the philosophical assumptions underlying inclusive education, mainstreaming, or integration. However, it seems that this exchangeable mixed use between integration and inclusion is not only prevalent in Algeria but in all the Arabic-speaking countries. Indeed, this point has been highlighted by Khochen-Bagshaw, who confirms that "'integration' and 'inclusion' have been used interchangeably in Arabic-speaking countries."[127]

The confusion that has been observed in research articles is also shared by the Committee on the Rights of Persons with Disabilities when reviewing the report on Algeria, which states that "there might be some confusion about the concept of inclusive education, which in Algeria seemed to be confounded with integrated education."[128] In the analysed set of articles, the term "integration" (الدمج) was used to describe the philosophical assumptions underlying inclusive education, mainstreaming, or integration.

In making a difference between the various types of available education for people with disabilities, Bessai distinguished between full and partial educational integration.[129] In other cases, the meaning behind the use of the word "integration" referred to inclusive education or mainstreaming; Bechatta and Chuiale, for example, state that educational integration refers to the process where a child is placed in a general classroom with a specific pedagogical plan in which this process can be either done fully or partially.[130] It was also noticed in an article written in Arabic that the researchers cited Hallahan and Kauffman who are against inclusive education particularly in their book *Illusion of Full Inclusion*.[131] This may be due to the lack of translated versions of how inclusive education works in Arabic as well as a lack of research publications in this field in Arabic-speaking countries.

From another angle, Bouhadj, Mansouri, and Mezari argued that inclusion (integration) has spread recently in many countries around the world, although it has been criticized by many researchers. They define inclusion (integration) as the process of

> [p]roviding all services and care for people with special needs in an environment far from isolation, which is the normal classroom environment in the regular school, or in a regular school classroom or in the so-called resource rooms, which provide services for people with special needs for some time.[132]

The definition provided by the authors does not clarify whether they refer to inclusive education, integration, or mainstreaming. The term they used in the article is *Al-damj* (الدمج), which has different translations depending on its use. To summarize, although there are researchers who have provided a clear understanding of inclusive education, it is still ambiguous and inconsistent, and this was a shared element in the major-ity of the selected papers. Overall, Khochen-Bagshaw concludes "that so many different terms [...] being used to refer to the same concept suggests that inclusive education is still open to, or vulnerable to, a wide interpre-tation in the Arabic language."[133]

Discussion

Throughout the analysis, regardless of which language was used, there were gaps and inconsistent use of certain concepts, fluctuating between inclusivity and exclusion as well as the dominance of "super-crip" and euphemistic attitudes. Using the most appropriate terminology is very crucial since some terms may be offensive, discriminatory, or exclusive, leading to emphasizing difference and categorization.

In viewing the story line of this research through a critical disabil-ity theory (CDT) lens, difference is not neglected but it should rather be valued. Looking at the selected articles, there were fluctuations in the terminologies used and in the position taken by the researchers between and within articles. Regarding positivity and negativity of the concepts used, language choice was mostly exclusive, as it did not show that indi-viduals' differences were embraced, which may lead to exclusion and discrimination.[134]

Also, language choice depicts the attitudes and perceptions that indi-viduals have toward disability, as the way disability is conceptualized may position people with disabilities in a powerless status.[135] Indeed, CDT perceives language as having the power of bringing "ideological implica-tions" and it is politically structured.[136] Although there were several gaps within the language used, Bessai pointed at the new conception of handi-cap and the reason behind the use of disability.[137]

The medical model was prevalent and predominant in most of the analysed articles. Disability was regarded as a problem and people with disabilities are people with problems that limit their accessibility to and performance of their daily activities. This has been accentuated by CDT in which Hosking argued that disability is traditionally interpreted as a "personal misfortune" by liberalists, and it should be remedied as a way to meet the societal norms and standards that derived from "nor-malcy" attitudes toward disability.[138] This perspective that was articu-lated by several authors, intentionally or unintentionally, delineates the principles of the medical model which views disability as "a medical condition."[139]

The third theme that was discussed in this chapter was person-first versus identity-first language. There was not a clear idea about which side of the debate the authors opted for but labeling and use of undesirable terms such as "mentally retarded," "mentally disabled," and "handicapped" was noticed. Researchers in this case can be considered as people in power who have picked certain concepts to describe people with disabilities. This status of power can be observed in labeling theory in which institutionalization of labels would be driven by the judgments that have been already established and those who are part of a particular group would be impacted by them.[140] Power is owned by institutions in which "organisations possess the capacity to label and deal with individuals as deviants."[141]

Inclusive education was also conceptualized and explained differently, mostly confused, and used interchangeably with integration or mainstreaming in the three selected languages. The Algerian choice of terminology has been regarded as inconsistent. Indeed, there is inconsistent use of terminology within the same paper, for instance: difference between integration and inclusion was sometimes misunderstood and mis-conceptualized by different authors in which some of them used the concepts interchangeably throughout the article.[142] Issues with inconsistency in terminology choice and use were also highlighted by the Committee on the Rights of Persons with Disabilities that reviewed the Algerian reports on the Convention on the Rights of Persons with Disabilities (see "Inclusion Versus Integration").[143] The way the terms have been translated may have been the reason behind this mixture between terms, which does not mean that their choices were wrong especially when it comes to Arabic. The terms were first introduced in English, which makes it difficult to find equivalent vocabulary that may have similar meaning.

Overall, the choices of terminology have been influenced by the medical model, which pathologizes disability. The way disability has been pictured does not show deconstruction of prejudice, but it rather highlights it. Unlike these wordings that were used, in some cases (intentionally or unintentionally) difference was appreciated and positively perceived while promoting and visualizing equality in a framework that is based on diversity.[144]

To conclude, when reading the selected papers, it seems that there are different factors that may have influenced researchers' choices of terminology. As it has been already discussed, the detour that has taken place in the world of disability terminology due to CRPD can be one of these factors. Indeed, the use of phrases such as *personnes handicapées*, أشخاص ذوي الإعاقة, or persons with disabilities demonstrate the influence of the CRPD (e.g., see Appendix 4.1, section K). Also, there were some direct translations from French to Arabic, which shows the influence of French literature on those who write in Arabic.[145]

Conclusion

This article has aspired to analyse the terminology that is used by Algerian researchers to refer to disability in three different languages (Arabic, French, and English). Inclusive education research is novel in Algeria and does not have a strong base due to the different languages used to refer to inclusion and disability. Through the analysis, it was disclosed that there is not an established way of reference or addressing disability in Algeria. Different authors used different concepts in which some used literal translation from French to Arabic, while others appear to have opted for concepts used by doctors and policymakers thus mirroring a medical model.[146] A conclusion cannot be completely made about these authors' attitudes and understanding of disability as, within the same text, different perspectives from individual and medical models were used. In the end, this chapter advocates the standardization of new terms that are respectful, take into consideration linguistic connotations, and better express the local culture.

Disability in the Algerian context and what terminology should be advocated

It is difficult to say what is suitable and what is unsuitable as this process requires a long process of research. I believe that people with disabilities should be asked about their preferred terminology in order to have an equitable terminology based on their own choices. For instance, there was a study conducted by Kenny et al. (2016) to explore autistic people's preferences of terminology.[147] This will not only promote inclusivity and equity but will provide people with disabilities an opportunity to be part of the process of decision-making.

The term "people with disabilities" (أشخاص ذوي الإعاقة) that has been embraced and promoted by CRPD has been used in different articles (see Appendix 4.1, section K). Attitudes regarding this expression are different as there are those who accept it and others who do not.[148] It is similar to the situation with the concept "persons with disabilities," which has been refused by advocates of "identity-first language" as well as those who preferred "people with special (educational) needs."

On the other hand, UAE has created its own terminology and currently uses "People of determination" (أصحاب الهمم), which gives a sense of "supercrip" that has been criticized by many scholars. Although this concept of "people of determination" (أصحاب الهمم) intends to glorify and motivate people with disabilities, it also undermines their abilities and makes them look less abled than others. This can be included in the idea of supercrip in which people with disabilities are seen as achievers and exemplars when they *overcome* their assigned disability. Arguments for refusal to use phrases such as "ذوي الهمم" (people of determination) is due to its euphemistic reason that has sought to motivate people with disabilities. Other words that have been regarded as euphemism in Arabic include "*al-fi'āt al-khāṣṣa* ('special groups'), *dhawū al-iḥtiyājāt al-khāṣṣa* ('people with special needs'), *al-afrād ghayr al-'ādiyyīn* ('abnormal individuals')."[149]

The word used in the French language official documents including CRPD (handicap, *personne handicapée*) is originally an English concept. Giami, Korpès, and Lavigne explained that "[i]n France the term 'handicap' is not only used as a noun, it is also used as an attribute to designate people living with disabilities in the following term: 'les personnes handicapées' (to be translated as 'handicapped persons')."[150] They also demonstrated the negativity associated with the word "handicapped" and that researchers are advised not to use it in research and scientific works.[151] Undeniably, there are negative associations connected with the word *un handicapée* ("disabled"). Interestingly, Giami, Korpes, and Lavigne surprisingly argued that while many countries avoid using the word "handicapped," it is still accepted and utilized in France.[152]

One solution that can be proposed in order to promote inclusive language is that instead of giving random labels, research should be conducted in which the opinion of people with disabilities themselves is taken into consideration in every context. For example, in some Western countries, there have been several studies within autism communities in which autistic people alongside their guardians and other professionals were asked about their preferred terminology.[153] I do not mean that we should adopt Western methods or concepts, but it is important to take into consideration the opinions of persons with disabilities as they are the focal point of this question.

Appendix 4.1

Section	Arabic	French	English	Terminology used by
A	(فئة) ذوي الاحتياجات الخاصة	Personnes aux/avec besoins spécifiques/ particuliers	People with special needs	Abbassi and Nait Bouda (2019) Azdaou and Ghouileme (2018) Bechatta and Chuiale (2018) Belaid and Sarnou (2019) Benguesmia and Chouial (2019) Bouhadj, Mansouri, and Mezari (2018) Berrekail (2018) Bessai (2018) Bessai (2019b) Bey and Abdel al-Rahman (2019) Bouazza and Belhasini (2018) Bouzid Baa and Mekhoukh (2019) Brahimi (2018) Chabi (2019) Elmahi and Mekki (2020) Fekih (2019) Ghedeir and Nesba (2018) Guersas and Ouadah (2018) Idri (2019) Kaci (2019) Kheddoussi (2018) Majkoune Hamdeche and Zellal (2015) Oumokrane, Bouraoui, and Chabi (2019) Riad and Daas (2019) Saad (2015) Saidi and Bouizem (2020) Zoreli (2019)

B	معاق / معوقين	*Des handicapés*	Disabled	Bechatta and Chuiale (2018) Belaid and Sarnou (2019) Bessai (2019a) Bouhadj, Mansouri, and Mezari (2018) Bouazza and Belhasini (2018) Boulkroun (2019) Boumediene and Kaid Berraha (2019) Bouraoui and Chabi (2019) Boutebal and Yahi (2018) Brahmi (2019 Elmahi and Mekki (2020) Kerbouche (2019) Kheddoussi (2018) Meziani (2019) Oubaziz (2019) Riad and Daas (2019) Saad (2015) Sabri and Ben Mostfa (2019) Saidi and Bouizem (2020)
C	N/A	*Déficience*	Impairment	Belaid and Sarnou (2019) Bessai (2018) Bessai (2019a) Bessai (2019b) Bouraoui and Chabi (2019) Boutebal and Yahi (2019) Bouzid Baa and Mekhoukh (2019) Brahmi (2019) Fekih (2019) Oubaziz (2019) Sabri and Ben Mostfa (2019)
D	معوقين عقليا، ذهنيا معاقين ذهنيا، عقليا	*Handicapés mentaux*	Mentally disabled (mentally unsound, mentally maladjusted, mentally handicapped)	Azdaou and Ghouileme (2018) Bassai (2018) Bassai (2019b) Bechatta and Chuiale (2018) Belaid and Sarnou (2019) Benamara (2019) Berrekail (2018) Bouazza and Belhasini (2018) Boulkroun (2019) Bouzid Baa and Mekhoukh (2019) Brahmi (2019) Elmahi and Mekki (2020) Oumokrane, Bouraoui, and Chabi (2019) Saidi and Bouizem (2020) Yaaloui and Bouakline (2019)

E	أقرانهم العاديين ("Their normal peers")	*Enfants normaux*	Normal children Ordinary students	Azdaou and Ghouileme (2018) Bechatta and Chuiale (2018) Bekkaoui and Kaiba (2019)) Belaid and Sarnou (2019) Belkadi Nahed (2015) Benamara (2019) Benguesmia and Chouial (2019) Bey and Abdel al-Rahman (2019) Boudari and Bouazza (2019) Boutebal and Yahi (2018) Bouzid and Mekhoukh (2019) Elmahi and Mekki (2020) Ghedeir and Nesba (2018) Idri (2019) Kheddoussi (2018) Saad (2015) Saidi and Bouizem (2020) Yaaloui and Bouakline (2019)
F	أمراض اللغة والتواصل ("Communication and language diseases")	N/A	N/A	Yaaloui and Bouakline (2019)
G	(الأطفال) المصابون (بالإعاقة\الصمم) ("Children suffering of disability/ Children with disabilities")	N/A	N/A	Abdel el-Slam and Qualleti (2018) Azdaou and Ghouileme (2018) Elmahi and Mekki (2020) Kabli (2018) Kharkhache and Bouatta (2016)
H	إعاقة ذهنية	*Handicap mental*	Mental disability	Azdaou and Ghouileme (2018) Boutebal and Yahi (2018) Bouzid Baa and Mekhoukh (2019) Elmahi and Mekki (2020) Yaaloui and Bouakline (2019)
I	متخلفون عقليا\ذهنيا ("Mentally retarded")	N/A	N/A	Bechatta and Chuiale (2018) Bey and Abdel al-Rahman (2019) Kabli (2018) Yaaloui and Bouakline (2019)
J	الأطفال في وضعية إعاقة ("Children in a situation of disability/ Children with disabilities")	*Enfants (personnes) en situation de handicap*	N/A	Benamara (2019) Bey and Abdel al-Rahman (2019) Bouzid Baa and Mekhoukh (2019) Guersas and Ouadah (2018) Kaci (2019) Oubaziz (2019)

K	أطفال ذوي الإعاقة أطفال من ذوي الإعاقة	*Enfants (personnes) handicapées* ("Persons with disabilities/ Disabled persons")	Children (persons) with disabilities	Arezki (2019) Bechatta and Chuiale (2018) Belaid and Sarnou (2019) Benamara (2019) Benguesmia and Chouial (2019) Berrekail (2018) Bessai (2018) Bessai (2019a) Bessai (2019b) Bey and al-Rahman (2019) Boulkroun (2019) Bouhadj, Mansouri, and Mezari (2018) Boumediene and Kaid Berraha (2019) Bouraoui and Chabi (2019) Boutebal and Yahi (2018) Bouzid Baa and Mekhoukh (2019) Brahmi (2019) Elmahi and Mekki (2020) Ghedeir and Nesba (2018) Guersas and Ouadah (2018) Idri (2019) Kaci (2019) Kerbouche (2019) Meziani (2019) Oubaziz (2019) Oumokrane, Bouraoui, and Chabi (2019) Riad and Daas (2019) Sabri and Ben Mostfa (2019) Sahli and Benaissi (2019 Saidi and Bouizem (2020) Yaaloui and Bouakline (2019) Zoreli (2019)
L	N/A	N/A	Mental retardation	Boutebal and Yahi (2018) Sabri and Ben Mostfa (2019)
M	N/A	*Enfants en difficulés (children in difficulties)*	N/A	Bessai (2019a) Bouzid Baa and Mekhoukh (2019) Brahmi (2019) Chabi (2019) Kerbouche (2019) Zoreli (2019)
N	N/A	N/A	Disabling health disorder	Bessai (2019

O	يعاني	*Souffre*	Suffering	Abdel el-Slam and Qualleti (2018) Arezki (2019) Bechatta and Chuiale (2018) Bessai (2018) Bessai (2019a) Bessai (2019b) Bey and Abdel al-Rahman (2019) Bouzid Baa and Mekhoukh (2019) Brahmi (2019) Fekih (2019) Guersas and Ouadah (2018) Idri (2019) Kabli (2018) Kaci (2019) Kerbouche (2019) Kharkhache and Bouatta (2016) Saidi and Bouizem (2020) Yaaloui and Bouakline (2019) Zoreli (2019)
P	الصم، البكم، معاق، متخلف ("Deaf (dumb (handicapped/ Disabled (backward/ retarded")	N/A	N/A	Bechatta and Chuiale (2018) Bey and Abdel al-Rahman (2019) Elmahi and Mekki (2020) Kabli (2018) Kheddoussi (2018) Majkoune Hamdeche and Zellal (2015) Riad and Daas (2019) Yaaloui and Bouakline (2019)
Q	N/A	*Enfants porteurs/ atteints de spina bifida* ("Children carrying (with/ have) spina bifida")	N/A	Bekkaoui and Kaiba (2019)
R	الطفل الحامل للثلاثي الصبغي ٢١ ("Child carrying (with) chromosome 21")	N/A	N/A	Yaaloui and Bouakline (2019)
S	N/A	N/A	Visual impairment Auditory impairment Impairment(s)	Ghedeir and Nesba (2018)
T	N/A	*Personnes porteurs de handicap*	N/A	Guersas and Ouadah (2018)

| U | الطلبة (الأشخاص) المعوقين الأطفال (المعاقين) المعوقين (بصريا، سمعيا، حركيا) | N/A | N/A | Belaadi (2015)
Belkadi (2015)
Benguesmia and Chouial (2019)
Berrekail (2018)
Ghedeir and Nesba (2018)
Saidi and Bouizem (2020) |
| V | أسوياء سليمين | N/A | N/A | Belaadi (2015)
Belkaid (2015) |

Appendix 4.2.

Number	Author(s)/ Date(s)	Title(s)	Language
1.	Abbassi, A. & Nait Bouda, F. (2019)	L'inclusion scolaire de l'enfant autiste : un droit, une thérapie et un prélude pour une intégration sociale	French
2.	Bekkaoui, R. & Kaiba, N. (2019)	Enseignement inclusif des enfants atteints de Spina Bifida dans la wilaya de Bejaia: État des lieux et perspectives	French
3.	Bessai, R. (2019a)	Le soutien psychopédagogique de l'enfant handicapé : Le rôle des SESSAD	French
4.	Nasser Bey & Ben Abdel Al-Rahman, 2019	Dawr al-nashaat al-badanee al-riyaadee fee damj al-'atfaal dhawee al-'e'aaqa al-ssam'eya wa al-dhehneyya ma'a al-atfaal al-'adeyeen fee al-madaares al-'omoumeya	Arabic
5.	Boutebal, Saad Eddine & Yahi, Samia, 2018	Inclusion of the children with disabilities among school in Algeria	English
6.	Bessai, Rachid (2019b)	The Role of Associations in the Process of Inclusive Education of Children with Disabilities Journal of Studies in Language.	English
7.	Bessai, Rachid (2018)	Access to Schooling for People with Special Needs in Algeria	English
8.	Guersas, Hocine and Ouadah, Lamri (2018)	Intégration des Étudiants Handicapés aux Établissements de L'enseignement Supérieur	French
9.	Arezki, H. (2019)	Projet: Mon accessibilité, mon autonomie	French
10.	Azdaou, C. & Ghouileme, H. (2018)	Istraateejeeyaat al-tasneef al-'ohadhee al-'achkaal al-handaseya 'end al-'atfaal al-mousaabeen bemotalaazemah	Arabic

11.	Bechatta, M. & Chuiale, S. (2018)	Athar al-damj al-madrsee fi mafhoum al-dhat lada almo'aq sam'eyan	Arabic
12.	Belaid, L. & Sarnou, H. (2019)	University for All: Including Special Needs Learners in Education	English
13.	Benamara, A. (2019)	Scolarité inclusive, entre concept et réalité	French
14.	Boudari, A. & Bouazza, S. (2019)	Mahaaraat al-hisaab 'enda al-tefl al-'asam: Diraasa moqaarana bayna 'atfaal som modmajeen fee al-madaares al-'aadeya w'atfaal som ghayr modmajeen feehaa	Arabic
15.	Boulkroun, F. (2019)	Widening the Circle: Differentiating Instruction through Explicit and Implicit Grammar Teaching for Inclusion Purposes	English
16.	Boumediene, H. & Kaid Berrahal, F. (2019)	Moving Forward in Inclusive Education: Approaches and Opportunities for Learners with Disabilities	English
17.	Bouzid Baa, S. & Mekhoukh, H. (2019)	Scolarisation des enfants à besoins spécifiques: d'un enseignement intégratif à un enseignement inclusif	French
18.	Chabi, T. (2019)	Le tutorat à l'université de Bejaia, Etat des lieux et perspectives	French
19.	Elmahi, Z. & Mekki, M. (2020)	Al-atfaal al-motamadrisoun min dawi al-'ahteyaajaat al-khaasa be al- Jazaa'er – bayna al-waaqe' wa al-tatalo'aat	Arabic
20.	Fekih, M. (March, 2019)	EFL Teachers' Awareness of Dyslexia in Algerian Middle Schools	English
21.	Kabli, K. (2018)	So'oubaat al-ta'alom lada talaameedh al-ta'leem al-'ebtedaa'ee beba'ḍ al-madaares al-abtedaa'eya -al-sana al-khaamesa ebtedaa'ee kanamoudhaj-: Deraasa maydaaneya Be Al-Blida	Arabic
22.	Kaci, F. (2019)	Handicapés : Entre Bonne Volonté et Triste Réalités	French
23.	Kerbouche, A. (2019)	Soutien et accompagnement de l'étudiant handicapé Algérien	French
24.	Kharkhache, C. & Bouatta, A. (2016)	Ta'theer al-'elaaj al-soloukee al-ma'refee 'alaa al-ḍaght wa 'estraateejeyaat al-ta'aamol lada abaa' al-'atfaal al-som: diraasa maydaneya be-madrasat sighaar al-som be-welaayat Al-M'Sila	Arabic
25.	Kheddoussi, K. (2018)	Al-seha al-nafseya ledhawee al-'ehteyaajaat al-khaasa wa 'aaleyaat damjehom	Arabic

26.	Majkoune Hamdeche, S. & Zellal, N. (2015)	Tqdeer al-dhaat lada al-atfaal al-som al-modmajeen w ghayr al-modmajeen fee al-madaares al-'aadeya: Deraasa maydaaneya moqaarana	Arabic
27.	Meziani, K. (2019)	Des situations d'apprentissage handicapantes à une conception ergonomique des situations d'apprentissage des élèves handicapés	French
28.	Oumokrane, H., Bouraoui, K. & Chabi, T. (2019)	Rendre efficients, les dispositifs d'inclusion pour les personnes avec besoins spécifiques	French
29.	Yaaloui, K. & Bouakline, C. (2019)	Deraasa moqaarana ledawr al-damj al-madrasee fe tahseen ektesasb ba'd al-mafaaheem al-makaaneya lada al-tefl al-haamel lethoulaathee al-sabghee 21 dhawee 8 elaa 12 sana	Arabic
30.	Zoreli, M.A. (2019)	L'Université de Bejaia: enseignement inclusive et solidarité-éthique, entre les traditions nourricières de bonnes pratiques et la camisole de force bureaucratique	French
31.	Kamel Bouraoui & Tayeb Chabi, 2019	Inclusive Education: Case of the Region of Bejaia.	English
32.	Ghedeir Brahim Mohammed and Nesba Asma (2018)	Adjusting Foreign Languages' Syllabuses to the Specific Academic Needs of Students with Special Needs	English
33.	Ibrahim Belaadi, 2015	Ishkaaliyat 'al-ta'arrof 'ala 'al-'atfaal al-mo'aaqeen dihniyan fee 'Al-Jazaa'er	Arabic
34.	Belkadi Nahed, 2015	Taqdeer 'al-daat 'enda 'al-morahiqaat 'al-mosaabaat be-e'aaqa sam'eyya motawaseta	Arabic
35.	Bouhadj, Mansouri, and Mezari (2018)	'Al-damj 'al-'akaadeemee le-'al-tfaal dawee 'al-'ehtiyajaat 'al-khaasa fee marhalat maa kabla 'al-madrasa: diraasa maydaneeya 'alaa mosatawaa mudeereyat 'al-tarbeya lewelaayat Bouïra	Arabic
36.	Saad Elhadj (2015)	'Etijahaat dawee ihtiyajaat 'al-khaasa nahwa tatbiqaat 'al-'argonoumyaa 'al-mokhassasa lahom wa 'atharohaa 'ala amnehom 'al-nafsee	Arabic
37.	Bouazza Rabha and Belhasini Warda, 2018	Moustawaa 'al-daght 'al-modrak ladaa 'ayyena men 'oumahaat 'al-'atfaal 'al-mo'aaqeen 'aqliyan	Arabic
38.	Saidi Fatima Zohra and Bouizem Aicha, (2020)	The legal care for rights of persons with special needs in Algerian legislation	English

39;	Berrekail and Benmostfa (2018)	Hoqouq dawee 'al-'ehtiyaajaat 'al-khaasa fee 'al-nedaam 'al-qaanounee 'al-Jaza'eree	Arabic
40.	Farid Benguesmia and Samia Chouial (2019)	Qera'a tahleeleya fee manaahej 'al-deraaseyya 'al-mowajaha nahwa 'al-'atfaal 'al-mo'awaqeen sam'eyan bel-Jaza'er	Arabic
41.	Hamdouche riad and Ahmad Daas (2019)	Legal Protection for People With Disabilities in the Arab Countries: A Case Study Algeria and Egypt	English
42.	Sahli Naima Bouhass and Benaissi Fawzia (2019)	Education For All: Promoting Inclusive Pedagogy Through Moocs To Advance Research Skills	English
43.	Brahmi	'Un modèle idéal-typique face aux entraves bureaucratiques.' In Actes du séminaire national organisé les 03 et 04 décembre 2016: L'enseignement inclusif pour l'intégration sociale en Algérie : Réalité et perspectives à la lumière des expériences aguerries, (2019), 163-168, (p.164)	
44.	Sabri, F. & Benmostfa, N. (2019).	Critical Pedagogy and Assessment of Educational Inclusion. *Journal of Studies in Language, Culture and Society, 1*(2), 163-168. E-ISSN: 2676-1750	
45.	Oubaziz, L. (2019).	Obstacles et difficultés des enfants en situation de handicap au cours de leur scolarisation [Obstacles and difficulties of children with disabilities during their schooling]. *In Actes du séminaire national organisé les 03 et 04 décembre 2016: L'enseignement inclusif pour l'intégration sociale en Algérie : Réalité et perspectives à la lumière des expériences aguerries* (pp.159-162). Béjaïa: Université Abderrahmane MIRA	
46.	Brahimi, K. (2018).	M'ouwiqat alershad liadwy ale'eaqah alsam'eyah alhamilyn lizar'e alqawqa'ey fi nadar kol men alawliya' walmokhtasyn [Obstacles to counselling for the hearing-impaired who carry cochlear implants in the eyes of both parents and professionals]. Journal of Studies in Orthophonia and Neuropsychology, 3(2), 56-69.	
47.	Abdel El-slam, K. & Qualleti, N.E. (2018).	Dawr alakhisa'ey alartofouni fi taqyim wa tatwir maharat altawasol lada altfal altwahodi (al'elaj alma'erfy alsoulouki) [The role of a specialist in evaluating and developing communication skills of an autistic child (cognitive behavioral therapy)]. *Journal of Studies in Orthophonia and Neuropsychology, 3*(3), 64-72.	

| 48. | Idri, N. (2019). | Integration of Learners with Special Needs: A socio-cultural clue to debate. *In Actes du séminaire national organisé les 03 et 04 décembre 2016: L'enseignement inclusif pour l'intégration sociale en Algérie : Réalité et perspectives à la lumière des expériences aguerries* (pp.109-118). Béjaïa: Université Abderrahmane MIRA | |

Notes

1. Some sections from this chapter are taken from the author's PhD: Working towards inclusive education for autistic children in Algeria: Investigating English as Foreign Language (EFL) Algerian students/graduates' knowledge of autism and their attitudes towards inclusive education for autistic children. The author would like to acknowledge the support of her supervisors Dr Ines Alves and Dr David Simmons from University of Glasgow for giving feedback on this piece. The author wrote this chapter while she was still a student at University of Glasgow.

2. Hosking, David L. (2008). "Critical Disability Theory. A Paper Presented at the 4th Biennial Disability Studies Conference at Lancaster University, UK, Sept. 2–4, 2008." *Journal of Consulting and Clinical Psychology*, 72(3), 467–478.

3. See, for instance, Bessai, Rachid (2019a). "Le soutien psychopédagogique de l'enfant handicapé: Le rôle des SESSAD." In Kaci, F. (ed.), *Actes du séminaire national organisé les 03 et 04 décembre 2016: L'enseignement inclusif pour l'intégration sociale en Algérie: Réalité et perspectives à la lumière des expériences aguerries*. Béjaïa: University of Béjaïa, 135–143; Idri, N. (2019). "Integration of Learners with Special Needs: A Socio-cultural Clue to Debate." In ibidem, 109–118.

4. Office of the United Nations High Commissioner for Human Rights (OHCHR) (2018). *List of Issues in Relation to the Initial Report of Algeria, Addendum: Replies of Algeria to the List of Issues*. Committee on the Rights of Persons with Disabilities. Twentieth session.

5. Le Roux, Cheryl S. (2017). "Language in Education in Algeria: A Historical Vignette of a 'Most Severe' Sociolinguistic Problem." *Language & History*, 60(2), 112–128.

6. Ibidem, 124.

7. Bentahila (1983) as cited in Belmihoub, Kamal (2018). "Language attitudes in Algeria." *Language Problems and Language Planning*, 42(2), 144–172.

8. Ibidem, 146.

9. Ibidem.

10. United Nations Educational, Scientific and Cultural Organization (UNESCO) (1972). *Country Education Profiles: Algeria*. Paris: Cooperative Educational Abstracting Service (CEAS), 3.

11. Micaud, Charles A. (1974). "Bilingualism in North Africa: Cultural and Sociopolitical Implications." *Western Political Quarterly*, 27(1), 93.

12. Ibidem, 95.

13. Ulama is an Algerian association that was founded by Abdelhamid Ibn Badis in 1931 when Algeria was colonized by the French. See Watanabe, Shoko (2018). "The Party of God: The Association of Algerian Muslim 'Ulama, in Contention with the Nationalist Movement after World War II." *International Journal of Middle East Studies*, 50(2), 271–290.

14. Micaud, "Bilingualism in North Africa," 95.
15. Ibidem.
16. Ibidem.
17. Benrabah, Mohamed (2004). "Language and Politics in Algeria." *Nationalism and Ethnic Politics*, 10(1), 59.
18. Bektache, Mourad (2018). "Officialization of the Amazigh Language in Algeria: Impact on Sociolinguistic Attitudes and Representations of Some Algerian Speakers." *Multilinguales*, 10(10).
19. Grandguillaume, Gilbert (2005). *Country Case Study on the Language of Instruction and the Quality of Basic Education: Policy of Arabization in Primary and Secondary Education in Algeria: Background Paper Prepared for Education for all Global Monitoring Report 2005, The Quality Imperative*. Paris: UNESCO, 13.
20. Benrabah, Mohamed (2007b). "Language-in-education Planning in Algeria: Historical Development and Current Issues." *Language Policy*, 6(2), 225–252.
21. Ibidem.
22. Rouabah, Siham (2020). *Language Shift or Maintenance in Tamazight: A Sociolinguistic Study of Chaouia in Batna, Algeria* (PhD thesis, University of Essex), 16.
23. Benrabah, "Language-in-education Planning in Algeria," 234.
24. Djebbari, Zakia (2016). "Language Policy in Algeria: An Outlook into Reforms." Online submission, 4.
25. Benrabah, "Language-in-education Planning in Algeria," 234.
26. Ibidem, 235.
27. Djebbari, "Language Policy in Algeria," 4.
28. Bektache, Mourad (2018). "Officialization of the Amazigh Language in Algeria."
29. Benrabah, (2004). "Language and Politics in Algeria," 74.
30. Ibidem.
31. Benrabah, Mohamed (2007a). "Language Maintenance and Spread: French in Algeria." *International Journal of Francophone Studies*, 10(1–2), 209.
32. Ibidem.
33. Medjahed, F. Z. (2010). "Teaching English in Algerian Secondary Schools: State of the Art." *Communication Science and Technology*, 9, 73.
34. Zakia Djebbari and Houda Djebbari, (2020). 'Language Policy in Algeria: An Outlook into Reforms.' *Al-Lisaniyyat*, 21(1)., 43.
35. Laib, 1993, p.7 as cited in Benrabah, 2007b, p. 233.
36. Bennoune, M. (2000). *Education, Culture et développement en Algérie. Bilan & perspectives du système éducatif*. Algiers: Marinoor-ENAG, 303, as cited in Benrabah, 2007b, p. 233.
37. Benrabah, M. (2007b) "Language-in-education Planning in Algeria," 233.
38. Queffélec, A. et al. (2002). *Le Français en Algérie. Lexique et dynamique des langues*. Brussels: Editions Duculot, 38, as cited in Benrabah (2007b), 233.
39. Miliani, Mohamed (2000). "Teaching English in Multilingual Context: The Algerian Case." *Mediterranean Journal of Educational Studies*, 6(1), 13–29.
40. Ibidem, 22.
41. Bellalem, Fouzi (2008). *An Exploration of Foreign Language Teachers' Beliefs about Curriculum Innovation in Algeria: A Socio-Political Perspective* (PhD thesis, King's College, London, and the University of London), 58.
42. Miliani, Mohamed (2001). "Teaching English in Multilingual Context," 23.

43. Ibidem.

44. Al-Sohbani, Yehia and Muthanna, Abdulghani (2013). "Challenges of Arabic-English Translation: The Need for Re-systematic Curriculum and Methodology Reforms in Yemen." *Academic Research International*, 4(4), 444.

45. Khochen-Bagshaw, Maha. 'Inclusive education development and challenges: Insights into the Middle East and North Africa region.' *PROSPECTS*, 49.3, (2020), p.157.

46. Khochen-Bagshaw, Maha (2020). "Inclusive Education Development and Challenges: Insights into the Middle East and North Africa Region." *PROSPECTS*, 49(3), 153–167.

47. See Richardson, Kristina (2012). *Difference and Disability in the Medieval Islamic World: Blighted Bodies.* Edinburgh: Edinburgh University Press.

48. Ibidem, 5.

49. Ibidem.

50. Ibidem.

51. Ghaly, Mohammed (2009). *Islam and Disability: Perspectives in Theology and Jurisprudence.* Abingdon: Routledge, 11.

52. Ibidem.

53. El-Ezza, Muhannad (2013). *Qol wala taqol fee majaal houqouq al-'achkhaas dhawe al-'e'aaqa.* United States Agency for International Development.

54. Al Hammadi, (2000) as cited in Zain, Ayman Mohammad and Al Doush, Alhaj Mohammad (2019). "Tachgheel 'ashaab al-hemam be al-qetaa' al-khaas be al-qanoun al-'emaaraatee: Deraasat moqaarana." *Kuwait International Law School Journal*, 8(2), 249.

55. Feys, Pieter (2015). *Interactive Storytelling in Critical Disability Studies: Interactive Storytelling as a Method in an International Postgraduate Course* (PhD thesis, Ghent University).

56. See Devlin, R.F. and Pothier, D. (2006). *Critical Disability Theory: Essays in Philosophy, Politics, Policy, and Law.* Vancouver: UBC Press, and Hosking, "Critical Disability Theory."

57. Becker (1963) as cited in Gold, Moniqueka E., and Richards, Heraldo (2012). "To Label or Not to Label: The Special Education Question for African Americans." *Educational Foundations*, 26(1–2), 144.

58. Bernburg, Jón Gunnar (2009). "Labelling Theory." In Krohn, Marvin D., Lizotte, Alan, and Hall, Gina Penly (eds.), *Handbook on Crime and Deviance.* New York: Springer, 204.

59. Babori, Ahcene and Aknouche, Nabil (2020). "Increasing the Visibility of Grey Literature in Algerian Institutional Repositories." *The Grey Journal*, 16, 43.

60. Ibidem, 50.

61. Mohamed-Amokrane, Zoreli (2019). "L'Université de Bejaia: enseignement inclusive et solidarité-éthique, entre les traditions nourricières de bonnes pratiques et la camisole de force bureaucratique." In Kaci, F. (ed.), *Actes du séminaire national organisé les 03 et 04 décembre 2016: L'enseignement inclusif pour l'intégration sociale en Algérie: Réalité et perspectives à la lumière des expériences aguerries.* Béjaïa: University of Béjaïa, 101.

62. Ibidem.

63. Ibidem.

64. Resp. United Nations General Assembly (UNGA) (2006, December 13). *Convention on the Rights of Persons with Disabilities and Optional Protocol.* New York: UNGA; El-Ezza, (2013). *Qol wala taqol fee majaal houqouq al-'achkhaas dhawe al-'e'aaqa.*

65. Braun, Virginia and Clarke, Victoria (2006). "Using Thematic Analysis in Psychology." *Qualitative Research in Psychology*, 3(2), 77–101.

66. E.g. Bechatta, M. and Chuiale, S. (2018). "Athar al-damj al-madrsee fi mafhoum al-dhat lada almo'aq sam'eyan." *Al-jamie Journal in Psychological Studies and Educational Sciences*, 3(1), 12–38; Majkoune, Hamdeche, S. and Zellal, N. (2015) "Tqdeer al-dhaat lada al-atfaal al-som al-modmajeen w ghayr al-modmajeen fee al-madaares al-'aadeya: Deraasa maydaaneya moqaarana." *Journal El-Bahith in Human and Social Sciences*, 7(19), 323–334; Yaaloui, K. and Bouakline, C. (2019). "Deraasa moqaarana ledawr al-damj al-madrasee fe tahseen ektesasb ba'd al-mafaaheem al-makaaneya lada al-tefl al-haamel lethoulaathee al-sabghee 21 dhawee 8 elaa 12 sana." *Journal of Studies in Orthophonia and Neuropsychology*, 4(1), 37–49.

67. National Youth Leadership Network (NYLN) and Kids as Self Advocates (KASA) (2006). *Respectful Disability Language: Here's What's Up!*; El-Ezza, (2013) *Qol wala taqol fee majaal houqouq al-'achkhaas dhawe al-'e'aaqa.*

68. Gernsbacher, Morton Ann et al. (2016) "'Special Needs' is an Ineffective Euphemism." *Cognitive Research: Principles and Implications*, 1(1), 1.

69. NYLN and KASA, (2006).

70. Boutebal, Saad Eddine and Yahi, Samia (2018). "Inclusion of the Children with Disabilities among School in Algeria." *International Journal of Business and Social Science*, 9(10), 26–31.

71. Nasser Bey, K. and Ben Abdel Al-Rahman, S.A. (2019). "Dawr al-nashaat al-badanee al-riyaadee fee damj al-'atfaal dhawee al-'e'aaqa al-ssam'eya wa al-dhehneyya ma'a al-atfaal al-'adeyeen fee al-madaares al-'omoumeya." *Journal of Sport System Magazine*, 6(1), 254.

72. Canadian Ministry of Civic Affairs and Immigration (2004). *Guide terminologique: Un vocabulaire approprié à l'égard des personnes handicapées de l'Ontario*. Toronto: Imprimeur de la Reine pour l'Ontario. See, for instance, Brahmi (2019). "Un modèle idéal-typique face aux entraves bureaucratiques." In Kaci, F. (ed.), *Actes du séminaire national organisé les 03 et 04 décembre 2016: L'enseignement inclusif pour l'intégration sociale en Algérie: Réalité et perspectives à la lumière des expériences aguerries*. Béjaïa: University of Béjaïa, 163–168.

73. Bessai, Rachid (2019b). "The Role of Associations in the Process of Inclusive Education of Children with Disabilities Journal of Studies in Language." *Culture and Society*, 1(2), 77–84; Bessai, Rachid (2018). "Access to Schooling for People with Special Needs in Algeria." *Sociology International Journal*, 2(5), 371–375.

74. Bessai, (2019b). "The Role of Associations in the Process of Inclusive Education of Children with Disabilities Journal of Studies in Language," 76.

75. Ibidem, 80. Bessai, (2018) "Access to Schooling for People with Special Needs in Algeria," 374.

76. Hamdouche and Daas (2019). "Legal Protection for People with Disabilities in the Arab Countries: A Case Study Algeria and Egypt." *Scientific Journal for Special Education*, 1(2), 108–109. https://search.mandumah.com/Record/1048432

77. Ibidem, 108.

78. Ibidem, 109.

79. Saidi, F. and Bouizem, A. (2020). "The Legal Care for Rights of Persons with Special Needs in Algerian Legislation." *Journal of Legal Studies*, 7(3), 626–627.

80. See Shakespeare, Tom (2003). "The Social Model of Disability." *The Disability Studies Reader*, 2, 197–204; Titchkosky, Tanya (2003). *Disability, Self, and Society*. Toronto: University of Toronto Press.

81. Majkoune, Hamdeche, and Zellal, "Tqdeer al-dhaat lada al-atfaal al-som al-modmajeen w ghayr al-modmajeen fee al-madaares al-'aadeya," 325.

82. E.g., Benamara, A. (2019). "Scolarité inclusive, entre concept et réalité." In Kaci, F. (ed.), *Actes du séminaire national organisé les 03 et 04 décembre 2016: L'enseignement inclusif pour*

l'intégration sociale en Algérie: Réalité et perspectives à la lumière des expériences aguerries. Béjaïa: University of Béjaïa, 37–46; Bouzid Baa, S. and Mekhoukh, H. (2019). "Scolarisation des enfants à besoins spécifiques: d'un enseignement intégratif à un enseignement inclusive." In ibidem, 25–36; Bekkaoui, R. and Kaiba, N. (2019). "Enseignement inclusif des enfants atteints de Spina Bifida dans la wilaya de Bejaia: État des lieux et perspectives." In ibidem, 151–156; Brahmi, (2019) "Un modèle idéal-typique face aux entraves bureaucratiques."

83. Tassoni, Penny (2003). *Supporting Special Needs: Understanding Inclusion in the Early Years.* London: Heinemann, 9.

84. Kharkhache, C. and Bouatta, A. (2016). "Ta'theer al-'elaaj al-soloukee al-ma'refee 'alaa al-ḍaght wa 'estraateejeyaat al-ta'aamol lada abaa' al-'atfaal al-som: diraasa maydaneya be-madrasat sighaar al-som be-welaayat Al-M'Sila." *The Journal of Social Sciences and Humanities*, 6(10), 176.

85. Bechatta and Chuiale, (2018) "Athar al-damj al-madrsee fi mafhoum al-dhat lada almo'aq sam'eyan," '*Al-jamie journal in Psychological Studies and Educational Sciences*, 3(1), 17.

86. Yaaloui and Bouakline, "Deraasa moqaarana ledawr al-damj al-madrasee fe tahseen ektesasb ba'd al-mafaaheem al-makaaneya lada al-tefl al-haamel lethoulaathee al-sabghee 21 dhawee 8 elaa 12 sana", *Journal of Studies in Orthophonia and Neuropsychology*, 4(1), 43.

87. Idri, (2019). "Integration of Learners with Special Needs," 110.

88. Fekih, Miloud (2019). *EFL Teachers' Awareness of Dyslexia in Algerian Middle Schools* [Conference presentation]. International Conference on Teaching, Learning and Education, Berlin, 4.

89. Guersas, Hocine and Ouadah, Lamri (2018). "Intégration des Étudiants Handicapés aux Établissements de L'enseignement Supérieur." *Majalat Ansena Lelbohouth Wa Al-Deraasaat*, 9(1), 445.

90. Brahmi, "Un modèle idéal-typique face aux entraves bureaucratiques," 164.

91. Belaid, Louiza, and Sarnou, Hanane (2019). "University for All: Including Special Needs Learners in Education." *Journal of Studies in Language, Culture and Society*, 1(2), 115–124, resp. 117, 115, 114, and 118.

92. Idri, "Integration of Learners with Special Needs: a socio-cultural clue to debate," 111.

93. Boutebal, Saad Eddine and Yahi, Samia (2018). "Inclusion of the Children with Disabilities among School in Algeria," *International Journal of Business and Social Science*, 9 (10), resp. 26, 27, and 28.

94. Belaid and Sarnou, "University for All," 115.

95. Amponsah-Bediako, Kofi (2013). "Relevance of Disability Models from the Perspective of a Developing Country: An Analysis." *Dev Country Stud*, 3, 121–132.

96. Ibidem, 124; Jackson, Mary Ann (2018). "Models of Disability and Human Rights: Informing the Improvement of Built Environment Accessibility for People with Disability at Neighborhood Scale?" *Laws*, 7(1), 3.

97. Ibrahim Belaadi, Ishkaaliyat (2015). "al-ta'arrof 'ala 'al-'atfaal al-mo'aaqeen dihniyan fee 'Al-Jazaa'er." *Journal of Human Sciences and Society*, 4, 55.

98. Ibidem, 56.

99. Ibidem, 57.

100. Gomes, M. (2018). "A Study of the Effectiveness of People-First Language." In *Proceedings of the 4th Annual Linguistics Conference at UGA*. Athens, Georgia: The Linguistics Society at UGA GA, 1–19.

101. Ibidem, 2.

102. Brown, Lydia (2011, August 4). "The Significance of Semantics: Person-first Language: Why it Matters." *Autistic Hoya.*
103. Ibidem.
104. National Youth Leadership Network and Kids as Self Advocates, *Respectful Disability Language*; El-Ezza, *Qol wala taqol fee majaal houqouq al-'achkhaas dhawe al-'e'aaqa.*
105. United Nations, (2007). *Convention on the Rights of Persons with Disabilities and Optional Protocol.*
106. El-Ezza, (2013). *Qol wala taqol fee majaal houqouq al-'achkhaas dhawe al-'e'aaqa.*
107. Ibidem.
108. Giami, Alain, Korpès, Jean-Louis, and Lavigne, Chantal (2007). "Representations, Metaphors and Meanings of the Term 'Handicap' in France." *Scandinavian Journal of Disability Research*, 9(3–4), 200.
109. Fekih, (2019). *EFL Teachers' Awareness of Dyslexia in Algerian Middle Schools*, resp. 2, 12, and 11.
110. Ibidem, p. 11, and Bouraoui, Kamel and Chabi, Tayeb (2019). "Inclusive Education: Case of the Region of Bejaia." *Journal of Studies in Language, Culture and Society*, 1(2), 91.
111. Belaid and Sarnou, (2019). "University for All," 115.
112. Ibidem.
113. OHCHR (2016, November 25). *General Comment No. 4 on Article 24—the Right to Inclusive Education.* Committee on the Rights of Persons with Disabilities. Fourteenth session.
114. Ibidem.
115. see Walton, Elizabeth, (2015). "The Language of Inclusive Education: Exploring Speaking, Listening, Reading and Writing"; Brown, Zeta, (2016). "Inclusive Education: Perspectives on pedagogy, policy and practice"; Armstrong, Felicity, Derrick Armstrong, and Len Barton, (2016). "Inclusive education: Policy, contexts and comparative perspectives".
116. Bouzid Baa and Mekhoukh, (2019). "Scolarisation des enfants à besoins spécifiques," 26.
117. Ibidem.
118. Boutebal and Yahi, (2018). "Inclusion of the Children with Disabilities among School in Algeria," 27–28.
119. Bessai, (2019b). "The Role of Associations in the Process of Inclusive Education of Children with Disabilities Journal of Studies in Language," 77.
120. Ibidem, 79.
121. Bouraoui and Chabi, (2019). "Inclusive Education: Case of the Region of Bejaia," 85.
122. Khochen-Bagshaw, "Inclusive Education Development and Challenges," 157.
123. Ibidem.
124. Ibidem.
125. Serridj, Amina (2017). *Waki'3 damj 'atfaal motalaazemat Down* (master's dissertation, University of Akli Mohand Oulhadj).
126. Ibidem, 6.
127. Khochen-Bagshaw, "Inclusive Education development and challenges," 162.
128. OHCHR, *List of Issues in Relation to the Initial Report of Algeria*, para. 5.
129. See Bessai, 2018. "Access to Schooling for People with Special Needs in Algeria."
130. Bechatta and Chuiale, "Athar al-damj al-madrsee fi mafhoum al-dhat lada almo'aq sam'eyan," 17–18.
131. Nasser Bey and Ben Abdel Al-Rahman, (2019). "Dawr al-nashaat al-badanee al-riyaadee fee damj al-'atfaal dhawee al-'e'aaqa al-ssam'eya wa al-dhehneyya ma'a al-atfaal al-'adeyeen fee al-madaares al-'omoumeya." *Journal of Sport Organisation*, 6(1), 251-266.

132. Bouhadj, Mezyan, Mansouri, Nabil, and Mezari, Fateh (2018). "Al-damj 'al-'akaadeemee le-'al-tfaal dawee 'al-'ehtiyajaat 'al-khaasa fee marhalat maa kabla 'al-madrasa: diraasa maydaneeya 'alaa mosatawaa mudeereyat 'al-tarbeya lewelaayat Bouïra." *International Journal of Specialised Education*, 7(12), 101.
133. Khochen-Bagshaw, "Inclusive Education Development and Challenges," 157.
134. Hosking, "Critical Disability Theory."
135. Ibidem.
136. Ibidem, 13.
137. Bessai, "The Role of Associations in the Process of Inclusive Education of Children with Disabilities Journal of Studies in Language," 76.
138. Hosking, "Critical Disability Theory," 6.
139. Ibidem.
140. Goode, E. (2014). "Labeling Theory." In Bruinsma, G. and Weisburd, D. (eds.), *Encyclopedia of Criminology and Criminal Justice*. New York: Springer, 2807.
141. Ibidem.
142. Bessai, "Le soutien psychopédagogique de l'enfant handicap."
143. OHCHR, *List of Issues in Relation to the Initial Report of Algeria, Addendum*.
144. Hosking, "Critical Disability Theory," 11.
145. e.g. Benamara, 2019; Bouzid Baa & Mekhoukh, 2019; Kaci, 2019; Nasser Bey & Ben Abdel Al-Rahman, 2019; Oubaziz, 2019.
146. E.g., Nasser Bey and Ben Abdel Al-Rahman, "Dawr al-nashaat al-badanee al-riyaadee fee damj al-'atfaal dhawee al-'e'aaqa al-ssam'eya wa al-dhehneyya ma'a al-atfaal al-'adeyeen fee al-madaares al-'omoumeya."
147. Kenny, L. et al. (2016). "Which Terms Should be Used to Describe Autism? Perspectives from the UK Autism Community." *Autism: The International Journal of Research and Practice*, 20(4), 442–462.
148. Al Hammadi, (2000) as cited in Ayman and Al Doush, "Tachgheel 'ashaab al-hemam be al-qetaa' al-khaas be al-qanoun al-'emaaraatee," 249.
149. Ghaly, *Islam and Disability*, 11.
150. Giami, Korpès, and Lavigne, "Representations, Metaphors, and Meanings of the Term 'Handicap' in France," 200.
151. Ibidem.
152. Ibidem.
153. See Kenny et al., "Which Terms Should be Used to Describe Autism?"

References

Al-Sohbani, Yehia and Muthanna, Abdulghani (2013). "Challenges of Arabic-English Translation: The Need for Re-systematic Curriculum and Methodology Reforms in Yemen." *Academic Research International*, 4(4), 442–450.

Amponsah-Bediako, Kofi (2013). "Relevance of Disability Models from the Perspective of a Developing Country: An Analysis." *Dev Country Stud*, 3, 121–132.

Armstrong, Felicity, David Armstrong, and Len Barton (2016). *Policy, Experience and Change: Cross-Cultural Reflections on Inclusive Education*. Routledge.

Babori, Ahcene and Aknouche, Nabil (2020). "Increasing the Visibility of Grey Literature in Algerian Institutional Repositories." *The Grey Journal*, 16, 3-51.

Bechatta, M. and Chuiale, S. (2018). "Athar al-damj al-madrsee fi mafhoum al-dhat lada almo'aq sam'eyan." *Al-jamie Journal in Psychological Studies and Educational Sciences*, 3(1), 12–38.

Bekkaoui, R. and Kaiba, N. (2019). "Enseignement inclusif des enfants atteints de Spina Bifida dans la wilaya de Bejaia: État des lieux et perspectives." In Kaci, F. (ed.), *Actes du séminaire national organisé les 03 et 04 décembre 2016: L'enseignement inclusif pour l'intégration sociale en Algérie: Réalité et perspectives à la lumière des expériences aguerries* (pp. 151–156). Béjaïa: University of Béjaïa.

Bektache, Mourad (2018). "Officialization of the Amazigh Language in Algeria: Impact on Sociolinguistic Attitudes and Representations of Some Algerian Speakers." *Multilinguales*, 10(10).

Belaid, Louiza and Sarnou, Hanane (2019). "University for All: Including Special Needs Learners in Education." *Journal of Studies in Language, Culture and Society*, 1(2), 115–124.

Bellalem, Fouzi (2008). *An Exploration of Foreign Language Teachers' Beliefs about Curriculum Innovation in Algeria: A Socio-Political Perspective* (PhD thesis, King's College, London, and the University of London).

Belmihoub, Kamal (2018). "Language Attitudes in Algeria." *Language Problems and Language Planning*, 42(2), 144–172.

Benamara, A. (2019). "Scolarité inclusive, entre concept et réalité." In Kaci, F. (ed.), *Actes du séminaire national organisé les 03 et 04 décembre 2016: L'enseignement inclusif pour l'intégration sociale en Algérie: Réalité et perspectives à la lumière des expériences aguerries* (pp. 37–46). Béjaïa: University of Béjaïa.

Bennoune, M. (2000). *Education, Culture et développement en Algérie. Bilan & perspectives du système éducatif*. Algiers: Marinoor-ENAG.

Benrabah, Mohamed (2004). "Language and Politics in Algeria." *Nationalism and Ethnic Politics*, 10(1), 59–78.

Benrabah, Mohamed (2007a). "Language Maintenance and Spread: French in Algeria." *International Journal of Francophone Studies*, 10(1–2), 193–215.

Benrabah, Mohamed (2007b). "Language-in-education Planning in Algeria: Historical Development and Current Issues." *Language Policy*, 6(2), 225–252.

Bernburg, Jón Gunnar (2009). "Labelling Theory." In Krohn, Marvin D., Lizotte, Alan, and Hall, Gina Penly (eds.), *Handbook on Crime and Deviance* (pp. 187–207). New York: Springer.

Bessai, Rachid (2018). "Access to Schooling for People with Special Needs in Algeria." *Sociology International Journal*, 2(5), 371–375.

Bessai, Rachid (2019a). "Le soutien psychopédagogique de l'enfant handicapé: Le rôle des SESSAD." In Kaci, F. (ed.), *Actes du séminaire national organisé les 03 et 04 décembre 2016: L'enseignement inclusif pour l'intégration sociale en Algérie: Réalité et perspectives à la lumière des expériences aguerries* (pp. 135–143). Béjaïa: University of Béjaïa.

Bessai, Rachid (2019b). "The Role of Associations in the Process of Inclusive Education of Children with Disabilities Journal of Studies in Language." *Culture and Society*, 1(2), 77–84.

Bouhadj, Mezyan, Mansouri, Nabil, and Mezari, Fateh (2018). "Al-damj 'al-'akaadeemee le-'al-tfaal dawee 'al-'ehtiyajaat 'al-khaasa fee marhalat maa kabla 'al-madrasa: diraasa maydaneeya 'alaa mosatawaa mudeereyat 'al-tarbeya lewelaayat Bouïra." *International Journal of Specialised Education*, 7(12), 100–106.

Bouraoui, Kamel and Chabi, Tayeb (2019). "Inclusive Education: Case of the Region of Bejaia." *Journal of Studies in Language, Culture and Society*, 1(2), 85–103.

Boutebal, Saad Eddine and Yahi, Samia (2018). "Inclusion of the Children with Disabilities among School in Algeria." *International Journal of Business and Social Science*, 9(10), 26–31.

Bouzid Baa, S. and Mekhoukh, H. (2019). "Scolarisation des enfants à besoins spécifiques: d'un enseignement intégratif à un enseignement inclusive." In Kaci, F. (ed.), *Actes du séminaire national organisé les 03 et 04 décembre 2016: L'enseignement inclusif pour l'intégration sociale en Algérie: Réalité et perspectives à la lumière des expériences aguerries* (pp. 25–36). Béjaïa: University of Béjaïa.

Brahmi (2019). "Un modèle idéal-typique face aux entraves bureaucratiques." In Kaci, F. (ed.), *Actes du séminaire national organisé les 03 et 04 décembre 2016: L'enseignement inclusif pour l'intégration sociale en Algérie: Réalité et perspectives à la lumière des expériences aguerries* (pp. 163–168). Béjaïa: University of Béjaïa.

Braun, Virginia and Clarke, Victoria (2006). "Using Thematic Analysis in Psychology." *Qualitative Research in Psychology*, 3(2), 77–101.

Brown, Lydia (2011, August 4). "The Significance of Semantics: Person-first Language: Why it Matters." *Autistic Hoya*. https://www.autistichoya.com/2011/08/significance-of-semantics-person-first.html

Brown, Zeta (2016). *Inclusive Education: Perspectives on Pedagogy, Policy and Practice*. Routledge.

Canadian Ministry of Civic Affairs and Immigration (2004). *Guide terminologique: Un vocabulaire approprié à l'égard des personnes handicapées de l'Ontario*. Toronto: Imprimeur de la Reine pour l'Ontario. https://forms.mgcs.gov.on.ca/dataset/23ae8def-a2fe-4bf2-b25c-75d181ca68e3/resource/9e6e767a-b78c-4810-b275-ce2c8320966e/download/on00400f.pdf

Devlin, R.F. and Pothier, D. (2006). *Critical Disability Theory: Essays in Philosophy, Politics, Policy, and Law*. Vancouver: UBC Press.

Djebbari, Zakia (2016). "Language Policy in Algeria: An Outlook into Reforms." Online submission.

El-Ezza, Muhannad (2013). *Qol wala taqol fee majaal houqouq al-'achkhaas dhawe al-'e'aaqa*. United States Agency for International Development. https://hcd.gov.jo/ebv4.0/root_storage/ar/eb_list_page/%D8%AF%D9%84%D9%8A%D9%84_%D9%82%D9%84_%D9%88%D9%84%D8%A7_%D8%AA%D9%82%D9%84_.pdf.

Fekih, Miloud (2019). *EFL Teachers' Awareness of Dyslexia in Algerian Middle Schools* [Conference presentation]. International Conference on Teaching, Learning and Education, Berlin.

Feys, Pieter (2015). *Interactive Storytelling in Critical Disability Studies: Interactive Storytelling as a Method in an International Postgraduate Course* (PhD thesis, Ghent University).

Gernsbacher, Morton Ann et al. (2016). "'Special Needs' is an Ineffective Euphemism." *Cognitive Research: Principles and Implications*, 1(1), 1–13.

Ghaly, Mohammed (2009). *Islam and Disability: Perspectives in Theology and Jurisprudence*. Abingdon: Routledge.

Giami, Alain, Korpès, Jean-Louis, and Lavigne, Chantal (2007). "Representations, Metaphors and Meanings of the Term 'Handicap' in France." *Scandinavian Journal of Disability Research*, 9(3–4), 199–213.

Gold, Moniqueka E. and Richards, Heraldo (2012). "To Label or Not to Label: The Special Education Question for African Americans." *Educational Foundations*, 26(1–2), 143–156.

Gomes, M. (2018). "A Study of the Effectiveness of People-First Language." In *Proceedings of the 4th Annual Linguistics Conference at UGA* (pp. 1–19). Athens, Georgia: The Linguistics Society at UGA GA.

Goode, E. (2014). "Labeling Theory." In Bruinsma, G. and Weisburd, D. (eds.), *Encyclopedia of Criminology and Criminal Justice.* New York: Springer. https://doi.org/10.1007/978-1-4614-5690-2_182

Grandguillaume, Gilbert (2005). *Country Case Study on the Language of Instruction and the Quality of Basic Education: Policy of Arabization in Primary and Secondary Education in Algeria: Background Paper Prepared for Education for all Global Monitoring Report 2005, The Quality Imperative.* Paris: United Nations Educational, Scientific and Cultural Organization (UNESCO).

Guersas, Hocine and Ouadah, Lamri (2018). "Intégration des Étudiants Handicapés aux Établissements de L'enseignement Supérieur." *Majalat Ansena Lelbohouth Wa Al-Deraasaat,* 9(1), 440–452.

Hamdouche and Daas (Unk.). "Legal Protection for People with Disabilities in the Arab Countries: A Case Study Algeria and Egypt." *Scientific Journal for Special Education,* 1(2), 105–120.

Hosking, David L. (2008). "Critical Disability Theory. A Paper Presented at the 4th Biennial Disability Studies Conference at Lancaster University, UK, Sept. 2–4, 2008." *Journal of Consulting and Clinical Psychology,* 72(3), 467–478.

Ibrahim Belaadi, Ishkaaliyat (2015). "al-ta'arrof 'ala 'al-'atfaal al-mo'aaqeen dihniyan fee 'Al-Jazaa'er." *Journal of Human Sciences and Society,* 4, 45–64.

Idri, N. (2019). "Integration of Learners with Special Needs: A Socio-cultural Clue to Debate." In Kaci, F. (ed.), *Actes du séminaire national organisé les 03 et 04 décembre 2016: L'enseignement inclusif pour l'intégration sociale en Algérie: Réalité et perspectives à la lumière des expériences aguerries* (pp. 109–118). Béjaïa: University of Béjaïa.

Jackson, Mary Ann (2018). "Models of Disability and Human Rights: Informing the Improvement of Built Environment Accessibility for People with Disability at Neighborhood Scale?" *Laws,* 7(1), 1–21.

Kenny, L. et al. (2016). "Which Terms Should be Used to Describe Autism? Perspectives from the UK Autism Community." *Autism: The International Journal of Research and Practice,* 20(4), 442–462. https://doi.org/10.1177/1362361315588200

Kharkhache, C. and Bouatta, A. (2016). "Ta'theer al-'elaaj al-soloukee al-ma'refee 'alaa al-daght wa 'estraateejeyaat al-ta'aamol lada abaa' al-'atfaal al-som: diraasa maydaneya be-madrasat sighaar al-som be-welaayat Al-M'Sila." *The Journal of Social Sciences and Humanities,* 6(10), 173–199.

Khochen-Bagshaw, Maha (2020). "Inclusive Education Development and Challenges: Insights into the Middle East and North Africa Region." *PROSPECTS,* 49(3), 153–167.

Le Roux, Cheryl S. (2017). "Language in Education in Algeria: A Historical Vignette of a 'Most Severe' Sociolinguistic Problem." *Language & History,* 60(2), 112–128.

Majkoune, Hamdeche, S. and Zellal, N. "Tqdeer al-dhaat lada al-atfaal al-som al-modmajeen w ghayr al-modmajeen fee al-madaares al-'aadeya: Deraasa maydaaneya moqaarana." *Journal El-Bahith in Human and Social Sciences,* 7(19), 323–334.

Medjahed, F. Z. (2010). "Teaching English in Algerian Secondary Schools: State of the Art." *Communication Science and Technology,* 9, 72–77.

Micaud, Charles A. (1974). "Bilingualism in North Africa: Cultural and Sociopolitical Implications." *Western Political Quarterly,* 27(1), 92–103.

Miliani, Mohamed (2000). "Teaching English in Multilingual Context: The Algerian Case." *Mediterranean Journal of Educational Studies,* 6(1), 13–29.

Mohamed-Amokrane, Zoreli (2019). "L'Université de Bejaia: enseignement inclusive et solidarité-éthique, entre les traditions nourricières de bonnes pratiques et la camisole de force bureaucratique." In Kaci, F. (ed.), *Actes du séminaire national organisé les 03 et 04 décembre*

2016: L'enseignement inclusif pour l'intégration sociale en Algérie: Réalité et perspectives à la lumière des expériences aguerries (pp. 83–107). Béjaïa: University of Béjaïa.

Nasser Bey, K. and Ben Abdel Al-Rahman, S.A. (2019). "Dawr al-nashaat al-badanee al-riyaadee fee damj al-'atfaal dhawee al-'e'aaqa al-ssam'eya wa al-dhehneyya ma'a al-atfaal al-'adeyeen fee al-madaares al-'omoumeya." *Journal of Sport System Magazine,* 6(1)), 251–266.

National Youth Leadership Network and Kids as Self Advocates (2016). *Respectful Disability Language: Here's What's Up!* https://www.aucd.org/docs/add/sa_summits/Language%20Doc.pdf

Office of the United Nations High Commissioner for Human Rights (OHCHR) (2016, November 25). *General Comment No. 4 on Article 24—the Right to Inclusive Education.* Committee on the Rights of Persons with Disabilities. Fourteenth session.

Office of the United Nations High Commissioner for Human Rights (OHCHR) (2018). *List of Issues in Relation to the Initial Report of Algeria, Addendum: Replies of Algeria to the List of Issues.* Committee on the Rights of Persons with Disabilities. Twentieth session.

Queffélec, A. et al. (2002). *Le Français en Algérie. Lexique et dynamique des langues.* Brussels: Editions Duculot.

Richardson, Kristina (2012). *Difference and Disability in the Medieval Islamic World: Blighted Bodies.* Edinburgh: Edinburgh University Press.

Rouabah, Siham (2020). *Language Shift or Maintenance in Tamazight: A Sociolinguistic Study of Chaouia in Batna, Algeria* (PhD thesis, University of Essex). https://repository.essex.ac.uk/28557/1/SihamRouabah%20Thesis.pdf

Saidi, F. and Bouizem, A. (2020). "The Legal Care for Rights of Persons with Special Needs in Algerian Legislation." *Journal of Legal Studies,* 7(3), 623–646.

Serridj, Amina (2017). *Waki'3 damj 'atfaal motalaazemat Down* (master's dissertation, University of Akli Mohand Oulhadj).

Shakespeare, Tom (2003). "The Social Model of Disability." *The Disability Studies Reader,* 2, 197–204.

Tassoni, Penny (2003). *Supporting Special Needs: Understanding Inclusion in the Early Years.* London: Heinemann.

Titchkosky, Tanya (2003). *Disability, Self, and Society.* Toronto: University of Toronto Press.

United Nations Educational, Scientific and Cultural Organization (UNESCO) (1972). *Country Education Profiles: Algeria.* Paris: Cooperative Educational Abstracting Service (CEAS).

United Nations General Assembly (UNGA) (2006, December 13). *Convention on the Rights of Persons with Disabilities and Optional Protocol.* New York: UNGA. http://www.un.org/disabilities/documents/convention/convoptprot-e.pdf

Walton, Elizabeth (2015). *The Language of Inclusive Education: Exploring Speaking, Listening, Reading and Writing.* Routledge.

Watanabe, Shoko (2018). "The Party of God: The Association of Algerian Muslim 'Ulama, In Contention with the Nationalist Movement after World War II." *International Journal of Middle East Studies,* 50(2), 271–290.

Yaaloui, K. and Bouakline, C. (2019). "Deraasa moqaarana ledawr al-damj al-madrasee fe tahseen ektesasb ba'd al-mafaaheem al-makaaneya lada al-tefl al-haamel lethoulaathee al-sabghee 21 dhawee 8 elaa 12 sana." *Journal of Studies in Orthophonia and Neuropsychology,* 4(1), 37–49.

Zain, Ayman Mohammad and Al Doush, Alhaj Mohammad (2019). "Tachgheel 'ashaab al-hemam be al-qetaa' al-khaas be al-qanoun al-'emaaraatee: Deraasat moqaarana." *Kuwait International Law School Journal,* 8(2), 235–277.

CHAPTER 5

The Transformations of Policies for the Blind in Algeria and Tunisia in the Twentieth Century (1918–1987)

Gildas Brégain

Abstract

This chapter focuses on North Africa, where blindness has long been a category with a particular social status. Since the twelfth century, some blind people had the opportunity to integrate into Koranic schools and mosques, and become reciters of the Koran at ceremonies, or become Imam. Thanks to this, a small minority of blind people were able to rise socially, and differentiate themselves from the majority, who had to rely on begging, family assistance, or community solidarity. This chapter addresses the gap on this topic in academic literature by analyzing and comparing the policies of assistance to the blind in two North African countries during the twentieth century: Algeria and Tunisia, during the colonial and post-independence period. It also examines the circulation of experts, ideas, and materials between these two countries, where since colonial times the authorities chose to divide government work by creating a sector of public action specifically dedicated to the blind. The chapter discusses the public action that included the creation of an administrative agency responsible for the issue, the allocation of specific social and economic benefits, and the funding of educational or vocational training institutions.

Keywords: Blindness, disability, North Africa, Algeria, Tunisia

Introduction

In North African countries, the blind have long been a category of disabled persons with a particular social status. Indeed, since the twelfth century, some blind people have had the opportunity to integrate in Koranic schools and mosques and to follow an oral teaching focused on memorizing the Koran and its interpretation. They could thus become reciters of the Koran at ceremonies, festivals, or major events, or become Imam. Thanks to this, some blind people were able to rise socially and differentiate themselves from others who were blind and disabled, living on begging, family solidarity, and community solidarity. Despite their particular social status within North African societies, the literature on their history remains extremely weak: only one article provides information on policies to assist the blind in colonized Algeria.[1]

This chapter aims to fill this historiographical gap by proposing to analyse the policies of assistance to the blind in two North African countries during the twentieth century. The adoption of a comparative perspective between Algeria and Tunisia seems relevant because these two countries have similar issues of a similar nature and intensity in the field of the blind (trachoma epidemics, employment, education, economic assistance), and share a relatively similar historical trajectory: Located under French colonial domination at the beginning of the twentieth century, these countries became independent in 1956 for Tunisia, and in 1962 for Algeria, while knowing authoritarian regimes. In addition, there are circulations (ideas, experts, materials) between Algeria and Tunisia during the colonial and post-independence period. However, these countries have distinct statuses within the French Empire: Algeria is a settlement colony, legally integrated into French territory since the first half of the nineteenth century and divided into three French departments (Orania, Algiers, *Constantinois*), while Tunisia is a protectorate country.

In both countries, since colonial times, the authorities have chosen to divide government work by structuring a sector of public action specific to the blind.[2] This structuring of the sector is based on the construction of a social problem specific to the blind (covering both the problems to be treated and the nature of the populations concerned). Community mobilizations promote the inclusion of this social issue on the agenda, which is then the subject of public action targeted at a limited number of beneficiaries: creation of an administrative agency responsible for the issue, allocation of specific social and economic rights, financing of educational or vocational training institutions dedicated solely to the blind, and so on. After independence, the Algerian and Tunisian governments continued to structure this sector specific to the blind. Interventionism in this social field is undoubtedly one of the elements on which the authoritarian regimes of both countries are based since it allows strong alliances with certain social sectors.

The analysis of long-term assistance policies for the blind (1920–1989) makes it possible to identify the genesis of this structuring of the sector, but also the first challenges to this specific structuring under the influence of the action of international organizations. Indeed, since the 1950s, the United Nations (UN) and the International Labour Organization (ILO) have been developing international action programmes based on the equalization of the rights of the various categories of persons with disabilities, the coordination of all sectors of disability (rehabilitation, special education, assistance to the blind and/or deaf, and so forth), and, since the late 1960s, on the idea of integrating children with disabilities into mainstream schools and workplaces.[3] These dynamics induce a trend toward the cyclical de-sectorization of sectoral disability policies, which places the actors involved in them in an unstable and changing position.[4] This dynamic of cyclical de-sectorization of sectoral disability policies was reinforced in the 1970s with the adoption by the United Nations of the Declaration of the Rights of Disabled Persons (1975) and the organization of the International Year of Disabled Persons (1981). This international dynamic has an impact on Algeria and Tunisia with a differentiated temporality and intensity.

The analysis of policies for the blind until the end of the 1980s raises questions about the persistence of the particularism of the blind cause in Algeria, which is perceptible to this day. Our study stops at a time of economic and social turmoil in both countries. The authorities repressed social protests and reacted by changing leaders (Ben Ali deposed Bourguiba in 1987) and by organizing an extremely slow, gradual, and totally controlled democratization of the regime, with the adoption of a new constitution (1989 in Algeria), the end of the single party (1989 in Algeria; 1988 in Tunisia).

The adoption of a comparative and transnational perspective makes it possible to better understand the specificity of each national case, and to better identify the appropriation of ideas from abroad and the role played by intergovernmental organizations in reorienting national policies. The objective of this chapter is to analyse how different dynamics (political changes, associative mobilizations, influence of transnational circulations) promote or not the strengthening of the specificity of the blind sector.

Our research is based on a cross-reference of different sources: the national archives of Algeria and Tunisia; the archives of the wilaya of Algiers and of the ILO, the World Health Organization (WHO), and United Nations Educational, Scientific and Cultural Organization (UNESCO); the national archives of the French overseas territories; and some associative reviews. These sources have many gaps; the post-independence documentation is generally commendable for independent governments and the post-independence period is less documented than the colonial period. Our sources rarely allow us to assess the quality of the services provided.

First, I will mention the upheavals brought about by French colonization on traditional policies for the blind; second, I will mention the gaps and continuities in these policies linked to the conquest of these countries' independence (1955–early 1970s); and, finally, mention the late and partial disappearance of the specificity of policies for the blind (mid-1970s–1987).

The construction of a specific sector of action for the blind during the colonial period

The disruption of traditional practices of assistance to the blind by colonization

Families and religious communities traditionally provided economic assistance to the blind. In the community, the *zakât* was a social tax with purifying virtues aimed at supporting the poor and those in need in the community, and blind people benefited from it. In Muslim countries of North Africa, blind people often got resources from a number of *Zaouïa* or *habous*. In the same way, blind Jews received the *tzedaka* ("alms to the poor"), which could be given in different ways (money, loans, job offer, and so forth). These forms of assistance inside the community were part of religious solidarity and continued to exist during the colonial period. In the same way, a number of blind Muslim children traditionally benefited from oral teaching in Koranic schools and mosques. Many blind people continue their studies by listening courses in Islamic law and science at the University of Zitouna in Tunisia, and at the Zawiya of Ben Yellès in Algeria. As a result, they could then make a living teaching or reciting the Koran during ceremonies, celebrations, or important events.

Many actors (doctors, blind people, religious people, association leaders) moved between the metropolis and the Algerian and Tunisian territories, and created new institutions (hospitals, eye clinics, special schools) inspired by institutional models in metropolitan France in the big cities (Algiers, Bône, Tunis). Indeed, these actors consider that it is necessary to remedy unemployment, begging, and idleness of the blind by providing them with education (for the European blind) and vocational training (for the Muslims and European blind).

Until the end of the 1940s, because of the very limited involvement of public authorities, the number of institutions founded on the model of French institutions was still low compared to the needs in both countries. But these innovative practices were disrupting traditional practices of assisting the blind.[5] The idea of a dichotomy between "French" or "European" and "traditional" practices must, however, be overcome by taking into account the new community and collective forms that appeared during the colonial period, and that "were anything but the survivors of tradition."[6] In Algeria, during the first half of the twentieth century, there was noticeable reinforcement of certain community systems of assistance, like the Muslim Charity Offices promoted by the French administration or the muslim subcomitee of the Association Valentin Haüy (AVH), an association managed by French citizens. In Bône, the local committee of the AVH created a Muslim subcommittee to organize an assistance policy in their favor.[7]

The creation of more extensive social and economic rights in Algeria

While in the metropolis many associations of the blind mobilized from the first decades of the twentieth century to obtain new rights, the creation of associations led by the blind seemed later in Algeria (1920s), and especially in Tunisia (1946). It is necessary to differentiate, on the one hand, between charitable associations run by European leaders—in Tunisia, the Cuenod group of friends of the blind (of Protestant orientation) and the Valentin Haüy Association (of Catholic orientation); in Algeria the AVH of Bône and the North African Association for the Education of the Blind of Algiers—and, on the other hand, the associations run by blind people: in Tunisia, the Union of the Blind of Tunisia (UAT), the Blind Association of Sfax, and so forth; in Algeria, the Federation of the Blind of Algeria (FAA), and so forth. In both countries, national blind associations are led by French blind (Adrien Aufraise for the UAT; André Balliste for the FAA), but there are local blind associations led by Muslim blind: the Blind Association of Relizane in Algeria; the Blind Association of Sfax in Tunisia (chaired by Ahmed Ben Adj Mahmoud Sahnoun). These associative movements are plural, massive, and demanding in Algeria since the 1930s, and in Tunisia since 1952. They generally claim a multitude of economic, social, and professional rights in the field of crafts (Algeria and Tunisia) or teaching (Tunisia).

These differences in the intensity of community mobilization can be explained by at least two factors: the importance of the French presence in Algerian cities, and the relatively large number of blind Algerian children sent to the metropolis for training (twenty-five Algerian children placed in metropolitan institutions during the period 1902–1946, against four Tunisians).[8] Once back in their countries, these educated young blind people promote the rights of the blind. They often hold positions as craft workshop teachers or Braille teachers, and/or hold senior positions in associations of the blind. André Balliste, a student at the Institut National des Jeunes Aveugles in Paris, then became president of the Federation of the Blind of Algeria, then president of the Federation of the Blind of North Africa (FAAN) formed in 1946.

However, a nuance needs to be made: there are informal, precarious groups of blind people who have never asked governments for official recognition; this is the case of groups of blind people who are legitimate and exclusive beneficiaries of the resources drawn from certain pious foundations (*habous* or *waqf*) in Tunisia. Some of these groups eventually became formalized: in 1946, several blind graduates teaching in Koranic schools joined together to form the Sfax Blind Association to defend their interests threatened by a decision of the colonial administration.

In both countries of the Empire, the blind do not de facto enjoy the rights conferred by the social legislation adopted in metropolitan France. From the 1910s onwards, they benefited only from the free help of the municipalities granted to the elderly and disabled without resources, in the form of hospitalization or limited economic assistance. From the 1930s onwards, Algerian associations of the blind put pressure on the authorities to adopt social legislation to protect the blind, similar to the legal actual provisions in mainland France.[9]

In both countries, despite the coercive colonial context, community leaders mobilize a diversity of means of action to win rights for the blind: charitable associations are content with interpersonal negotiations between elites and respectful demands to the authorities, but associations run by the blind employ more radical means of action from the late 1940s onwards, using letter harassment and critical questioning of the authorities. Moreover, André Balliste, the president of FAAN, does not hesitate to publicly denounce the scandalous inaction of the colonial authorities, and to invoke French imperial citizenship.[10] Algeria's associative leaders also have greater political support from parliamentarians of the French Union and communist parliamentarians.[11] In both countries, the struggle of community leaders is reinforced by the inclusion of the issue of the blind on the agenda by UNESCO from 1949 (with its programme for the standardization of Braille in regional areas), then by the United Nations from 1952 (with its international rehabilitation programme for the blind).[12] The action of these international organizations forces the French authorities to provide information on their action in this field in the territories of North Africa and therefore to act in order to be able to produce expertise on the subject.

The blind in Algeria have managed to conquer economic and social rights earlier than the blind in Tunisia.[13] The use of protest measures, the multiple political support acquired, and Algeria's specific legal status (divided into French departments) explain this precocity of the rights conquered, and their greater extension. It should be noted here that the social conquests obtained by the blind in Algeria are then instrumentalized by Tunisian blind community leaders—with the support of FAAN leader André Balliste, esteemed by the Director of Public Education of the Tunisian colonial administration, Lucien Paye, to demand the application of similar measures in their country.[14] As early as 1952, the UAT asked the government to grant a pension to blind people who were not working, an increase for the permanent assistance of a third person, and a compensation allowance for blind workers.

The administrative authorities of both countries easily agree to adopt measures that do not generate any expenditure: the introduction of a disability and blindness card, the regulation of the use of white canes, the allocation of reserved places on railways and public transport and the creation of an advisory committee in the General Government on issues related to the protection of blind people and the prevention of blindness. This administrative committee began to operate in 1950 in Algeria and in March 1954 in Tunisia. The legislative measures of both countries assign responsibility for the organization of the work of the blind to certain ministries and ensure commercial opportunities for certain productions of the blind, by forcing public services and establishments to purchase certain objects manufactured by blind workers as a priority. In Tunisia, while the associations wanted to obtain a monopoly in this area, the Tunisian text only provides, at the request of the Government Expenditure Section, for a preferential right, as in Algeria.[15] Moreover, while ATU claims the reserve of workstations for blind switchboard operators, the legislation does not provide for it.

But the Tunisian administration refuses to grant a pension to the blind in Tunisia and a compensation allowance for blind workers, while the Algerian administration refuses to grant it after multiple pressures. Decision No. 52–038 legitimizes the granting of a compensation allowance to blind workers, and a pension to blind civilian non-working people, "the amount of which is equal to one-sixth of the allowance paid in Algeria to old workers in the non-agricultural sector."[16] This pension is substantially increased (150 percent) "when the disabled person needs the constant help of a third person." In Tunisia, the subject was studied by officials of the Ministry of Health and the Ministry of Labour during 1953. But the two ministries refused to assume any responsibility in this field until 1954, then the Ministry of Health was finally charged with assuming this responsibility. Subsequently, the Ministry of Health and the Finance Department mutually relieve each other of the financing of these assistance allowances.[17] The situation does not unblock before the declaration of independence. The French Ministry of Foreign Affairs, and the Residence, do not wish to grant economic allowances that could generate considerable expenses. This French control over the decisions of the protectorate also crystallizes the oppositions on multiple themes.[18] However, the members of the Blind Association of Sfax are mobilizing with the Habous Administration to obtain new economic benefits, but we do not know the outcome of these negotiations.

A more developed specialized educational system for teaching Braille in Algeria

During the colonial period, associations chose to promote the teaching of French Braille (and Arabic Braille from the 1950s onwards), which was legitimized by transnational networks for the well-being of the blind. As Table 5.1 shows, two specialized schools for teaching Braille were created in Algeria, one by the AVH in 1920 in Algiers, and the other by the FAA in Oran in 1941.

Table 5.1: Braille teaching institutions in North Africa in the early 1950s

	Number	Total capacity of reception	Date of creation of educational institutions	Place	Body responsible for the institution
Algeria	2	From 16 to 40 depending on the years	1920 (La Scala)	Algiers	North African Association
		About ten	1941 (Louis Braille)	Oran	FAAN
Tunisia	1	18	1955	Tunis	Public Instruction Directorate

The main objective of these schools is to help blind European Catholic children, but they also welcome some Muslim and Jewish children who are generally poor and/or orphans. On the other hand, no such school appeared in Tunisia until Pierre Mendès France recognized Tunisia's autonomy in 1954. In 1946, the Tunisian Ministry of Health and the Directorate of Public Education jointly studied the project to create a school for the blind, but this project did not succeed, the Directorate of Public Instruction considering that this problem was not a priority compared to "the schooling of normal children."[19]

In the following years, however, the administration agreed, as in Algeria, to finance the sending to metropolitan institutions (or to Villa Scala) of half a dozen blind children from poor families. In addition, existing associations (AVH of Tunis, UAT, Blind student Association) provide Braille classes for a few young blind people. The AVH thus provides Braille classes to the ten blind adults who work in its workshop in Tunis. In 1953, Mohamed Rajhi, a young teacher who had learned Braille, gave evening classes to about twenty blind young people (3 hours a week) and forty blind adults (3 hours a week).[20] While the Directorate of Public Instruction of the Tunisian Residence granted Mohamed Rajhi the right to teach in his ordinary school in 1953, it delayed the opening of a specialized class, while offering a grant to Mohammed Rajhi to continue his work. The pressure from associations (UAT, Blind student Association, Dr Cuenod Group, FAAN) contributes to overcoming the resistance of the administration. On March 21, 1955, the Directorate of Public Instruction opened a mixed class for eighteen blind children in Tunis, taught by a Tunisian teacher (Rajhi) and a specialized and qualified French teacher, Miss Alpin. The creation of this day school class is seen as the recognition of the right of the blind to free public education.[21] However, the project to open a class in Sfax is not being carried out, particularly because it is impossible to find a qualified teacher from French institutions.[22] Only three evening classes are created in Sfax by the Blind Student Association, thanks to public subsidies. These three courses in French and Arabic Braille benefit about forty students and are taught by a blind man who does not have a specialized diploma, Mohamed Rajhi's former student.[23]

The later and reduced nature of the special education system in Tunisia is explained both by the difference in legal status with Algeria and by the small number of potential beneficiaries who are French citizens in Tunisia (approximately 91,000 French citizens in Tunisia in 1931; against approximately 900,000 in Algeria). School provision remains concentrated in the few urban areas (Algiers, Oran, Tunis), which then have more than 100,000 inhabitants, mainly Europeans and Israelites.[24]

The low financial support provided by both governments for the development of special education in Braille is easily explained by the prevalence of the idea that assistance to the blind is a private initiative, as in metropolitan France, where public authorities are only there to support this initiative. As a result, associations are forced to resort to quests, lotteries, or charity balls. The decision of Lucien Paye, Director of Public Instruction, to open a public class in Tunis is probably explained by his personal convictions, having been convinced of the validity of this assistance project by André Balliste, who he met during an international and highly regarded congress.

In a colonial context, intra-imperial movements play a fundamental role in providing the trained professionals and equipment necessary for the functioning of the classes. In Algiers, it is the French Lucie Ros, a blind woman from Larnay, who teaches Braille at Villa Scala. The Tunisian Mohamed Rajhi travels to Paris every year from 1951 to visit institutions for the blind (Institut National des Jeunes Aveugles (INJA) and Association

Valentin Haüy (AVH)) to document himself and collect Braille books and specialized equipment. Other circulations outside the imperial framework are worth mentioning: The American Foundation for Overseas Blind distributes American paper books and tablets to FAAN.[25]

The development of vocational training in handicrafts and the loss of traditional Koranic teaching jobs

Table 5.2: Vocational training and employment institutions for the blind in North Africa in the early 1950s.

	Number	Reception capacity	Institutions	Date of creation	Cities	Trades taught
A L G E R I A	5	30	Institut municipal des aveugles laborieux	1924	Alger	Basketry, brushmaking
		10	AVH Workshop	Early 1940's	Oran	Basketry
		60 in1960	Société des aveugles d'Oran	1942	Oran	
		24 in 1960	Union des aveugles travailleurs	Early 1940's	Oran	Basketry
		?	AVH Workshop	Early 1940's	Bône	
T U N I S I A	2	6	Mr Aron-Baruch' Workshop	1933	Hammam-Lif	Chair wickerwork, brushing
		18	AVH Workshop	1938	Tunis	

As Table 5.2 shows, in both countries, the associations for or of the blind organize some professional workshops, sooner in Algeria (Algiers in 1924; Bône in the early 1940's) than in Tunisia (Tunis in 1938, Hammam Liff in 1933). Unlike Algerian workshops, Tunisian workshops are very precarious, and Hammam Liff's workshop closes a few years after its creation. The offer of professional rehabilitation is not discriminatory; they accept Muslims, Jews, and Christians. The objective is to get these blind people out of "humiliating" begging by offering them a dignified and remunerative professional activity. These workshops promote the professional training of the blind in basketry, flesh canning, and brushing. The privileged professional orientation of blind people toward low-skilled crafts is explained by the choices of association leaders to replicate in the same way certain vocational education experiences organized in the metropolis, and by the qualifications already acquired by students who have attended school in metropolitan institutions. In Tunisia, it is a former student of the Villa Scala School (Algiers) who teaches the job of brush maker to the children of the Hammam-Lif school.[26]

The supply of vocational training remained limited throughout the colonial period. There is a minority of beneficiaries (less than 100 in Algeria, and less than 30 in Tunisia, which can be explained by the lack of funds; the difficulty of finding raw materials, especially during the Second World War; and the difficulty of selling goods made by the blind). The amplification of the action of the AVH of Tunis is made thanks to the financial support of the Countess of Hautecloque. More marginally, Algerian and Tunisian associations promote the integration of a few blind people as switchboard operators. In the absence of a major action in favour of employment, many blind people were left without paid work, a lot of them choosing to beg to live.

In addition, in Tunisia, blind Muslims have lost a qualified professional opportunity as teachers in Koranic schools. Following the application of a decree on modern Koranic schools (in 1944) leading to the end of the financing of blind teachers, the public education administration ceased to finance blind teachers in Koranic schools and recommended the dismissal of these blind teachers. Blind teachers are then deemed "unable, because of their blindness, to keep a classroom running, especially in primary schools."[27] Reacting to this measure, which threatened their professional future, the blind graduates created an association and mobilized from 1946 to 1956 to obtain both the retention of teachers in their positions and the access of young graduates to new teaching positions. The *Direction de l'instruction publique* was initially firmly opposed to this, but the administrative harassment of the association and the political pressure exerted on other actors (Prime Minister, and so on) led the *Direction de l'instruction publique* to qualify its position and allow the retention of a few blind people in their positions. Finally, in 1949, she stated, "The Administration intends to maintain its assistance to existing teachers until they are extinguished. But there can be no question of recognizing the right of the Modern Koranic Schools to recruit new ones who would benefit from the same generosity; a teacher can only properly ensure his service to the extent that he enjoys all his physical and intellectual faculties."[28] The Public Instruction directorate seems to adopt here an attitude similar to that adopted earlier by the French administration toward the disabled and blind, prohibited from teaching in primary and secondary schools with the same argument.[29]

In both countries, a new sector of public action was built during the colonial period, the sector of assistance to the blind, which acquired materiality through the creation of educational and professional institutions dedicated exclusively to the blind, and later, from the late 1940s, through the organization of an administrative body in charge of steering public policy on assistance to the blind. While public authorities make little contribution to the promotion of educational and professional infrastructure, they have been undertaking trachoma control campaigns since the 1920s in Algeria and the 1930s in Tunisia. During this period, Algeria was a model for policies to assist the blind in the other two North African countries (Tunisia, Morocco).

The assistance policies linked to the conquest of independence (1956–mid-1970s)

Tunisian independence activists gained the independence of their country in March 1956, while Algerians finally conquered it only in 1962, after several years of war against the French army. This war considerably changed the hierarchy of the categories of disabled people, because the 100,000 Mujahideen of the War of Independence obtain preferential rights from the new regime (right to a pension, employment, access to rehabilitation centers, vocational rehabilitation). The blind (approximately 60,000) are

no longer the only category of disabled people assisted by public authorities, unlike Tunisia, where the blind (approximately 20,000) continue to
be the only ones to be assisted.[30]

The two countries initially followed a relatively similar political trajectory: the new governments officially opted for socialism (from 1962
in Algeria, between 1962 and 1969 in Tunisia), and organized an authoritarian regime, with the establishment of a single party (the National
Liberation Front (FLN) in Algeria, *Neo Destour* in 1963 in Tunisia) and
the prohibition of freedom of association. Both countries are adopting a
policy of social planning and modernization (significant investment in
education, health, employment, and so on), allowing strong alliances with
certain sectors of society and the consolidation of regimes.[31] Both governments quickly consider the issue of the blind as a priority social issue, as it
is a means of proving the activism and effectiveness of the nationalist government, unlike the French colonial action that is caricatured as non-existent. These policies thus offer an additional source of political legiti-
macy. Ahmed Ben Bella, President of the Algerian Government Council, is
Honorary President of the ONAA. On March 23, 1963, he declared: "Blind
brothers, you will never know humiliation and charity, you must participate in the construction of our country because the Algerian revolution
is human and social."[32] In both countries, the new governments insist on
the "conquest of citizenship" of the blind through their action. This prioritization of the issue of the blind is facilitated by the participation of
several actors of the blind cause within the independence movements in
both countries, who facilitate the connection between association representatives and political leaders. However, the prioritization of the issue of
the blind at the expense of other categories of disabled people then con-
tradicts one of the new requirements of international disability policy,
namely, to treat all categories of persons with disabilities equally.

The rapid creation of a single organization of blind people controlled by the political authorities

In both countries, the conquest of independence led to a considerable
change in the associative structure of the blind, with the creation of a single organization of the blind controlled by the political authorities, with a
monopoly on the associationism of the blind. This new associative structure is similar to that imposed by political authorities in other sectors

(women, children, and so forth), where we also observe the unification of associative movements and their placing under the supervision of political parties.[33] In both cases, the former private associations (FAA, UAT, AVH, and so on) are dissolved, and all their infrastructures and resources are entrusted to the newly created organization, which has a monopoly on blind associationism: the National Union of the Blind of Tunisia (UNAT) created in 1956 and formalized in 1961 in Tunisia; the National Organisation of the Algerian Blind (ONAA) created in March 1963 in Algeria. These two national organizations quickly obtained public utility status (in January 1964 for the ONAA; in 1961 for the UAT). They are politically controlled by the pro-independence political parties that govern the country: the Front de libération nationale in Algeria), and the Parti destourien in Tunisia.[34] Their flexibility is very limited, the public authorities control the activity of associations, and their leaders are appointed by political parties and ministers of social affairs. While the ONAA is run exclusively by blind people, this is not the case with UNAT, which is run by a committee composed of blind and sighted people. One of the pillars of UNAT, its Secretary General, Mohammed Rajhi, is a sighted educator and a former Destourian activist.

In its statutes, the ONAA is conceived as an association "by and for the blind," opposed to all solutions that include "a spirit of paternalism or that disregard the real possibilities or legitimate rights of people who are blind." The first president of the ONAA (until 1984) is a blind man from the war of independence, Mustapha Djelloul, who is a member of the National Assembly set up by Ben Bella in 1964. He has great prestige in the country and manages to meet regularly with the president to demand the development of programs for the blind.[35] UNAT is chaired first by Mr. Bâtonnier Taieb Miladi, constituent deputy and former president of the committee for the defence of the interests of the blind in Tunis, but Mohammed Rajhi quickly took over the management of the association by holding the position of Secretary General and then after 1971 President. Several UNAT leaders are Destourian activists.

With the support of the ministries concerned, these two associations developed multiple activities, relating to economic and social assistance (provision of food aid, clothes, and so forth), education and vocational training, and medical assistance. UNAT's activities are strongly supported by the Minister of Health and Social Affairs Ahmed Ben Salah, and Wassila Bourguiba quickly becomes Honorary President of UNAT. In their public speeches, UNAT leaders like Ben Salah regularly insist on the achievement of citizenship for the blind through government action.

UNAT and ONAA received substantial public subsidies at the end of the 1950s. In Tunisia, they also benefit from the revenues related to the White Cane Campaign (national quest). In July 1972, UNAT became the beneficiary of an annual contribution of 20 millimes per cinema and theatre place (by increasing the price) during the first half of March each year, as part of the White Cane campaign, thanks to the adoption of Law No. 72–591.

Thanks to their monopoly and extensive action, these organizations are able to become large management associations that are fully integrated into the state's social action system. These associations become transmission belts for political parties, supervising the population and promoting state nationalism.[36] However, they use their flexibility to exploit the state and increase their activities, or to promote individual interests. It is therefore undeniable that the social action developed by these organizations is used to manufacture political consent, following the example of the associative action developed in other authoritarian regimes such as Francoism at the same time.[37] However, the work of the two organizations during the first decade was largely empirical, and they did not have permanent specialized staff to lead special education and vocational rehabilitation projects in the regional sections, which is why they sought the expertise of intergovernmental bodies (ILO, UN) during the 1960s.

The legitimization of the specific rights of the blind

In Algeria and Tunisia, the leaders of the ONAA and UNAT are campaigning for the recognition of the specific rights of the blind.[38] In both countries, associations are asking for the guarantee of the sale of products manufactured by the blind, and the reserve of a compulsory hiring quota.[39] In Tunisia, Mohamed Naceur invokes the 1944 ILO recommendation to demand the application of a mandatory hiring quota of disabled for employers, and the introduction of a priority right of access to certain jobs.[40] In Algeria, the ONAA manages relatively easily and very quickly to have a social protection legislation adopted, thanks to the intervention of its President Mustapha Djelloul—also a deputy from Oran—in the

National Assembly. The bill was unanimously adopted by the Assembly on June 4, 1963 without any debate.[41]

In both countries, following the mobilization of associations, legal provisions were adopted in the 1960s and 1970s that legitimized certain specific rights for the blind: Act No. 63–200 of June 8, 1963 in Algeria and its regulatory decree No. 63437 of November 1963; in Tunisia the decree of December 25, 1957 and Act No. 5 of March 8, 1968 with its regulatory decree of January 4, 1969; Act No. 71–27 of June 14, 1971 and the regulatory decree of March 23, 1972.[42] These laws repeal laws adopted during the colonial period, and generally only extend previously acquired rights (with exception of the right to education). However, the new governments consider that state intervention is essential to ensure their education, rehabilitation, and social reintegration.

Once regulated, these laws provide several economic rights and benefits to the blind: compensation for non-workers blind (Algeria) and in Tunisia "special allowances of any kind" by the 1968 law, a temporary compensatory benefit for blind workers (whose productivity is reduced because of their disability) paid by the National Social Security Fund; the payment of scholarships to trainees in need or those called upon to carry out training courses outside specialized centers (scholarships paid to the centers). The number of blind people receiving these allowances is much higher in Algeria than in Tunisia. In Algeria, in 1975, about 40,000 blind people received a modest allowance. In Tunisia, UNAT distributes small amounts of money and housing assistance to some of its members who are severely disabled (blind deaf, tuberculosis patients). But it does not call for the generalization of a pension system for the blind, "convinced that, in the current economic situation of the country, the severity of the problem of the blind makes it impossible for a country such as ours to provide direct financial assistance at too high a cost."[43] Another argument is put forward by management: "To allow them to benefit from a special regime would encourage them to consider themselves as idlers, as balls that society drags along."[44]

These laws also grant free access or reductions in public transport, exemption from any fee on radio receivers, and discounts on the price of tickets for cultural events. These laws also define blindness, determine the distribution of the "blind" disability card, the use of the white cane, and institute free and compulsory education and vocational rehabilitation of young blind people in the Algerian case, and admission to specialized schools and vocational training institutions in the Tunisian case. In the Tunisian case, admission to vocational training and rehabilitation centers is subject to the successful completion of psychotechnical examinations. Algerian and Tunisian legislation determines the obligation for administrations to purchase products manufactured by the blind in order to secure the commercial outlets of products manufactured by the blind (article 11 of the 1968 law in Tunisia; article 10 of the 1963 law in Algeria). Tunisian legislation, on the other hand, also gives blind persons the possibility of being placed in reserved jobs in industry and commerce: article 8 of the 1969 decree stipulates, "The placement of trainees in jobs in industry and commerce [public and private sector] shall be a priority within the limit of a percentage to be fixed by decree." This measure only partially satisfies the UNAT management, which called for "a law setting at least 10% of jobs for the blind in industrial companies, administrations, public institutions and local authorities," and the protection of blind people's production against competition from imported products.[45] Moreover, no implementing decree was issued in the following decade.

In both countries, these laws determine the creation of an advisory committee on the social protection of the blind and the prevention of blindness (within the Ministry of Social Affairs in Algeria, and within the State Secretariat for Youth, Sports, and Social Affairs in Tunisia), in which participate UNAT and ONAA. In Algeria, special administrative commissions are also set up in each department to evaluate the distribution of disability cards and the use of a white cane. In Tunisia, employment committees for the blind and visually impaired as well as guidance are established within the State Secretariat for Youth, Sports, and Social Affairs.

These legislations only partially satisfy the associative claims. In August 1964, delegates to the ONAA congress called for the adoption of social legislation in favor of all categories of physically disabled people, "especially the blind," as well as a 40 percent reduction in the amount of rents for low-income housing.[46] Throughout the 1960s, UNAT leaders called for "the creation of a law requiring that a percentage of switchboard positions be reserved for the blind." [47] Their request was defended by one ILO expert but was not successful.

Necessity of International Assistance for Strengthening Specialized Education

The new regimes do not choose to upgrade the traditional system of oral education for blind children in Koranic schools but instead choose to continue to upgrade the system of special education in Braille, which they consider more appropriate. Mustapha Djelloul, the president of the ONAA, gave a speech devaluing the oral instruction system, saying it is "hard and painful for the teacher [...]; difficult and even more painful for the student." He highlights the advantages of the Braille method, a system "adapted and adopted today in all the languages of the world, making it a universal writing."[48]

Table 5.3: Educational institutions for the blind in North Africa in the late 1960s

	No.	Cities and towns	Institutions (date of creation)	Types of education	Number of students
Algeria	2	Algiers	Villa Scala	Primary school	120
		Oran	El Achour (1967)		?
Tunisia	2	Bir Kassaa/ Tunis	En-Nour (1959)	Primary/ Secondary	300
		Sousse	Institute (1962)	Secondary school	50

As table 5. 3. shows, as soon as it was created, the ONAA decided to recover the existing school infrastructures in Algiers (Villa Scala) and Oran to create two schools. Villa Scala had about sixty students in 1964. To accommodate more students, the authorities organized the renovation of an old children's sanatorium in Algiers to transfer the students from Villa Scala and welcome new ones. In 1967, the transfer of the students from Villa Scala to the new building in El Biar proved to be a real public scandal, as nothing was planned to re-case the young lung patients.[49] In Tunisia, thanks to the support of the administrations, UNAT is redeveloping old apartments to organize a new school infrastructure in Bir Kassaa in 1959, the Institut En-Nour. Directed by Mohammed Rajhi, this En-Nour Institute initially welcomed about a hundred students, then nearly 300 students in 1968. In addition, UNAT created a secondary and technical education structure in 1962 in Sousse, which welcomes about fifty students in Secondary. The management of the Institute is entrusted to a well-known Destourian activist, Youssef Jedai. In Tunisia, these schools for the blind are attached to the Education Secretariat and follow the official school curricula, unlike Algeria, where these two schools are attached to the Public Health Department. Indeed, when drafting the bill on the social protection of the blind in Algeria, the Minister of Public Health wishes to obtain their connection, arguing that the blind are sick and invoking the French model.[50] The President of the ONAA is opposed to this, claiming a link to the National Education, but does not succeed.

In both countries, the size of schools is still insufficient to meet all needs, and associations do not have the necessary funds to carry out their school projects. This is particularly the case for the ONAA, which failed to establish a third school in Constantine in the 1960s.

In both countries, independence is accompanied by the departure of French specialist teachers (in Tunisia the only qualified teacher, in Algeria several teachers). In Algeria, the conquest of independence was accompanied by the exclusion of religious sisters from the responsibility of teaching at the Villa Scala school. These multiple departures, combined with new recruitment needs linked to the increase in the number of pupils, led to a considerable shortage of specialized teachers. At Villa Scala, in 1966, for 120 students, there are only two teachers and three coaches, whereas double is necessary. Calls for recruitment are made through various channels (diplomatic, press, personal letters, trip of the headmaster of the Algiers school to INJA) in France, Belgium, and Switzerland. In August 1964, the Ministry of Social Affairs of the Algerian Republic requested fifteen French teachers specializing in the teaching of young blind people to be recruited under technical cooperation for the new school year. The French Ministry of Health replied in the negative to this request, given the small number of lay teachers in place. Finally, some teachers (including one Belgian) are recruited through two-year common law contracts. This deficit in qualified human resources visibly persists until the end of the 1970s in Algeria. These schools also lack many Braille books and teaching materials (globe, rulers, and so forth) to operate. In Tunisia, the choice is made to recruit teachers, most of whom are not qualified, and to employ some sisters to educate the blind.

To compensate for this lack of equipment and specialized teachers, the association leaders are forced to seek international assistance. In the context of the 1960s, during which Algeria embodied the "Mecca of revolution" and Tunisia also pursued a socialist path thanks to Minister Ben Salah, it is interesting to note that associative leaders and political leaders did not choose to seek international assistance from socialist countries.[51] Their approach remained above all pragmatic, and the assistance requested could come from both capitalist countries (USA, Germany, and so forth) and socialist countries.[52] While ONAA leaders solicit donations of specialized equipment from a few foreign organizations (Swiss Federation of the Blind, AFOB), the Tunisian Mohammed Rajhi adopted a different strategy by seeking UNESCO's assistance as early as 1954 (in order to benefit from its international assistance voucher program), and then establishing regular collaborations with AFOB, the International Federation of the Blind, and a West German organization for the blind during the 1960s. As a result, the ONAA receives only occasional international aid, while Tunisian institutions receive more and more substantial and sustainable international aid. From 1954 to 1960, the Tunis School for the Blind received UNESCO assistance vouchers from many French secondary schools, which enabled it to purchase adapted equipment (tablets, cubarithms, and so forth).[53] A twinning is then established between the Marburg Institute and the Sousse Institute. Nevertheless, this international aid remains largely insufficient and sometimes symbolic, such as the offer of some Optacon (OPtical to TActile CONverter) by the West German organization.

UNAT's collaboration with AFOB was strengthened in the 1960s, with the joint organization of Franco-African and Malagasy seminars to train educators for the blind, attended by leaders from the Maghreb and some African countries. The Tunisian government, unlike Algeria, supports Mohammed Rajhi's efforts to organize international training seminars and then to create in October 1974 an international school for the training of blind educators called the African Centre for Research and Training of Senior Officials in Education and Rehabilitation of the Blind.[54] This makes it possible to establish diplomatic relations and collaboration agreements with the Maghreb countries (Morocco, Algeria, Libya) and other African (Senegal) or Arab (Saudi Arabia) countries. Tunisia printed the Koran in unified Braille in 1975, and immediately exported it to Saudi Arabia. The objective of these actions is to increase its *soft power*, by appearing as a leader country of the Third World countries in this field of social policy.

The conservation of the orientation of the blind toward brushing and telephone switchboard in Algeria, and Diversification of vocational training in Tunisia

In 1955, the ILO adopted a Recommendation on the Rehabilitation of Disabled Persons (No. 99), which sets new guidelines for the employment of disabled persons. In the context of the Cold War, the representatives of the governments of the Anglo-Saxon countries and the leaders of private companies succeeded in giving priority to economically liberal solutions, by promoting the principle of selective placement and the solution of sheltered workshops, and by obtaining the devaluation of the solution of mandatory hiring quotas for the disabled within administrations and private companies.[55] On the other hand, the representatives of the socialist countries promote the principle of cooperatives for the disabled as one of the best solutions to employment. Moreover, the cooperatives of disabled workers in Poland were established as an international model to be followed by the ILO in the 1950s and 1960s.

Given the socialist orientation pursued by independent Algeria and Ben Salah in Tunisia, it is not surprising to note that, in the 1960s, ONAA and UNAT opted to promote the organization of blind workers' cooperatives, drawing on the experience of cooperatives in socialist countries. In both countries, these associations organize accelerated professional training (three months) in brushing for the unqualified and illiterate blind (often beggars). They then facilitate the integration of these blind people into the labour market by organizing cooperatives of brush workers. In Algeria, ONAA leaders perceived the brushing industry as very profitable. The number of brush workers working in cooperatives increased considerably, from 60 in 1965 to 500 in 1976, thanks to the creation of cooperatives in several cities. This growth is made possible by securing the sale of brushes to administrations. In Tunisia, UNAT has been supporting the creation of the Tunisian professional cooperative for the blind since 1956. Benefiting from considerable subsidies from the government, this cooperative employs about fifty blind brushcutter workers in 1959, then more than 190 workers in 1966, spread over three different centers (Tunis, Sousse, Sfax). Another cooperative unit appeared in Gafsa in the following years. However, this number is highly fluctuating, and due to difficulties in replenishing supplies, workers only work half the year. Two other agricultural cooperatives are created in Sidi Thabeit and Beja. However, by 1970, UNAT had no longer any agricultural land available for trained young farmers.[56]

To improve the productivity of cooperatives, the two countries are sending some workers (Mohammed Souamès in Algeria; Béchir Denden and Salah Djaziri in Tunisia) to specialize in the mechanical manufacture of brushmaking and mattress making abroad with the help of the ILO. If the Algerian is sent to France and Switzerland, Tunisians are sent to Switzerland and Poland respectively, the latter being chosen only by default of other possibilities. The ILO then provided a mechanical machine to the cooperative of the blind in Sousse. While Algeria continued to develop blind workers' cooperatives in the early 1970s, Tunisia was on a different path, due to the abandonment of the socialist project by the government in 1969.[57] The government's choice of a more liberal economic orientation led UNAT leaders to change the status of cooperatives of blind workers to that of sheltered workshops, which is more in line with the model of countries where the liberal economy dominates.[58] While the Tunisian blind working in sheltered workshops have a specific status and do not have the rights of ordinary workers (annual leave, bonuses, social security, retirement and so forth), we ignore the status of workers in Algerian cooperatives, and the reality of self-management of these cooperatives.

The ONAA also refers several dozen blind people to the profession of telephone switchboard operators by organizing three-month internships under the guidance of a former ILO scholarship holder, Lounes Mokrétar, who trained at the AVH in Paris. In 1976, seventy blind people were telephone switchboard operators in Algeria.[59]At the same time, thirty-five blind people are teachers. The ONAA wishes to diversify professional opportunities by creating agricultural and massage therapist training courses, but these projects are delayed due to lack of resources. A few students are sent abroad to train as massage therapists. On the other hand, UNAT is able to organize more diversified vocational training thanks to significant international support. UNAT provides training in foreign languages, telephone switchboards, shorthand typists, metal work, knitting, and so forth. Following a request from the Tunisian government, an ILO expert Paul Grosse is helping to develop the vocational rehabilitation center for the blind in Sousse. It encourages the operation of a physiotherapy section in Sousse and improves the selective placement policy. However, the expert's work is hampered on the spot by personal conflicts with the management of the Sousse center.[60] UNAT created in 1968 a pilot vocational and rural rehabilitation center for the recently blind in Sidi Thabet (with the help of the USA government), a Higher School of Physiotherapy for the Blind in 1969 in Sousse (aid from Belgium government), a vocational training center in Kairouan in July 1968, and in 1973 a Higher School of Interpretation and Translation for the Blind in Sousse.

In both countries, the conquest of independence led to a considerable change in the associative structure of the blind, with the creation of a monopolistic organization of the blind controlled by political power. UNAT and ONAA decided to continue teaching Braille and training the blind as brushers. However, UNAT quickly distinguished itself by the diversification of its vocational training courses, and the shift toward liberal approaches to professional integration in the early 1970s (sheltered workshops, selective placement). Tunisia is now a polarizing center for the diffusion of techniques of rehabilitation in North Africa. As proof, the Tunisian Mohamed Rajhi is sent to Algeria and Morocco by the ILO to advise these governments on vocational rehabilitation policies to be implemented. In 1977, he became Vice-President of the World Council for the Welfare of the Blind.

The late and partial disappearance of the specificity of policies for the blind (1975–1987)

In the mid-1970s, the first steps toward a new orientation of policies to assist the blind were taken under the impetus of intergovernmental bodies, which urged states to develop intersectoral coordination policies, to equalize the rights of categories of disabled persons, and to develop integration policies based on standardization (integration of students with disabilities into mainstream schools and vocational training centers).

A desectorization of public policies on disability since 1981 in Tunisia, almost non-existent in Algeria

The dynamics of cyclical desectorization in the field of disability, which became apparent in the 1970s and 1980s, impacted the two North African countries with varying intensity and temporality. This dynamic of cyclical desectorization is earlier and stronger in Tunisia than in Algeria. In Tunisia, the government equalizes the rights of the various categories of disabled persons and establishes a coordinating body for disability policies, the High Council for Social Affairs (Ministry of Social Affairs), by signing Act No. 81–46 of May 29, 1981 on the promotion and protection of the disabled. The International Year of Disabled Persons (IYDP) seems to be a pivotal period in affirming the ability of the blind to determine themselves. In March 1981, about fifty blind people protested in downtown Tunis to demand the democratization of UNAT, the exclusion of Mohammed Rajhi from the leadership, and the possibility of electing a blind man to the leadership of UNAT.[61] The organization of this demonstration is the culmination of a long series of protests (petitions, press articles) by blind UNAT employees and members against the uncompromising attitude of the management. Until then, the management has always responded with contempt and firmness, firing blind protesters (Ali Sassi, Youssef Ez-Zine). In March 1981, the blind demonstrators obtained the support of the Ministry of Social Affairs, which excluded Mohammed Rajhi and placed a blind man at the head of UNAT.

In Algeria, however, the ongoing process of equalizing rights between the different categories of people with disabilities does not in practice include the blind. The ONAA on the one hand and the Ministry of Health on the other are fighting for and obtaining the provisional preservation of the specificity of the blind sector. The Ministry of Health manages to keep the supervision of the ONAA and the specialized schools until 1982. The ONAA manages to keep the specific professional rights allocated to them. During the IYDP, Mohammed Rajhi, an ILO expert working in Algeria, advised the Algerian government to create a public body to coordinate all policies to assist people with disabilities, without this being applied.[62] A national committee for the IYDP was set up in 1981, without bringing together all the ministries. This attempt of inter-ministerial coordination of sectoral disability policies remains very limited, as it comes up against the will of several ministries (Health, Labour, and Social Affairs, Former

Mujahideen) to maintain complete autonomy. The following year (1982), it led to the transfer of the ONAA's supervision to the State Secretariat for Social Affairs, thus making it possible to group several categories of disabled people under the same supervision. The blind then lose some of the benefits previously granted by the Ministry of Health (40 percent reduction in the amount of their rent).

Strengthening specialized education for the blind, despite enrollment problems

While the international dynamic, since the 1960s, has been aimed at promoting the integration of blind children into mainstream education, the two countries have pursued radically different policies, consolidating the education of blind children in specialized institutions. Although AFOB emissaries (Paul Langan, Jean Sainte-Croix) tried in the 1960s to promote this solution of integrated education in Algeria and Tunisia, this idea remained in its infancy for the following two decades, despite its legitimization by the Franco-African seminar of educators for the blind in Tunis in 1963.[63] In Tunisia, an attempt to integrate several blind children into the mainstream school system in 1963 did not subsequently become widespread.[64] In both countries, there is no massive increase in investment in special education facilities, leading to a relatively stable number of students.

In Algeria, the ONAA requires the development of specialized schools, and finally manages to open a third school in Constantine in 1977. In December 1980, the FLN Central Committee defended the development of specialized schools. Other actors challenge this orientation, in particular the Union of the physically disabled of the wilaya of Algiers, which is against segregating education and is in favor of educating handicapped children alongside "normal" children.[65] In Tunisia, the new orientation set by the law adopted in 1981, determining that "[e]ducation and rehabilitation shall be carried out as far as possible in ordinary educational establishments and, failing that, in specialized establishments," does not change this policy oriented toward the specialized school environment. In 1987, 260 blind people were taught at the En Nour Institute, and about a hundred students attended secondary school at the Institut de Sousse, thanks to the opening of new sections (Letters, Sciences, and Maths). In

1988, these students signed a petition to demand the possibility for students to study in "normal" secondary schools.[66]

In both countries, during the 1980s, there was still a lack of teachers specialized in teaching Braille, and a lack of equipment. To compensate for this lack, the management of the Institut de Sousse requires students to write their copy in black script, in order to be able to hire teachers who do not know Braille. In 1988, out of about thirty teachers, only twelve mastered Braille. That year, the students of Sousse mobilized to protest the impossibility of writing copies in Braille, by systematically returning their homework in Braille.[67]

Fossilization of the orientation of the blind toward brushing in Algeria, and diversification of vocational guidance for the blind in Tunisia

In Algeria, the ONAA wishes to diversify the vocational training of the blind, and to promote their placement in the mainstream labor market. Several dozen blind receive vocational training in ordinary vocational training centers, and since 1981 several dozen others have been receiving vocational training at the new National Vocational Training Centre for the Physically Disabled in Téfeschoun (*wilaya* of Blida). Due to employers' prejudices, very few qualified blind people find employment in the labor market (such as switchboard operators). To remedy this, ONAA leaders are demanding job quotas for the blind in government and private companies. Their claim was legitimized by the FLN's Economic and Social Commission in 1980 but was not successful.

Faced with the lack of employment for the blind in the labor market, the ONAA seeks to ensure the sale of products made by the blind. In the mid- to late 1970s, the ONAA and the Ministry of Social Affairs signed an agreement granting the ONAA the exclusive right to produce several items (brushes and brooms, tweezers). This monopoly allows the company (Entreprise nationale des Brosses or ENABROS) to enjoy great commercial success and to create more cooperatives of blind brushers. Whereas there were 500 blind brushers in 1976, there were 3,600 at the end of the 1980s.[68] Brushing now symbolizes the professional ability of the blind, as shown by the stamp issued by Algeria in 1976 (Fig. 5.1).

الجزائر لإعادة إدراج المكفوفين

1.20

REINSERTION DES AVEUGLES

ALGERIE

MOHAMED TEMMAM

Figure 5.1: Stamp issued by Algeria in 1976

This fossilization of professional opportunities toward brushing occurred despite the emergence of voices (FLN; Union des handicapés moteurs de la wilaya d'Algers; ILO expert Mohammed Rajhi) challenging the restriction of professional opportunities for blind people to brush, and wishing to promote other professional training (agricultural, switchboard operators, and so on).[69]

In Tunisia, UNAT leaders are pursuing their policy of diversifying the vocational training of its members. Several hundred blind people benefited from vocational training in the 1980s in the center of Sidi Thabet or in other training centers (Sousse, and so forth). However, it is possible to observe a deterioration in the quality of the professional training provided by the School of Physiotherapy for the Blind in Sousse and the Higher School of Blind Translators and Interpreters, due to the opening of these schools to sighted students. Several dozen blind people also benefit from vocational training in ordinary centers, as provided for in the law of May 29, 1981. UNAT continues to run production centers and agricultural farms, and organizes a factory to produce cleaning products. But by the mid-1970s, due to the large number of graduates, the integration of blind graduates into the labor market was becoming increasingly difficult (apart from physiotherapy and interpreting). Those who are trained in metal processing do not find employment upon leaving, as do a substantial proportion of those who are trained in carpentry and switchboard work.[70] In 1987, more than 300 blind UNAT graduates remained unemployed.[71] To offer jobs to blind graduates, UNAT leaders are calling on the authorities to adopt measures to guarantee certain professional opportunities (switchboard operators, brush making). The authorities granted the cooperatives of the blind a monopoly on the import of coconut fibre in 1977, and obliged public administrations to purchase cleaning products manufactured by the blind as a matter of priority. Nevertheless, in 1987, the President of UNAT conceded that UNAT had great difficulty in selling the products of these centers. Moreover, the Beja textile cooperative closed its doors in 1978.

UNAT leaders are campaigning for measures that would reserve a low quota of jobs for the blind. In July 1980, the authorities considered a bill giving priority to employment for the blind as switchboard operators,[72] but did not adopt a resolution on the subject until the late 1980s. The 1981 law legitimizes the existence of sheltered workshops "for disabled people who cannot enter the normal employment system" and prohibits any discrimination on the grounds of disability to access employment in the public or private sector (under certain conditions). But the decrees regulating this law were not published during the 1980s, and UNAT complained about it. In addition, blind people are still unable to access teacher positions in primary and secondary schools.

UNAT's placement policy is less effective than that developed in Algeria from a quantitative point of view: at the end of the 1980s, there were fewer than 1,200 blind people in paid employment in Tunisia, compared to more than 3,000 in Algeria thanks to their placement in brush makers' cooperatives.

Conclusion

Algeria and Tunisia are experiencing trajectories of policies for the blind that have diverged significantly since the 1970s. During the colonial period, Algeria was a model for the policies of assistance to the blind for Tunisia and Morocco. In both countries, under pressure from associations, the colonial authorities are late in granting certain specific rights to the blind, without doing the same for other categories of disabled people.

The Algerian blind then conquer substantial economic rights (pension rights and increase), unlike the Tunisian blind. After the proclamation of independence, the Algerian and Tunisian authorities grant specific rights to the blind by adopting new legislative texts, which confirm the rights already acquired. Both countries organize cooperatives of blind workers inspired by socialist experiences. However, UNAT quickly distinguished itself by the diversification of its vocational training, and the shift toward liberal approaches to professional integration in the early 1970s (sheltered workshops, selective placement), the coordination of sectoral disability policies, and the adoption of legislation granting rights to people with disabilities in 1981.

Tunisia is now a polarizing center for the diffusion of techniques of rehabilitation in North Africa. Tunisia therefore applies the main international recommendations on disability, but it fails in guaranteeing jobs for qualified blind people, unlike its Algerian neighbor, which is pursuing the development of cooperatives for the blind and thus succeeds in providing low-skilled jobs for more than 3,000 blind people at the end of the 1980s.

The cyclical de-sectorization and the loss of the specificity of the rights granted to the blind took place at the beginning of the 1980s in Tunisia, and much later in Algeria due to the many forms of resistance associated with the loss of economic and professional privileges. The change in economic orientation from socialism to economic liberalism from 1989 onwards led to real changes in the employment of the blind. Now facing competition from foreign production, ENABROS is facing increasing economic difficulties, which are leading to a gradual decline in the number of blind workers, followed by the definitive closure of blind brush makers' cooperatives in 2009.

The conquest of independence in both countries led to the—partly involuntary—break with dependence on France in the field of social protection for the blind, in favor of a multipolar dependence (and not focused on socialist countries). This breakdown of dependency links with France is mainly the result of cyclical factors that led Algerian and Tunisian leaders to seek available resources elsewhere. Unlike Algerians, Tunisian community leaders made great demands for international aid during the 1960s. In this way, they succeeded in making Tunisia the leading Arab country in terms of social protection for the blind in the 1970s.

Notes

1. Brégain, Gildas (2016). "Colonialism and Disability: The Situation of Blind People in Colonised Algeria." *ALTER, European Journal of Disability Research*, 10(2), 148–167.
2. Muller, Pierre (2010). "Secteur." In Boussaguet, Laurie, Jacquot, Sophie, and Ravinet, Pauline (eds.), Dictionnaire des politiques publiques. Paris: Presses de Sciences Po, 591–599.
3. Brégain, Gildas (2018). *Pour une histoire du handicap au XXe siècle: Approches transnationales (Europe et Amériques)*. Rennes: PUR.
4. Dobry, M. (2009). "Révolutions, crises, transitions." In Fillieule, O., Mathieu, L., and Pechu, C. (eds.), *Dictionnaire des mouvements sociaux*. Paris, Presses de Science Po, 479–483.
5. Brégain, "Colonialism and Disability."
6. Djerbal, Daho (2014). "De la difficile écriture de l'histoire d'une société (dé)colonisée. Interférence des niveaux d'historicité et d'individualité historique." *NAQD, Revue d'études et de critique sociale*, 3(2), 228.
7. Brégain, "Colonialism and Disability."
8. Statistics compiled from the archives of the National Institute for Young Blind People, the Valentin Hauy Association, the Val Mandé Institute, and the colonial archives in Paris.
9. The law of July 14, 1905, art. 30 of the 1930 Finance Act, ordinance of July 3, 1946, law No. 49–1094 of August 2, 1949.
10. Brégain, "Colonialism and Disability."
11. Ibidem.
12. Brégain, *Pour une histoire du handicap au XXe siècle*.
13. In Algeria, the decree of September 8, 1947, decision No. 52–038 of July 2, 1952, the decree of August 26, 1952, and the decree of August 22, 1953; in Tunisia, the Beylical Decree of May 15, 1952.
14. Archives of the wilaya of Algiers (DZ-AWA), 1Z53/190. *Union des Aveugles de Tunisie*, Statutory Assembly of 1955 (n.d.).
15. National Archives of Tunisia (ANT), SG/5, 293, file 10. Letter, November 30, 1951, Tunis, A. *Declère* to the general resident of France in Tunis.
16. Decision No. 52–038.
17. DZ-AWA, 1Z53/2190, FAAN, ordinary GA of 1955, activity report.
18. El Mechat, Samia (2017). "Le protectorat en Tunisie ou la réforme à contre-coeur 1945–1954." *Outre-Mers, Revue d'histoire*, 396–397(2), 51–67.
19. ANT, SG/2, 252, file 15. Letter, Tunis, January 8, 1951, from the Minister of Public Health to the Prime Minister of the Kingdom of Tunisia.
20. UNESCO Archives (AUNESCO), 36 A653 (611) 146. Letter, Mohamed Rajhi, Tunis, February 1, 1955, entitled "General Concepts on the Education of the Blind in Tunisia."
21. DZ-AWA, 1Z53/2190. FAAN, AG ordinaire de 1955, *compte rendu d'activité*.
22. Ibidem, "Assemblée générale ordinaire de 1956, *Compte rendu d'activité*." March 11, 1956.
23. AUNESCO, 36 A653 (611) 146 Tunisia. Letter, Tunis, February 9, 1956, Mohamed Rajhi à Philippe Roux.
24. Ganiage, Jean (1994). *Histoire contemporaine du Maghreb de 1830 à nos jours*. Paris: Fayard, 460.
25. DZ-AWA, 1Z53/2190. FAAN, *Rapport moral*, of Sunday May 23, 1948.
26. *Le Valentin Haüy* (1934), 2(2), 40.

27. ANT, E 509–472, dossier 1. Letter, Tunis, February 24, 1949, Director of Public Education and Fine Arts, Lucien Paye, to the Prime Minister in Tunis.

28. Ibidem.

29. Brégain, Gildas (2019). "De l'interdiction faite à Jacques Lusseyran d'enseigner dans le secondaire (décret du 1er juillet 1942)." In Chottin, Marion, Roussel, Céline, and Weygand Zina (eds.), *Jacques Lusseyran, Entre cécité et Lumière*. Paris: Editions Rue d'Ulm, 67–86.

30. Seklani, Mahmoud (1967). *La mortalité et le coût de la santé publique en Tunisie depuis l'après-guerre, Vol. 1*. Tunis: Université de Tunis.

31. Ben Néfissa, Sarah (2011). "Mobilisations et révolutions dans les pays de la Méditerranée arabe à l'heure de 'l'hybridation' du politique. Égypte, Liban, Maroc, Tunisie." *Revue Tiers Monde*, 5(HS), 5–24.

32. Djelloul, Mustapha (1963). "L'indépendance et les aveugles." *Vue et Lumière. Revue de l'organisation nationale des aveugles algériens*, 1, 5.

33. Belaïd, H. (2004). "Bourguiba et la vie associative pendant la période coloniale et après l'indépendance." In Camau, M., Geisser, M., and Geisser, V. (eds.), *Habib Bourguiba: la trace et l'héritage*. Paris: Karthala, 325–339.

34. Tainturier, Pierre (2017). *Associations et révolution au prisme du local: le cas de Tozeur en Tunisie* (PhD thesis, Conservatoire national des arts et metiers).

35. International Labour Office (ABIT) Archives, RH 1–68, jacket 1. Paul J. Langan, AFOB, August 9, 1965, "Report on Algeria".

36. Gallissot, René (1999). "Mouvements associatifs et mouvement social: le rapport Etat/société dans l'histoire maghrébine." *Insaniyat*, 8, 5–19.

37. Molinero, Carmen (2011). *La captación de las masas: Politica social y propaganda en el regimen franquista*. Madrid: Catedra.

38. Djelloul, "L'indépendance et les aveugles," 7.

39. ABIT, RH 1–68, jacket 1. ONAA National Congress held in Ben-Aknoun on August 27, 28, and 29, 1964.

40. *L'aveugle du maghreb arabe* (1960, November), III.

41. Law No. 63–200 of June 8, 1963, on the social protection of the blind in Algeria.

42. See, resp. the *Official Gazette of the Tunisian Republic* (1968, March 8–12), 249–250. Ibidem (1969, January 17–24), 91–92. Ibidem (1972, March 24–28), 373.

43. National Union of the Blind of Tunisia (1973a). *L'aveugle au travail*. Tunis: Impression UGTT, 16.

44. Tunis National Library, Braille Library Archives, Rajhi Collection (BNT-ABB, FR), box 1972–1966. (1966, July 20). *A l'institut En-Nour, les professeurs sont parfois, eux aussi, des aveugles. La Presse*.

45. Ibidem.

46. ABIT, RH 1–68, jacket 1. ONAA National Congress held in Ben-Aknoun on August 27, 28, and 29, 1964.

47. *L'aveugle du maghreb arabe*, Tunis, September 1960, XI.

48. Djelloul, "L'indépendance et les aveugles," 9.

49. ABIT, RH 1–68, jacket 1. Letter dated September 12, 1967, Palaiseau, Descoubes to Mr Schircks.

50. Ibidem. ONAA, Teaching young blind children, for the Algerian government.

51. Byrne, Jeffrey James (2016). *Mecca of Revolution: Algeria, Decolonization and the Third World Order*. Oxford and New York: Oxford University Press.

52. Archives nationales de Pierrefitte, France (ANP), 19760177/106. Copy of a letter, Algiers, August 4, 1964, from the Minister of Social Affairs (the Director of Cabinet Areski Azi) to the High Representative of France in Algeria.

53. A cubarithm is a plastic tray containing a grid of square holes and a box of plastic cubes with Braille numbers on them and helps in the teaching of arithmetic.

54. This center, unique in the French-speaking African sphere, trains about a hundred trainees (physiotherapists, interpreters, teachers, and instructors) from various French-speaking African countries in ten years. Chaired by Wassila Bourguiba, it receives grants from the Tunisian government and technical support from UNESCO and the International Labour Organization (ILO).

55. Brégain, *Pour une histoire du handicap au XXe siècle.*

56. BNT-ABB, FR, box 1972–1966. (1970, July 9). *En vue d'une meilleure intégration des aveugles à la vie sociale et économique. La Presse.*

57. Chouikha, Larbi and Gobe, Eric (2015). *Histoire de la Tunisie depuis l'Indépendance.* Paris: Editions La découverte, Repères.

58. National Union of the Blind of Tunisia, *Actions et réalisations.*

59. ABIT, RH 1–68, jacket 1. Document entitled "People's Democratic Republic of Algeria" (1976). "Information submitted to WCWB office in Stockholm."

60. Ibidem, TAP 0881(D) 2. Letter, Mrs. Ben Hamida, Deputy Director of the Blind Centre to the Director of Vocational Training, Tunis.

61. BNT-ABB, FR, box 2004–1980 (1981, March 17). *Marche pacifique à Bab Benat. Des aveugles revendiquent un congrès extraordinaire. La Presse.*

62. International Labour Organization (ILO) (1981). *Report to the Government of the People's Democratic Republic of Algeria on the Rehabilitation, Vocational Training, and Employment of Persons with Disabilities.* ILO, 8.

63. ABIT, RH 1–68, jacket 1. Paul J. Langan, AFOB, August 9, 1965, "Report on Algeria."

64. BNT, BB-FR, box 1965–1960. Article entitled *"Regards sur l'Union nationale des aveugles de Tunisie,"* March 1963. The name of the newspaper is not cited.

65. AAA, 370. (1980 or 1981). *Comité d'entente des handicapés moteurs Algériens/Union des Handicapés moteurs de la wilaya d'Alger, Scolarité des Handicapés: Eléments de réflexion.* Alger: FLN Central Committee, 6.

66. BNT, BB-FR, box 2004–1980. (1988, February 15). *"Ils ne demandent pas l'impossible." Dialogue,* 697.

67. Ibidem. (1988, February 15). *"Lycée des non voyants de Sousse: Ils manquent de tout." Dialogue,.*

68. Hamadou, Farida (2009, October 11). *"Quel sort pour les 185 travailleurs? Dissolution de L'epih (Ex-ENABROS)."* El Watan.

69. ABIT, RH 1–68, jacket 1. FLN, *Comité central, Rapports et résolutions du séminaire pour un programme national d'intégration des personnes handicapées du 14 au 16 mars 1981.*

70. BNT, BB-FR, box 2004–1980. W. Sfar W. and Ouaer, M. (1981, January 11–17). *"Le dossier noir des aveugles."* Le Phare.

71. Ibidem. (1987, February 2). *"Entretien avec Yahia Yahia, President de l'UNAT."* Dialogue.

72. Ibidem. (1980, July 25). *Mohammed Mzali préside la réunion du Conseil des Ministres. La presse.*

References

Belaïd, H. (2004). "Bourguiba et la vie associative pendant la période coloniale et après l'indépendance." In Camau, M., Geisser, M., and Geisser, V. (eds.), *Habib Bourguiba: la trace et l'héritage* (pp. 325–339). Paris: Karthala.

Ben Néfissa, Sarah (2011). "Mobilisations et révolutions dans les pays de la Méditerranée arabe à l'heure de 'l'hybridation' du politique. Égypte, Liban, Maroc, Tunisie." *Revue Tiers Monde*, 5(HS), 5–24.

Brégain, Gildas (2016). "Colonialism and Disability: The Situation of Blind People in Colonised Algeria." *ALTER, European Journal of Disability Research*, 10(2), 148–167.

Brégain, Gildas (2018). *Pour une histoire du handicap au XXe siècle: Approches transnationales (Europe et Amériques)*. Rennes: PUR.

Brégain, Gildas (2019). "De l'interdiction faite à Jacques Lusseyran d'enseigner dans le secondaire (décret du 1er juillet 1942)." In Chottin, Marion, Roussel, Céline, and Weygand Zina (eds.), *Jacques Lusseyran, Entre cécité et Lumière* (pp. 67–86). Paris: Editions Rue d'Ulm.

Byrne, Jeffrey James (2016). *Mecca of Revolution: Algeria, Decolonization, and the Third World Order*. Oxford and New York: Oxford University Press.

Chouikha, Larbi and Gobe, Eric (2015). *Histoire de la Tunisie depuis l'Indépendance*. Paris: Editions La découverte, Repères.

Djelloul, Mustapha (1963). "L'indépendance et les aveugles." *Vue et Lumière. Revue de l'organisation nationale des aveugles algériens*, 1-5.

Djerbal, Daho (2014). "De la difficile écriture de l'histoire d'une société (dé)colonisée. Interférence des niveaux d'historicité et d'individualité historique." *NAQD, Revue d'études et de critique sociale*, 3(2), 213–231.

Dobry M. (2009). "Révolutions, crises, transitions." In Fillieule, O., Mathieu, L., and Pechu, C. (eds.), *Dictionnaire des mouvements sociaux* (pp. 479–483). Paris: Presses de Science Po.

El Mechat, Samia (2017). "Le protectorat en Tunisie ou la réforme à contre-coeur 1945-1954." *Outre-Mers, Revue d'histoire*, 396–397(2), 51–67.

Ganiage, Jean (1994). *Histoire contemporaine du Maghreb de 1830 à nos jours. Paris:* Fayard.

Gallissot, René (1999). "Mouvements associatifs et mouvement social: le rapport Etat/société dans l'histoire maghrébine." *Insaniyat /*19–5 ,8, إنسانيات.

Hamadou, Farida (2009, October 11). "*Quel sort pour les 185 travailleurs? Dissolution de L'epih (Ex-ENABROS)*." *El Watan*. https://www.djazairess.com/fr/elwatan/139736

International Labour Organization (ILO) (1981). *Report to the Government of the People's Democratic Republic of Algeria on the Rehabilitation, Vocational Training, and Employment of Persons with Disabilities*. ILO.

Le Valentin Haüy (1934), 2(2).

Molinero, Carmen (2011). *La captación de las masas: Politica social y propaganda en el regimen franquista*. Madrid: Catedra.

Muller, Pierre (2010). "Secteur." In Boussaguet, Laurie, Jacquot, Sophie, and Ravinet, Pauline (eds.), *Dictionnaire des politiques publiques (pp. 591–599)*. Paris: Presses de Sciences Po.

National Union of the Blind of Tunisia (UNAT) (1973a). *L'aveugle au travail*. Tunis: Impression UGTT.

Seklani, Mahmoud (1967). *La mortalité et le coût de la santé publique en Tunisie depuis l'après-guerre, Vol. 1*. Tunis: Université de Tunis.

Tainturier, Pierre (2017). *Associations et révolution au prisme du local: le cas de Tozeur en Tunisie* (PhD thesis, Conservatoire national des arts et metiers).

CHAPTER 6

Disability, Humanitarian Diplomacy, and the Roman Catholic Church in Modern Palestine

Maria Chiara Rioli

Abstract

This chapter discusses an instance of religious humanitarianism: the mission of the Dorothean nuns who arrived in Palestine from Italy in 1927 and opened the Effeta school for deaf Palestinian children in 1971. Based on extensive archival material, the chapter explores the history and practices toward deaf children carried out by the Dorothean nuns. The chapter discusses the international circulation of medical and rehabilitation ideas and practices, and it reveals that Catholic humanitarianism in the Middle East was embedded in political and diplomatic relations between Israel, Jordan, Italy, the United Nations Relief and Works Agency for Palestine Refugees in the Near East, and, since the 1990s, the Palestinian authority. By pointing to the cooperation between the Effeta school and the Palestinian authorities, it also nuances the idea that at the end of the twentieth century secular and Catholic forms of welfare toward disability run separately.

Keywords: Palestine, religious humanitarianism, Roman Catholic Church, disability

Introduction[1]

On June 30, 1971, Cardinal Maximilien de Fürstenberg, Prefect of the Vatican Congregation for the Oriental Churches, arrived in the city of Bethlehem from Rome to celebrate the inauguration of a school. This school, located on the road historically linking Jerusalem and Hebron, was called Effeta ("Be opened!" in Aramaic)[2] and it remains until today a Pontifical Institute dedicated to Paul VI and run by a congregation of Roman Catholic sisters of Italian origin, the Teaching Sisters of St. Dorothy, Daughters of the Sacred Hearts, who are better known as the Dorotheans (Fig. 6.1). Initially planned as a school for Palestinian girls and a house of retreat for nuns, during its construction and after Pope Paul VI's pilgrimage to Jordan and Israel in January 1964 it was transformed into a school for Palestinian deaf children, boys and girls, some of them refugees, mainly from East Jerusalem, the West Bank (especially the Hebron and Bethlehem areas), and the Gaza Strip.

The choice of Bethlehem for this pontifical institution was not accidental: the town has extreme importance for Catholicism in the region, traditionally, as birth place of Jesus, but also historically, due to the presence of the largest Roman Catholic community in Palestine and the activism of the friars of the Franciscan Custody of the Holy Land, the most ancient Catholic congregation in the region.[3] Beside the Custody itself, the foundation of the Effeta school relates to the history of the main Roman Catholic institutions operating in the so-called "Holy Land" and their involvement and practices in assistance to persons with disability. The Latin Patriarchate—the Roman Catholic diocese—was created in 1099 during the Crusades and then re-established in 1847 by Pope XI.[4] It covers the areas corresponding nowadays to Israel, the occupied Palestinian territory (East Jerusalem, the West Bank, and the Gaza Strip), Jordan, and Cyprus. It was and still is responsible for a network of schools, hospitals, and infrastructures for assistance of pupils and adults, including with disability.

In the Effeta school establishment, together with the Latin Patriarchate, the Apostolic Delegation of Jerusalem and Palestine played a relevant role, as the Holy See's seat in the region.[5] Moreover, Effeta was also connected to the Pontifical Mission for Palestine, the main Vatican humanitarian agency devoted to assisting Palestinian refugees, created in 1949 by Pius XII, in the aftermath of the 1947–1949 war and the fleeing and expulsion of more than 750,000 Palestinians.[6] The history of Effeta offers a perspective for revisiting the forms of collaboration or competition between Christian institutions—more specifically, Catholics and Protestants—but also religious and non-religious organization, as in the case of the relations between Effeta and the United Nations Relief and Works Agency for Palestine Refugees in the Near East (UNRWA), established in 1949 and operational since 1950.[7]

Figure 6.1: The Effeta school in Bethlehem in 1971, the year of its inauguration

In an epoch marked by profound transformations and dramatic upheavals in the region—the new importance of Palestine during the late Ottoman period in the late nineteenth century and early twentieth; the First World War and the creation of the British Mandate (1918–1948); the reality emerging after the 1948 War, with the establishment of the Israeli State and the issue of Palestinian refugees; and, since 1967, the Israeli occupation of East Jerusalem, the West Bank, and the Gaza Strip—numerous Roman Catholic institutions and congregations addressed or excluded people with disability through schools, hospitals, and pastoral care.

Effeta is set in this history and at the same time presents a particular aspect: it constitutes the unique educational entity to persons with disability—in this case, deaf children—whose foundation was directly requested by the Vatican, as made evident by the characterization of "Pontifical" for this institute. It thus contains in its establishment and mission some strands of the Holy See's vision and goals in the region. At the same time, as this chapter will outline, the following developments in the methodologies used for training and education of deaf children, the gradual autonomy it gained, and the way the institute navigated the wars and conflicts in the region since its foundations in the 1970s to nowadays highlight how this experience was not a mere derivation dependent to the Holy See, but represented an original experiment for the nuns, the families, and the students who worked in and attended it.

This chapter explores the history and the practices toward deaf children carried out by the Dorotheans in Bethlehem. The Effeta school was not the first place in the region where the Dorotheans assisted people with disability. Almost twenty years after their arrival in Palestine in 1927, they were asked to serve in the Bethlehem psychiatric hospital by the British Mandate authorities. In the 1970s, the Apostolic Delegation asked the nuns to open what then became the Effeta school. These developments are intertwined with the history of disability in twentieth-century Palestine, before and after the watershed years of 1948 and 1967, and in the longer history of modern Palestine. It is also interconnected with questions related to the history of Catholic humanitarianism in the Middle East, the international circulation of medical and rehabilitation ideas and practices, as well as political and diplomatic relations between Israel, Jordan, the Vatican, Italy, and, since the 1990s, the Palestinian Authority.

While the history of disability remains underdeveloped in the history of Christianity, including the history of the Roman Catholic Church,[8] religious congregations played a pivotal role in caring and controlling persons with disability throughout the medieval, modern, and contemporary periods. Christianity has the incarnation of Jesus at the very core of its dogmas. The body is central in this doctrinal configuration. The negation or subjugation of the body to the soul, although significantly present in some of the first Christian authors, contrasts with the view of other fundamental Christian main references. This conflictual relation with the body is crucial in the complex history of Christian assumptions and practices toward disability. Disability was considered for centuries as a sign of punishment for personal or family's sins. However, other visions of disability have been historically elaborated within Christianity: a mystery, a test to measure the faith of individuals and families, a condition for the manifestation of God, a sign to inspire people. Interpretations of Hebrew Bible, Gospels, and Pauline letters have reinforced the stigma of a separated—although in some way "chosen"—minority.

Since the 1960s–1970s, feminist, liberation, and contextual Christian theologies have been devoting growing attention to disability to unpack the image of God as Father, and the related vision of the human as minor, child, made disable by sin. This vision also historically had been intertwined with the essentialization of disability and infantilization of the person with disability, depicted as a baby or a child, incapable and innocent. This was not a prerogative of Christian interpretations of disability, but Christian institutions and norms strengthened and crystallized it not only in the forms of assistance, but also in limiting access to sacraments. More recent attempts of reframing theologies and sacramental practices on disability and developing inclusive pastoral care are pursued and debated within Christianity, as in the case of the 2023 Synod of Bishops of the Roman Catholic Church.[9]

Approaching case studies like Effeta where the directives from the Roman Catholic institutions and practices developed in Europe were received and performed by missionary congregations in non-Christian areas, shed lights on the similarities and variations in interpreting disability, assistance to persons with disability, and their own forms of agency and activism. Effeta's history can also be approached through the angle of the history of humanitarianism and humanitarian diplomacy in its entanglements with cultural diplomacy in the Middle East and its entanglements with Europe. Historiography has devoted attention to elaborating various definitions of humanitarianism. As Silvia Salvatici, one of the most prominent historians of humanitarianism, has clarified, "when we talk about 'international humanitarianism' we are referring to the organised help for individuals who are victims of war, natural disasters or disadvantaged economic circumstances in the countries in which they live. The overall deployment of the help is promoted by specific institutions and organisations, is regulated by ad hoc legislation, and nowadays uses operating standards recognised at a supranational level."[10]

The reflection on the humanitarianism category builds over the experience of Christian, Jewish, and Muslim organizations during the centuries.[11] Humanitarian diplomacy is deeply connected with cultural diplomacy. Karène Sanchez Summerer devoted seminal studies to the elaboration of a cultural and humanitarian diplomacy by Christian institutions and mission in modern Palestine. Cultural diplomacy—as well as humanitarian diplomacy—is not merely a form of "soft power." It relates to "the activities of states and institutions operationalising culture as a means to wield power and communicate ideologies, but also Arab associations and individuals as cultural diplomats themselves."[12] As highlighted by Nisa Ari, "as a ubiquitous, though often perfunctory, term in the fields of art history, cultural studies, non-profit and humanitarian studies, and international relations, the concept of the cultural sector has yet to be historicised or positioned in relation to dominant frameworks of cultural diplomacy."[13]

Effeta interplays religious, cultural, and humanitarian diplomacy with disability. To unfold these connections, the history of the Dorotheans will be analysed and framed within the wider Roman Catholic missionary historical framework in the Levant, interrogating the unexplored archives of the congregation in Vicenza and the documents collected at the Effeta institute in Bethlehem, as well as the Latin Patriarchate archives in Jerusalem and Italian Foreign Office archives in Rome. The role of the Dorotheans in the psychiatric hospital in Bethlehem from 1946 and the foundation of the Effeta school for deaf children in the late 1960s and early 1970s will then be retraced to underline commonalities and specificities of these experiences and to draw initial observations and reflections on the interconnection between history of disability, humanitarian diplomacy,[14] and Catholic congregational action in modern Palestine.

Disability in modern Palestine: archival traces of a silenced story

Historically, disability is a multifaceted notion that has encompassed profoundly different meanings, conditions, and representations. In the modern age, it is intertwined with the concepts of normalcy, health, pathology, mentality, race, ethnicity, law, citizenship, poverty, victimhood, and social dis/order, and can be approached through several lenses, including biological, cultural, and political. Where to find the traces of people, including children, with disability? This is a far from an obvious question. The word "archive" itself contains an irreducible ambiguity: while it refers to objects, defining a record or a series of record, meaning a source of information, with a permanent value, it also means a place of custody, a repository, a place of safekeeping, an institution with an access regime. An extensive scholarship has worked on the redefinition of the notion of archive, from rigid category to a more inclusive concept.

Ecclesiastical archives contain a multitude of records that enable us to approach and unpack the perceptions and practices in defining and dealing with disability by charities, humanitarian, health, and educational actors. The Dorotheans' archives in Vicenza and Bethlehem differ in the documentation: the Generalice House is an institutional archive, similar for structure to congregations' archives, and it contains the documentation addressed to and coming from the Holy See and a rich collection of photographs. The Bethlehem archive concentrates on the Effeta school and contains documentation produced on site. They both preserve on papers produced by the nuns and the Vatican institutions. Traces of documents produced by the students and the families is less visible, although not completely absent.

These archives shed light on the transformation of the notion of disability in the twentieth century and as it was applied by an Italian Roman Catholic congregation in the Palestinian context. The emergence of the "disability lexicon" is relevant to identifying the emergence and the transformation of this concept within Arab societies: if in English there is a difference in the historical use of terms like "handicapped," "mentally defective," "retarded," "cripple," "subnormal," "invalid," or "insane," in Arabic the words "disability" (*i'āqa*) and "disabled" (*mu'awwaq*) appeared during the twentieth century, in place of "people with defects" or "people with blights."[15] Thus, Muslim societies and institutions played a pivotal role in the elaboration of the category of disability.

A growing scholarship have focused on the history of medicine, diseases, and epidemics in the region, providing significant scholarship on the history of mental and physical health. In particular, due to its growing political importance within the Ottoman Empire during the nineteenth century, to Zionist ambitions and to its cultural and religious relevance, Jerusalem, its different communities (Palestinian Arab, Jewish, Armenian, Syrian, Greek, Ethiopian components, among others), and Palestine more widely, and the Jewish medical service in particular, have been the subject of numerous and innovative studies in the field of the history of medicine.[16] Some contributions have offered insights into the elaboration of Hebrew and Arabic sign language. In 1932 a school for deaf people was established in Jerusalem.[17] This school was created by the Alliance israélite universelle, already present in Palestine since 1870 with a network of schools for boys and girls. Since the late 1920s, an Italian deaf Jew, Leone Levy, devoted his efforts to creating a school for deaf children, then opened in the early 1930s.

Christian congregational institutions, composed and ruled by Arab and non-Arab—especially European—religious and lay staff, who were responsible for an extensive network of schools and orphanages, enrolled children with disability among their pupils in their schools and orphanages, not only from Christian but also Muslim and Jewish families, underlining the mixedness and diversity that characterized education enrollment in the region in the late Ottoman period. In this framework, the case of the activities of a specific Roman Catholic congregation—the Dorotheans—deepens questions related to the history of disability, the history of humanitarianism, and the history of Christianity, from the Mandate period through the storm of 1948 and to the aftermath of the June 1967 war.

Between a crusade and offering assistance: the Dorotheans in Palestine

The Teaching Sisters of St. Dorothy, Daughters of the Sacred Hearts, were established by Antonio Farina (1803–1888), bishop of Treviso and Vicenza from 1850 to his death, in the Habsburg-ruled Kingdom of Lombardy–Venetia, which, in 1866, became part of the Kingdom of Sardinia and later the Kingdom of Italy.[18] One of the main areas of charitable intervention by the Farina and the congregation he initiated was the education of deaf children. In this activity, Farina was inspired by Antonio Provolo (1801–1842), founder of the religious congregation of the Society of Mary for the Education of the Deaf and of the "Institute for the education of deaf-mute" in Verona, a town close to Vicenza. In his numerous publications, Provolo provided the theoretical basis for an oral method teaching children to recognize lip movements and shapes and concentrating also on developing the pupils' voice. This methodology garnered considerable attention and was applied by other religious schools in the region and beyond.[19]

These foundations were part of a wider expansion of Roman Catholic assistance activity, which included the education of the deaf. During the nineteenth century, more than twenty-five special institutes with this purpose were established in Italy, mainly by Roman Catholic initiatives and congregations, as in the case of the Daughters of the Providence founded in Modena by Severino Fabriani.[20] Some of these foundations were exclusively dedicated to deaf boys and girls, while others include this activity with other pastoral goals, including the Dorotheans.

The mission to educate deaf boys and girls was seen as a means to instruct them in Catholic doctrine: a significant number of treatises and manuals on the catechism for the deaf-mute were published and circulated widely across Italy and beyond. The mission saw as a complementary objective the education of deaf-mute boys and girls—especially girls—in moral content, thus creating a bulwark against the "errors of modernity," as defined by Pius IX in his Syllabus. Due to their condition, the deaf-mute were seen to be particularly prone to these errors.

Farina was indebted in his methodology to Provolo. A few decades after Provolo's death, experiments with the oral method grew and became sufficiently widespread in Lombardy and Veneto, leading the latter to prevail over the previously prevalent mime gesture method. In 1873 the first congress of Italian teachers of deaf-mutes endorsed the oral method as the preferred method, a decision strengthened at the Second International Congress on Education of the Deaf in Milan in 1880. The oral method was considered more respectful:

> The Congress, considering the incontestable superiority of speech over signs in restoring the deaf mute to society and in giving him a more perfect knowledge of language, declares that the oral method ought to be preferred to that of signs for the education and instruction of the deaf and dumb.[21]

Farina reappropriated Provolo's teachings and re-elaborated them in the didactics offered in the congregation's schools that grew in number at the turn of the century.

As was the case in other Roman Catholic congregations, in the early twentieth century religious congregations opened up to missionary enterprises. In 1924, on the request of the Congregation of Saint Joseph (also known as the Murialdine Fathers), founded by Leonardo Murialdo, the Dorotheans started their first mission in Ecuador, in the province of Napo.[22] Two years later, in October 1926, the Mother General, Sister Azelia Dorotea Farinea, was informed about the intention of the Latin Patriarch of Jerusalem, Luigi Barlassina,[23] to request the sending of nuns as missionary collaborators in the boys' orphanage that the Latin Patriarchate intended to open in Rafat.[24] This project, which aimed to create a Catholic alternative to Jewish agricultural colonies in Palestine,[25] was of "direct interest" to Barlassina.[26] In November 1926, the Dorotheans General Council accepted Barlassina's proposal to destinate four sisters to this new mission. Mother General Azelia was also motivated by the goal of "redeeming the Upper Room in Jerusalem," the site traditionally identified as the location of Jesus's Last Supper. The Christian Cenacle had been transformed into a mosque by the Ottomans in the sixteenth century.[27] Azelia aimed at "snatching that sacred place from the hands of those who did not know its value."[28]

The first sisters left on April 7, 1927, from Venice, aboard the Lloyd Triestino steamer *Palacky*. The costs for the journey were covered by an Italian senator, Ernesto Schiaparelli.[29] Upon arrival at Jaffa, they went to Jerusalem, visited the Holy Sepulchre and the Cenacle, and on May 5 they moved to set up house in preparation for the opening of a school for poor children in Rafat, where the orphanage dedicated to Our Lady Queen of Rafat was assigned to them. The "spirit of a Crusade"[30] for the vaguely defined "redemption of the Upper Room" that motivated the missionary enterprise was gradually put aside as the priorities and tasks of care and apostolate work, particularly in Rafat, became more pressing. The sisters were mainly involved in running the Rafat orphanage, teaching catechism, and caring for the sick in nearby villages through a home-based clinic.[31]

Since the late 1920s, Palestine experienced increasing levels of violence. Especially after the 1929 riots,[32] the uncertainty about the future also reverberated in the chronicles of the Dorotheans in Rafat. The events of the 1936–1939 revolt were marked as foundational in the memory of the congregation.[33] After the entry of Italy in the Second World War in June 1940, the Deir Rafat orphanage became an internment camp for Italian priests and seminarists, and its educational activities interrupted.

In the years immediately before the 1948 catastrophe, the Dorotheans had turned their work more openly to the assistance to persons with psychiatric issues. In 1946 Dr R. H. Bland, Assistant Director of Medical Services, requested the Latin Patriarch to provide some nuns for service at the psychiatric hospital in Bethlehem and Barlassina nominated the Dorotheans for this task. This demand stemmed from internal discussions within the British government on Palestine. In 1946, the Assistant Senior Medical Officer shared with the assistant chief secretary, D.C. Thompson, concerns "about the difficulties we encounter in staffing our mental hospitals with suitable and contented nurses." According to the Assistant Senior Medical Officer, "few girls in Palestine appear to have a vocation for dealing with the Mentally Sick and so the service of these unfortunate suffers greatly."[34] Following one of the tropes of the orientalist discourse, the Assistant Senior Medical Officer judged Arab girls to be "unsuitable" for caring for this type of patient, in contrast to the mostly European Christian congregations: "it has occurred to me that if Religious orders could be interested in this aspect of medicine in Palestine great good would result."[35]

The British were not the first to engage with the field of psychiatry in Palestine. Colonial psychiatry in Palestine was part of a longer history of psychiatry in the region, grounded in the legacies of the Ottoman period. During the late Ottoman period, Palestinians had access to a variety of medical and non-medical approaches for the treatment of mental illness. These existing frameworks, along with the experiences and institutions that shaped them, significantly influenced the British response to mental health after their occupation of Palestine in 1917 and the establishment of the mandate in 1920.

In 1922 and 1932, the first two government mental hospitals were established outside Bethlehem. During the 1930s, especially after the 1931 census that included an analysis of the "insane" population in Palestine, the British increased the production of colonial knowledge on psychiatry. During the 1930s and the 1940s, a range of therapies utilizing work, drugs, and electricity were introduced into both private and government-run mental institutions in Palestine.[36]

The request of the British mandate's department of health formulated in 1946 to the Latin Patriarch for services of religious personnel for the first government mental hospital in Bethlehem was situated in the context of professionalization of doctors, nurses, and attendants employed in mental hospitals in Palestine. In the late 1910s and early 1920s, regulations and a full syllabus for the training of nurses were published.[37] Moreover, the department of health was probably motivated by other reasons in opting for religious personnel: the Arab nurses were increasing their claims in terms of respect of rights in salary and work-time. Religious personnel was considered less expensive and less active in requesting better conditions of work.

On July 23, 1946, in a Jerusalem under curfew the day after the King David Hotel bombing by the Irgun Zionist militia,[38] a group of six sisters, escorted by policemen, left Jerusalem to start their service at the psychiatric hospital in Bethlehem, which was under the authority of the Department of Health of the British Mandate authorities. In a report of the congregation reassessing the first ten years of work, the sisters noted that they were requested "for the care of demented patients in the most agitated ward." The working hours, the report continued, "were fair and balanced. The Sisters had 3 hours off per day and holidays. In 1947, 4 more nurse sisters entered; those who did not have a diploma studied privately for 3 years, took their exams and were promoted."[39]

In order to take care of patients, the sisters studied Arabic and English, and, according to internal documents, received "lessons in psychiatry, first aid, psychology," also with the aim of "getting to know the local mentality and customs better" and improving relations with the local staff (Fig. 6.2). The chronicles and internal reports do not neglect to underline the very difficult relations with nurses and orderlies of Arab origin, especially after the 1948 War.

The Palestinian War also had profound consequences for religious communities. In September Deir Rafat, including its monastery, was mostly blown up by the Israeli army.[40] In 1949 the sisters were able to reopen the kindergarten for a small number of children. The ambitions to "reconquest" the Upper Room, which passed to Israeli control in 1948, were a distant memory.

According to the nuns, the Bethlehem hospital's passage to Jordanian control aggravated their conditions, and conflict with Arab nurses became more frequent: "The Sisters' situation becomes critical, the work increases and they are often not paid and the relationship with the Arab nurses is difficult. Sometimes they [the Sisters] are on the verge of withdrawing but they resist to do good to the poor sick."

Figure 6.2: The community of sisters in the Bethlehem governorate psychiatric hospital in 1948

In 1957, the hospital housed 250 people, with fifty-seven nursing staff and ten nuns. During the June 1967 war, the hospital was bombed: "Today is Bethlehem's turn. From 11 to 12 a.m. they bombed our hospital. As soon as we could, we ran to the shelter during the short stop [...] It felt like hell," the chronicle of the hospital community recorded on June 6, 1967.[41]

Unexpected voices: the establishment of Effeta

The 1960s were a decade of revolution and change also for global Catholicism. The election of Pope John XXIII in 1958 and the holding of the Second Vatican Council in 1962–1965 brought about tremendous transformations in the Roman Catholic Church and its relations with religions, cultures, and societies, including the complex drafting and approval of the Nostra Aetate declaration on the relations of the Church with non-Christian religions.[42]

During Vatican II, Paul VI, who succeeded John XXIII after his death in June 1963, announced in the 1963 Christmas message the first papal pilgrimage to the Holy Land.[43] Paul VI visited Jordan and Israel on January 4–6, 1964. This event was a benchmark in the Holy See's diplomacy in the region. This was the first papal journey to the State of Israel, which had no formal relationship with the Holy See, and to Jordan.[44] The Hashemite Kingdom sought to benefit from the journey in two main ways: to promote an unprecedented boost to tourism and to present Jordan as the Holy Land, strengthening the efforts to legitimize Jordanian control over the holy places in Jerusalem and Bethlehem.[45]

Following the pope's visit, the Holy See sought to create two institutions meant as symbols of his visit. The pilgrimage had its most groundbreaking moment in the encounter between Paul VI and Constantinople Patriarch Athenagoras at the Holy Sepulchre. Therefore, the first proposal to continue these ecumenical efforts was the construction of Tantur Ecumenical Institute, a theological institution aiming at combining ecumenical commitment with the desire to contribute to dialogue with Judaism and Islam, promoting research and meetings for a peaceful resolution of the Israeli–Palestinian conflict without taking political positions.[46]

Paul VI conceived the pilgrimage also an act of proximity to the poor and especially the refugees of the region, following a centuries-dated tradition of pilgrimages to the "Holy Land."[47] According to Vatican documentation, during his travel to Jordan, Palestine, and Israel, Paul VI was moved by the numbers of deaf he noticed. This fed the idea of creating an institution to assist and educate deaf-mute children. In the first negotiations, a piece of land that the Jordanian government had offered after the pope's visit was initially identified. This portion of land was located in the area of ʿAzariya—the biblical Bethany—in East Jerusalem, but various difficulties arose that prevented its use.

In this phase, Apostolic Delegate Pio Laghi (1969–1973) was reluctant to erect a new structure. He sent the Dorotheans the proposal to transform the scope of the new nursery school into a "school for deaf-mute girls" they were building in Bethlehem at that time.[48] The building under construction was initially meant to respond to the ambition of the Mother General, Sister Irma Zorzanello,

> to offer the female youth of the Land of Jesus a place for spiritual encounters (moments of prayer, spiritual retreats, study days, conferences); to give the children so loved by Jesus, in a model kindergarten, a sound Christian education; to give its Religious, in need of spiritual and physical rest, an oasis of peace and serenity.[49]

The land chosen was part of a property owned by the Daughters of Charity of Saint Vincent de Paul, one of the main female congregations in the Holy Land. The land was situated in Bethlehem, on the road connecting Jerusalem and Hebron, very close to the Patriarchal Seminary in Beit Jala. The Dorotheans had purchased the 6,790-square-meter plot in 1965. The plans for the new building were drawn up by the architect al-Ghazzawi, who was originally from Bethlehem, and the construction was entrusted to the contractor Handal, also from Bethlehem. On December 8, 1966, Patriarch Alberto Gori, an Italian friar, laid the foundation stone.

Bethlehem was symbolically perfect for a pontifical school for children: the identification between the deaf children and the baby Jesus was powerful in communicating the care of the Holy See for the "Holy Land" and mobilizing in terms of potential donations from abroad. Since the nineteenth century, the city, historically containing the largest Roman Catholic community in the Franciscan friars' parish, had knew emigration to the Greater Syria and to the Americas.[50]

The establishment of Effeta represented an evolution of the forms of direct and indirect activism by the Roman Catholic Church in the area toward families with persons (children, young, and adults) with disability: from financial incentives that historically the Franciscan friars distributed to family and individuals and assistance through assistance institutions and programs, to the foundation of a stable structure with pontifical approval and supervision.[51] The 1967 War on June 5–10 marked another radical change for the inhabitants of the Bethlehem region, with the territory falling under Israeli occupation.[52] Due to the new political and administrative situation, the construction work could not be resumed until March 26, 1968, after all outstanding issues with the previous architect and contractor had been settled, and it was entrusted to the architect Yitzhak Moshe Lewkowicz,[53] who had already worked on the Basilica of the Annunciation in Nazareth, and the contractor Samih Noufi from Nazareth.[54]

In 1970, when the Dorotheans received from the Apostolic Delegate the request to modify this house into an educational institution for deaf-mute children, the sisters hesitated and transmitted the Vatican proposal to the Generalate of the sisters in Vicenza.[55] The Apostolic Delegate expressly chose the Dorotheans for their previous experience assisting the deaf.[56] Pio Laghi addressed his request to the Mother General. In the Apostolic Delegation's view, the original plan to create a nursery school, "designed in 1964 when the local political situation was challenging," was "now not [...] very appropriate in its fringe concerning childhood," while a diocesan endeavor would be, according to Patriarch Gori, "plausible in front of the population; and finally, very humanitarian."[57]

The proposal was accepted. The cost estimate soon turned out to be ambitious, which generated a series of difficulties between the congregation, the Patriarchate, and the Holy See. The initial estimate of 165,000 Italian lira (corresponding to about 265 million US dollars) proved insufficient to cover all expenses, which were finally estimated at 200 million. Patriarch Alberto Gori demanded that the congregation cover the difference. In January 1971, the Mother General, albeit with some reservations, decided to take out a loan of 53,000 Italian lira from the Vatican Bank.[58]

The close relationship of the new work with Italy and, in particular, Veneto was not only evidenced by the provenance of the sisters or the foundation's financial affairs. The structure was designed with clear references to the Generalate in Vicenza and specific strands of the twentieth-century Italian artistic vision in church construction. This resulted in the Institute chapel, decorated with a fresco of the nativity by a Veneto artist, Giuseppe Modolo.

Training and teaching at Effeta

The explicit connection with Italy regarding the training of the staff for the start-up of the school was highly significant. While the economic negotiations were still in progress, the issue of recruiting teachers, finding the necessary equipment to start lessons and training staff was the subject of exchanges between the congregation and the Patriarchate: it was agreed to organize a training course for the first teachers in Veneto, from September 1970 to May 1971. In a letter to the Mother General, the patriarch informed her that "three indigenous candidates" had applied to work in the new school: "two sisters graduated from Beit Jala: aged 27 and 25, respectively, and one from Bethlehem, aged 23." He specified that "the one from Bethlehem also speaks Italian, the other two do not, but speak French" and that "the three girls teach but have no official diplomas." For the sisters of the congregation assigned to the school, on the other hand, an intensive study of Arabic was required "to deal with families, staff, etc."[59]

The training took place in Mogliano Veneto. Not only was the specialization acquired in Italy: the equipment also came from the Italian company Amplifon.[60] The agreement stated that only "Arabic-speaking girls" would be received. As for the Pontifical Mission for Palestine's commitment, it undertook

> to offer an adequate sum to ensure the assistance [...] of the Religious in charge of the work, the financial treatment of the technical staff [...] and service personnel, and to offer each girl an adequate monthly sum that can be adjusted to ensure the pupils: food, clothing, medical care, and education.[61]

Significantly, the nuns removed from the words "preferring those from Palestinian refugee families" and "giving preference to those of Christian origin" from the first drafts. The agreement foresaw that the institute, "within the limits permitted by its own regulations, will take into account the existence of UNRWA in Palestine and its work in favour of deaf-mutes from Palestinian refugee families."[62]

At the time of its inauguration, the house had fourteen rooms with three beds for girls; a dormitory with twenty beds for children; ten bedrooms for nuns and teachers; eight classrooms, four of which were equipped with electronic equipment supplied by Amplifon; the kitchen and refectories. Included were spaces for workshops, a gymnastics room, an outpatient clinic, and a silent room for hearing tests. It also had a playground with forty olive trees. Many materials were sent from Italy: The Effeta archives contain lists of children toys, blackboards, bricks, and remnants for children clothes.[63]

The summer of 1971 was devoted to the selection and admission of students, which involved an educational team consisting of the sisters, teachers, a doctor, and a social worker meeting with parents and children. For the first year twenty-four students were accepted, divided into two sections (4–5 years, 6–7 years). The first students underwent an initial audiometric test, carried out at the Tel Ha-Shomer audiology center. Classes started on September 4, 1971 (Fig. 6.3 and Fig. 6.4). In 1977 the Institute enrolled eighty-three hearing-impaired children (thirty boys and fifty-three girls), aged 5 to 14, twenty-one Christians and sixty-two Muslims, some of them from refugee camps. Students came from the Jerusalem area, the West Bank (Nablus, Tubas, Tulkarem, Jenin, Ramallah, Jifnah, Taybeh, Beit Sahour, Beit Hanina, Bethlehem, Beit Jala, Sourbaher, and Jericho), Gaza, and a few from Jordan.

Figure 6.3: The first classes in 1971

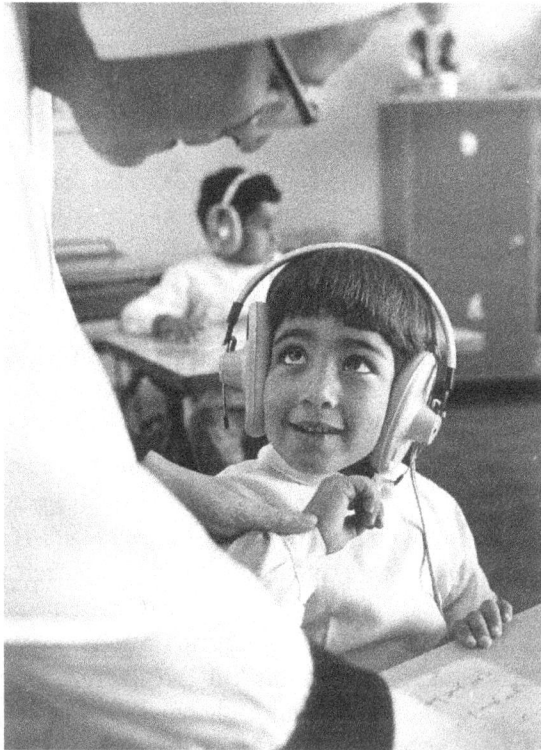

Figure 6.4: Child at Effeta school with Sr Gaetana Grandi, 1971

The teaching community was composed of twelve members: a social worker, four specialized religious teachers and six lay teachers, led by the superior of the Institute. The education provided involves the audio-phonetic education of the hearing impaired by means of the oral-acoustic method and included for almost all pupils two years of kindergarten and the complete primary cycle. The teaching was conducted in Arabic, but the pupils were also introduced in English. The program also included learning knitting, sewing, typing for the girls, and various trades for the boys. For the girls, training was given in the Institute itself. Therefore, they were initiated early on in knitting, crochet, and embroidery. For the boys, a collaboration was established with Salesian Fathers in Bethlehem. The analysis of Effeta's history also relates to the transformation and "modernization" of the concept of disability, in the not unproblematic entanglement of educational and religious policies in Palestine. It also includes the linguistic features, an element deeply articulated by Karène Sanchez Summerer but still underrepresented in studies. Effeta staff confronts with the question of languages in two main ways: first, in the forms of the oral method to adopt, and, second, in the choice of languages to be taught. Roman Catholic schools traditionally taught the national languages predominant in the different congregations (especially Italian, French, and Russian), with some classes in Arabic. However, English became synonymous of "modernization" and grew its importance also in Roman Catholic schools, in parallel with the reinforcement of the Arabic. In the Effeta case, we see this multilingualism operating in a video published in 1979 by UNRWA.[64] This is a fourteen-minute documentary, entitled *My name is Fadwa*, entirely devoted to the Effeta school and the collaboration with UNRWA. In this video, deaf children are shown learning Arabic, English, and some words of Italian. While the voice-over states that "with love and care from skilful hands, new worlds and imagination can be opened up and explored," the teacher has one pupil mime a sentence in Italian: "*Prendi un bacio, prendi un fiore e tutto l'affetto del mio cuore*" ("Take a kiss, take a flower and all the affection of my heart"), and then has them all repeat aloud "*buona festa madre!*" ("Happy feast, Mother!") (Fig. 6.5).[65]

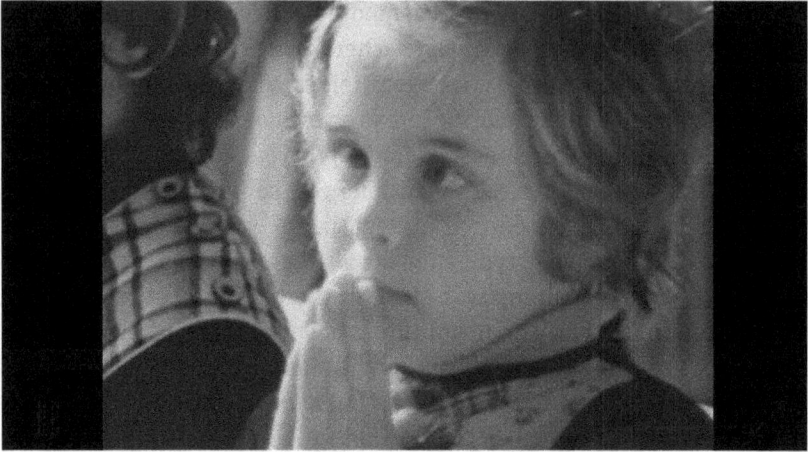

Figure 6.5: Still from the 1979 UNRWA documentary *My Name is Fadwa*

In the 1980s–1990s, the school opened secondary school sections, and the teaching methods were significantly revised:

> [T]he school offered boarding for up to 60 children. They only went home once a month. With the social worker I had hired, we visited and studied the territory of origin of the children, with the topographical map, with the odometer. We met the families and the villages. We ascertained that some children could go home, and we convinced some families that this was their child, and he had the right to go home. The current boarding school has 15 children, the motivation is only geographical remoteness, but going home at the weekend is compulsory. Work has been done on the children's autonomy.[66]

The Dorotheans also continued their work during the first Intifada (1987–1990). Since the 1990s and in the framework of the—then failed—Oslo peace process, the sisters-initiated relations with the Palestinian Authority. Currently, the plan for the training proposal is worked out together with the educational system of the Palestinian Ministry of Education.

The second Intifada and in particular the siege of Bethlehem (April 2–May 10, 2002) represented dramatic moments in the contemporary history of the institute: "We could see the tanks blocking the cars. We had 7–8 girls aged 13–14, they started shooting. We took refuge in the pantry. We spread mats on the floor. When it became dark, we thought we were going to die, they were shooting hard."[67] The construction of the wall and the checkpoints further limited the possibility of having students from northern Palestine (Fig. 6.6).[68]

Figure 6.6: View from the Effeta Institute during the siege of Bethlehem in 2002

Although the Dorotheans community in the Bethlehem psychiatric hospital was closed in 1996, the Dorotheans still run the Pontifical Institute Effeta. In 2022–2023, the school hosted about 200 students, among them sixteen UNRWA-registered refugees.[69] The school is still funded in collaboration with the Dorotheans, the Congregation for the Oriental Churches and the Pontifical Mission for Palestine,[70] and juridically recognized by the Palestinian Authority according to the norms of the Comprehensive Agreement between the State of Palestine and the Holy See.[71] Since the mid-2010s, the Italian Ministry of Foreign Affairs and the John Paul II Foundation have offered grants to support new projects.

Unfolding the disability in religious and humanitarian diplomacy

When dealing with the history of disability in modern Palestine, and specifically of religious humanitarian enterprises, the limited extension of scholarship makes it difficult to draw general remarks. However, the history of pupils, teachers, and nuns studying, working, and praying in a remote—although Pontifical—school in the town of Bethlehem confirms, contexts, and nuances a number of approaches, scholarship, and common sense when dealing with the multiple of concepts on the ground: religion, humanitarianism, disability, and refugeedom.

The humanitarian effort by the Dorothean sisters in Palestine presents classic elements of the Roman Catholic approach to mission and to disability: the shift from conversionist attitudes, as expressed in the first ideas of mission in the Holy Land and the departure toward Palestine, to a vision characterized by the desire to share the life with a people, characteristic of the theology of mission elaborated during and in the aftermath of the Second Vatican Council. This clearly emerges from the sources analysed in the different registers used at the departure to Palestine by the first nuns in the 1920s and the arguments employed in the 1960s–1970s in support of the foundation of the Effeta school. The concept itself of disability used by the sisters and the Latin Patriarch when dealing with the patients in the psychiatric hospital profoundly differ from the lexicon used when describing the pupils of the Effeta school.

The study of these experiences represents a still silent chapter of modern history of Palestine. In this case, it allows to go beyond the existing literature on European and generally European and North American missions, contributing to strengthening the need for new scholarship on history of disability in the Middle East, and, more broadly, in "non-Western" contexts. It also nuances the idea that at the end of the twentieth century secular and Catholic forms of welfare state toward disability run separately, as expressed in the forms of cooperation between the Effeta school and the Palestinian Ministry of Education. It also confirms the passage from confrontation and competition—with the British authorities, with Jewish, Arab, and non-Catholic Christian agencies—to respect and collaboration. This should not be confused with the shift between an age of perpetual conflict to another marked by harmony. The history of the region clearly attests the permanence of tensions and divisions and the overall complexity in dealing. However, new models of relations between religious and state organizations clearly emerge in the second half of the twentieth century. Its history and the history of the Dorotheans in Palestine is part of the framework of humanitarian diplomacy carried out by the Holy See and by Catholic institutions in the "Holy Land." It endows a case study of the transformation of the paradigm in humanitarian action toward persons, including children, with disability. The

Sisters' task in the psychiatric hospital in Bethlehem, assigned in 1946 by the British Mandate authorities and the Latin Patriarchate during the troubled years of the discussion over the future status of Palestine, embodied the role of disciplinary control over the "alienated," as they are often referred to in the sources. This experience also highlights the complexity of relations between foreign and Arab staff, a common trope in religious chronicles and ecclesiastical archives, especially during a time of the revendication of positions of power by the local clergy and religious members of Christian communities in the wider Arab nationalist movement.

The foundation of the Effeta school illuminates a further phase in the humanitarian diplomacy toward people with disability in the region. The initiative taken by the Holy See and realized by the Dorotheans encountered financial and political difficulties, and required a complex mediation with different actors, from Jordan to the Palestinian Authority ministries and officers. In the communications with potential donors, the deaf becomes the hearing person. The methods adopted to teach students profoundly changed over the years. Moreover, in the Effeta school disability and refugeedom are both present in the status of some students and in the institutions involved in the agreements, such as UNRWA.

To enter the Effeta school means revisiting archives and collections, retracing the history of documents and collections produced by or concerning the voices—and silences—of people with disability, unpacking the strategies of preservation and destruction of records by public and private institutions and their goals, involving in the discussion archives, but also agencies, museums, and associations, and conducting a fruitful methodological review of all the disciplines invested. It means "to live with these young people for a moment, to read what they read, and to see what they had to learn, learn with, and learn against," revisiting in this way the history of childhood—from subject to agent—and of childhood with disability in Palestine.[72]

New protagonists emerge in the history of Effeta: the students themselves, their narratives within and beyond the schools, their trajectories. Today, some of them are authors of artistic exhibition where they communicate their life experiences through paintings and other media. In one of the paintings realized by an alumna, she portrays herself as strangled by the wall. Through these paintings, the wall becomes a second—or first—form of disability and cause of impossibility to speak. The sources they compiled during and after their school time realized by the pupils become the present records of the tragic reality of the occupation and segregation.

Despite a restrictive daily reality that did not include many alternatives, the interplay between disability, cultural and educational missions, humanitarian diplomacy, and refugeedom remains open to the study of experiences and forms of agency.

Notes

1. This research has received funding under the project DHABILITY (FAR-FOMO).
2. This verb is contained in the Gospel of Mark (7:34), in the narrative of Jesus healing a deaf mute (7:31–37): "Then Jesus left the vicinity of Tyre and went through Sidon, down to the Sea of Galilee and into the region of the Decapolis. There some people brought to him a man who was deaf and could hardly talk, and they begged Jesus to place his hand on him. After he took him aside, away from the crowd, Jesus put his fingers into the man's ears. Then he spit and touched the man's tongue. He looked up to heaven and with a deep sigh said to him, 'Ephphatha!' (which means 'Be opened!'). At this, the man's ears were opened, his tongue was loosened, and he began to speak plainly. Jesus commanded them not to tell anyone. But the more he did so, the more they kept talking about it. People were overwhelmed with amazement. 'He has done everything well,' they said. 'He even makes the deaf hear and the mute speak.'"
3. For new approaches on the history of Betlehem, see Norris, Jacob (2023). *The Lives and Deaths of Jubrail Dabdoub: Or, How the Bethlehemites Discovered Amerka*. Stanford: Stanford University Press; Norris, Jacob (2019). "Dragomans, Tattooists, Artisans: Palestinian Christians and Their Encounters with Catholic Europe in the Seventeenth and Eighteenth Centuries." *Journal of Global History*, 14(1), 68–86.
4. On the history of the Latin Patriarchate, see Pieraccini, Paolo (2006). *Il ristabilimento del Patriarcato latino di Gerusalemme e la Custodia di Terra Santa: La dialettica istituzionale al tempo del primo patriarca, mons. Giuseppe Valerga* (1847–1872). Cairo and Jerusalem: resp. Franciscan Centre of Christian Oriental Studies and Franciscan Printing Press.
5. On the modern history of Christianity in Palestine, see Pieraccini, Paolo (2019). "Catholic Missionaries of the 'Holy Land' and the Nahda." *Social Sciences and Missions*, 32(3–4), 311–341, as well as numerous chapters in Dalachanis, Angelos and Lemire, Vincent (eds.) (2018). *Ordinary Jerusalem, 1840–1940: Opening New Archives, Revisiting a Global City*. Leiden: Brill; in particular, see Ancel, Stéphane (2018). "The Ethiopian Orthodox Community in Jerusalem: New Archives and Perspectives on Daily Life and Social Networks, 1840–1940." In Dalachanis, Angelos, and Lemire, Vincent (eds.), *Ordinary Jerusalem, 1840–1940: Opening New Archives, Revisiting a Global City*. Leiden: Brill, 50–74; Gerd, Lora and Potin, Yann (2018). "Foreign Affairs through Private Papers: Bishop Porfirii Uspenskii and His Jerusalem Archives, 1842–1860." In ibidem, 100–117; Dalachanis, Angelos, and Tselikas, Agamemnon (2018). "The Brotherhood, the City and the Land: Patriarchal Archives and Scales of Analysis of Greek Orthodox Jerusalem in the Late Ottoman and Mandate Periods." In ibidem, 118–136; and Papastathis, Konstantinos (2018). "Diplomacy, Communal Politics, and Religious Property Management: The Case of the Greek Orthodox Patriarchate of Jerusalem in the Early Mandate Period." In ibidem, 223–239. See also

Sanchez Summerer, Karène (2016). "Linguistic Diversity and Ideologies among the Catholic Minority in Mandate Palestine: Fear of Confusion or Powerful Tool?" *British Journal of Middle Eastern Studies*, 43(2), 191–205; Haiduc-Dale, Noah (2013). *Arab Christians in British Mandate Palestine: Communalism and Nationalism, 1917–1948*. Edinburgh: Edinburgh University Press; Robson, Laura (2011). *Colonialism and Christianity in Mandate Palestine*. Austin: University of Texas Press; Maggiolini, Paolo (2011). *Arabi Cristiani di Transgiordania. Spazi politici e cultura tribale (1841–1922)*. Milan: FrancoAngeli; Chatelard, Géraldine (2004). *Briser la mosaïque: Les tribus chrétiennes de Madaba, Jordanie, XIXe–XXe siècle*. Paris: CNRS; O'Mahony, Anthony (ed.) (2003). *The Christian Communities of Jerusalem and the Holy Land: Studies in History, Religion and Politics*. Cardiff: University of Wales Press; O'Mahony, Anthony (ed.) (1999). *Palestinian Christians: Religion, Politics and Society in the Holy Land*. London: Melisende. On the relations between Christians, Muslims, and Jews in Palestine from the end of the nineteenth century to the First World War, see Freas, Erik (2016). *Muslim–Christian Relations in Late Ottoman Palestine: Where Nationalism and Religion Intersect*. London: Palgrave Macmillan, and the seminal book by Campos, Michelle U. (2011). *Ottoman Brothers: Muslims, Christians, and Jews in Early Twentieth-Century Palestine*. Stanford: Stanford University Press.

6. On the creation of the Pontifical Mission for Palestine, see Rioli, Maria Chiara (2020). *A Liminal Church: Refugees, Conversions, and the Latin Diocese of Jerusalem, 1946–1956*. Leiden: Brill.

7. For a historical appraisal on UNRWA's establishment and management, see Feldman, Ilana (2018). *Life Lived in Relief: Humanitarian Predicaments and Palestinian Refugee Politics*. Oakland: University of California Press; Feldman, Ilana (2017). "Humanitarian Care and the Ends of Life: The Politics of Aging and Dying in a Palestinian Refugee Camp." *Cultural Anthropology*, 32(1), 42–67; Feldman, Ilana (2016). "Punctuated Humanitarianism: Palestinian Life between the Catastrophic and the Cruddy." *International Journal of Middle East Studies*, 48(2), 372–376.

8. On Christian theology and disability, see Creamer, Deborah Beth (2009). *Disability and Christian Theology: Embodied Limits and Constructive Possibilities*. New York: Oxford University Press. For some historical reflections on the Catholic Church, see Schianchi, Matteo (2022). "Chiesa e disabilità. Un lungo rapporto non troppo controverso." In Fontana, Alberto and Merlo, Giovanni (eds.), *A sua immagine? Figli di Dio con disabilità*. Milan: La vita felice, 93–100.

9. The operational document—the *Instrumentum laboris*—preparing the 16th General Assembly of the Synod of Bishops, stated that "there are widespread reports of a variety of practical and cultural barriers that exclude persons with disabilities, which must be overcome," including among the questions for synodal reflections: "What physical and cultural barriers do we need to break down so that people with disabilities can feel that they are full members of the community?" See Holy See, Sixteenth Ordinary General Assembly of the Synod of Bishops (2023, October). *Instrumentum Laboris: For the First Session*. Vatican: Press Office of the Holy See. The synthesis report at the conclusion of the synodal works affirmed: "In the promotion of the co-responsibility of all the baptised for mission we recognise the apostolic capacities of persons with disabilities. We want to better value the contribution to evangelisation offered by the immense richness of their humanity. We recognise their experiences of suffering, marginalisation, and discrimination, sometimes occurring even within the Christian community." See Holy See, Sixteenth Ordinary General Assembly of the Synod of Bishops (October 4–29, 2023). *A Synodal Church in Mission: Synthesis Report*. Vatican: Press Office of the Holy See.

10. Salvatici, Silvia (2019). *A History of Humanitarianism, 1755–1989: In the Name of Others*. Manchester: Manchester University Press, 15–16.

11. See Paulmann, Johannes (ed.) (2016). *Dilemmas of Humanitarian Aid in the Twentieth Century.* Oxford: Oxford University Press; Barnett, Michael and Stein, Janice (eds.) (2012). *Sacred Aid: Faith and Humanitarianism.* Oxford: Oxford University Press; Barnett, Michael (2011). *Empire of Humanity: A History of Humanitarianism.* New York: Cornell University Press.

12. Sanchez Summerer, Karène and Zananiri, Sary (2021). "Introduction." In Sanchez Summerer, Karène and Zananiri, Sary (eds.), *European Cultural Diplomacy and Arab Christians in Palestine, 1918–1948: Between Contention and Connection.* Cham: Palgrave, 12.

13. Ari, Nisa (2021). "Competition in the Cultural Sector: Handicrafts and the Rise of the Trade Fair in British Mandate Palestine." In Sanchez Summerer, Karène and Zananiri, Sary (eds.), *European Cultural Diplomacy and Arab Christians in Palestine, 1918–1948: Between Contention and Connection.* Cham: Palgrave, 217–218.

14. On this concept and its application in the Middle East and specifically Palestine, see Kévonian, Dzovinar (2004). *Réfugiés et diplomatie humanitaire: Les acteurs européens et la scène proche-orientale pendant l'entre-deux-guerres.* Paris: Publications de la Sorbonne; Sanchez Summerer, Karène and Okkenhaug, Inger Marie (2023). "The Role of Protestant Missionaries during the Great Arab Revolt in Jerusalem and South Palestine (1936–1939): Towards Humanity?" *British Journal of Middle Eastern Studies,* 52 (1), 139-158. For the Catholic case in the nineteenth century, see, for example, Stornig, Katharina (2016). "Between Christian Solidarity and Human Solidarity: Humanity and the Mobilisation of Aid for Distant Children in Catholic Europe in the Long Nineteenth Century." In Klose, Fabian and Thulin, Mirjam (eds.), *Humanity: A History of European Concepts in Practice from the Sixteenth Century to the Present.* Göttingen: Vandenhoeck and Ruprecht, 249–266. For the Protestant case, see Becker, Judith (2008). "Conceptions of Humanity in the Nineteenth-Century German Protestant Missions." In Klose, Fabian and Thulin, Mirjam (eds.), *Humanity: A History of European Concepts in Practice from the Sixteenth Century to the Present.* Göttingen: Vandenhoeck and Ruprecht, 107–129; Löffler, Roland (2008). *Protestanten in Palästina: Religionspolitik, sozialer Protestantismus und Mission in den deutschen evangelischen und anglikanischen Institutionen des Heiligen Landes, 1917–1939.* Stuttgart: Kohlhammer.

15. Scalenghe, Sara (2014). *Disability in the Ottoman Arab World, 1500–1800.* New York: Cambridge University Press, 1–2.

16. Simoni, Marcella (2010). *A Healthy Nation: Zionist Health Policies in British Palestine (1930–1939).* Venice: Cafoscarina; Sufian, Sandra (2007). *Healing the Land and the Nation: Malaria and the Zionist Project in Palestine, 1920–1947.* Chicago: University of Chicago Press; Sufian, Sandra (2002). "Arab Health Care during the British Mandate, 1920–1947." In Barnea, Tamara and Husseini, Rafiq (eds.), *Separate and Cooperate, Cooperate and Separate: The Disengagement of the Palestine Health Care System from Israel and Its Emergence as an Independent System.* Westport: Praeger, 9–30; Reiss, Nira (1996). "British Public Health Policy in Palestine, 1918–1947." In Kottek, Samuel S. and Waserman, Manfred (eds.), *Health and Disease in the Holy Land: Studies in the History and Sociology of Medicine from Ancient Times to the Present.* Lewiston: Edwin Mellen Press, 301–327; Reiss, Nira (1991). *The Health Care of the Arabs in Israel.* Boulder: Westview Press.

17. Danan, Ariel (2010). "L'École des sourds-muets de Jérusalem: Un cas particulier dans l'histoire de l'Alliance israélite universelle." In Bocquet, J. (ed.), *L'enseignement français en Méditerranée: Les missionnaires et l'Alliance israélite universelle.* Rennes: Presses universitaires de Rennes. For a broad picture, see also Rietveld-van Wingerden, Marjoke and Westerman, Wim (2009). "'Hear,

Israel': The Involvement of Jews in Education of the Deaf (1850–1880)." *Jewish History*, 23(1), 41–56.

18. Sterbini, Gina Giannarosa (1988). "L'Istituto delle Suore Maestre di S. Dorotea Figlie dei Sacri Cuori, dalla fondazione alla morte del Farina (1836–1888)." In Bassani, Albarosa Ines (ed.), *Il vescovo Giovanni Antonio Farina e il suo Istituto nell'Ottocento Veneto*. Rome: Edizioni di storia e letteratura, 455–512.

19. On Provolo's method, see Gecchele, Mario (2008). "L'abate Antonio Provolo e l'istruzione dei sordomuti a Verona." In Sani Roberto (ed.), *L'educazione dei sordomuti nell'Italia dell'800: Istituzioni, metodi, proposte formative*. Turin: Società Editrice Internazionale, 345–380; Butturini, Emilio (2001). *Istituzioni educative a Verona tra '800 e '900*. Verona: Mazziana; Rossi, Mario (2001). *Dal canto alla parola: La musicopedagogia di Antonio Provolo*. Milano: FrancoAngeli; Shurman, Dvora (1999). "Antonio Provolo: Hero or Villain?" *Journal of Deaf Studies and Deaf Education*, 4(1), 69–72; De Giorgi, Fulvio (1999). *Cattolici ed educazione tra Restaurazione e Risorgimento: Ordini religiosi, antigesuitismo e pedagogia nei processi di modernizzazione*. Milan: EDUCatt Università Cattolica.

20. See Sani, Roberto and Saladini, Paola P. (2001). *Un ecclesiastico ed educatore nella Modena della Restaurazione: Severino Fabriani (1792–1849)*. Rome: Città Nuova.

21. See Gallaudet, Edward M. (1881). "The Milan Convention." *American Annals of the Deaf and Dumb*, 26(1), 1–16.

22. According to a later booklet, one that was internal to the congregation, "the first band of Sisters, ready to fearlessly face risks and sacrifices, left Vicenza for that distant country. Mother Azelia followed them with love, suffered with them, was happy for their happiness." The Sisters of Saint Dorothy (1977). Cinquant'anni nella terra del Signore. Le Suore M. di S. Dorotea figlie dei SS. Cuori a ricordo del loro 50° anno di missione in Terra Santa. N.p., 7.

23. On Luigi Barlassina, Latin Patriarch of Jerusalem from 1920 to 1940, see Pieraccini, Paolo (1998a). "Il patriarcato latino di Gerusalemme (1918–1940): Ritratto di un patriarca scomodo. Mons. Luigi Barlassina." *Il Politico*, 63(2), 207–56; Pieraccini, Paolo (1998b). "Il patriarcato latino di Gerusalemme (1918–1940): Ritratto di un patriarca scomodo. Mons. Luigi Barlassina." *Il Politico*, 63(4), 591–640.

24. Archive of the Latin Patriarchate of Jerusalem (ALPJ), 1.8, LB-AG, Ste Dorothée, 1926–1965, Sr Azelia Dorotea Farinea to Patriarch Barlassina, Vicenza, October 27, 1926.

25. Archivio storico-diplomatico del Ministero degli affari esteri (ASDMAE), *Affari Politici*, Siria, 1568, 1523, Italian Consul in Jerusalem Tritonj to the Italian Foreign Minister Carlo Schanzer, Jerusalem, November 18, 1921.

26. ALPJ, 1.8, LB-AG, Ste Dorothée, 1926–1965, Patriarch Barlassina to Sr Farinea, [Jerusalem], November 3, 1926.

27. Since the second half of the nineteenth century, the various Custos of the Franciscan Custody of the Holy Land made their claims for the Cenacle the object of an international campaign. Historically, the first Franciscans to arrive in the Holy Land after the final defeat of the Crusaders (1291) settled near the Cenacle.

28. "Meditating [Mother Azelia] on the Passion, her thoughts turned with particular emotion to the CHRIST where Jesus, before beginning the painful drama that would lead him to Calvary, had left himself, as a gift to his own, in the Eucharist. [...] 'I will send my daughters there,' she said, 'and they will live not far from that sacred place; they will visit it often, pray and sacrifice themselves for its recovery, sighing for the day when it can be given back to the Catholic Church in its rightful possession'." Ibidem, 8.

29. Archive of the Latin Patriarchate in Jerusalem, Sr Ubaldina Capovilla to Patriarch Luigi Barlassina, Vicenza, April 3, 1927.

30. This reference to a "cultural Crusade" aimed at "reconquering hearts" was recurrent in the Italian Catholic press. See Zanini, Paolo (2012). *"Aria di crociata': I cattolici italiani di fronte alla nascita dello Stato d'Israele (1945–1951)."* Milan: Unicopli.

31. Letter from Mother Azelia, dated March 23, 1936, republished in The Sisters of Saint Dorothy, *Cinquant'anni nella terra del Signore*, 18: "My beloved daughters, I remind you that all your sacrifices must have only one aim: the redemption of the Upper Room!" letter, March 23, 1936.

32. See Cohen, Hillel (2015). *1929: Year Zero of the Arab-Israeli Conflict*. Waltham, MA: Brandeis University Press.

33. The documentation highlights the effect of shock after the death of the Salesian director of Beit Jemal, Mario Rosin, who was killed on his way back from a meeting with the sisters in Rafat. On the Salesian Fathers, see Pieraccini, "Catholic Missionaries of the 'Holy Land,'" 311–334.

34. Archive of the Teaching Sisters of St. Dorothy, Daughters of the Sacred Hearts, Vicenza (ADS), "Betlemme, Ospedale Mentale, 1946–1996," Assistant Senior Medical Officer to Assistant Chief Secretary D.C. Thompson, copy, February 16, 1946.

35. Ibidem.

36. Chris Sandal-Wilson comprehensively unpacked the social and cultural history of mental illness in his *Mandatory Madness: Colonial Psychiatry and Mental Illness in British Mandate Palestine* (Cambridge, Cambridge University Press, 2024).

37. On nursing in British Mandate Palestine, see Shatz, Julia (2018). "A Politics of Care: Local Nurses in Mandate Palestine." *International Journal of Middle Eastern Studies*, 50, 669–689.

38. On July 22, 1946, the Jewish terrorist organization Irgun Zvai Le'umi (National Military Organisation) bombed the King David Hotel in Jerusalem, killing ninety-one persons and injuring seventy others. The hotel housed the British Mandate military headquarters, intelligence stations, and government secretariat. The dead included forty-one Arabs, twenty-eight Britons, and seventeen Jews, as well as two Armenians, a Russian, an Egyptian, and a Greek national. See Hoffman, Bruce (2015). Anonymous Soldiers: The Struggle for Israel, 1917–1947. New York: Knopf.

39. ADS Betlemme, Ospedale Mentale, 1946–1996, handwritten report entitled "Betlemme, Ospedale Mentale, 1946–1957."

40. Morris, Benny (2004). *The Birth of the Palestinian Refugee Problem Revisited*. Cambridge: Cambridge University Press, 355.

41. ADS Betlemme, Ospedale Mentale, 1946–1996, "Quaderno 12," "Cronistoria 1966–1968," June 6, 1967.

42. Lamdan, Neville and Melloni, Alberto (eds.) (2007). *Nostra Aetate: Origins, Promulgations, Impact, on Jewish-Catholic Relations*. Münster: LIT Verlag.

43. Il primo messaggio natalizio del Sommo Pontefice Paolo VI (23 dicembre 1963). (1963, December 25). *L'Osservatore Romano*, 1.

44. See Mazzini, Elena (2009). "Terra Santa o Israele? Alcune Considerazioni Intorno al Viaggio Di Paolo VI (Gennaio 1964)." *Archivio Storico Italiano*, 167(4), 645–668. On Vatican–Israeli and Vatican–Jordan relations, see Zanini, Paolo (2017). "Vatican Diplomacy and Palestine, 1900–1950." *Jerusalem Quarterly*, 71, 120–131; Bialer, Uri (2005). *Cross on the Star of David: The Christian World in Israel's Foreign Policy, 1948–1967*. Bloomington: Indiana University Press; Breger, Marshall J. (ed.) (2004). *The Vatican-Israel Accord: Political, Legal and Theological Contexts*. Notre Dame: Notre Dame University Press; Minerbi, Sergio I. (1988). *Il Vaticano, la*

Terra Santa e il Sionismo, 1895–1925. Milan: Bompiani; Ferrari, Silvio (1991). *Vaticano e Israele dal secondo conflitto mondiale alla Guerra del Golfo*. Florence: Sansoni; Pieraccini, Paolo (1997). *Gerusalemme: Luoghi Santi e comunità religiose nella politica internazionale*. Bologna: EDB; and Fabrizio, Daniela (2004). *Identità nazionali e identità religiose, diplomazia internazionale, istituzioni ecclesiastiche e comunità cristiane in Terra Santa fra Otto e Novecento*. Rome: Studium.

45. Katz, Kimberly (2005). *Jordanian Jerusalem: Holy Places and National Spaces*. Gainesville: University Press of Florida, 124–129.

46. On the history of Tantur Ecumenical Institute, see Guasco, Alberto (2017). "L'istituto ecumenico di Tantur: Appunti e problemi per una storia (1963–1978)." *Cristianesimo nella storia*, 38(1), 221–246; Guasco, Alberto (2017). "Tantur. Un crocevia del cammino verso l'unità: L'Istituto ecumenico di Tantur tra Roma, Ginevra e Gerusalemme (1963–1978)." *Schweizerische Zeitschrift für Religions- und Kulturgeschichte*, 111, 215–227.

47. Cozzo, Paolo (2022). *In Cammino: Una storia del pellegrinaggio Cristiano*. Rome: Carocci.

48. ADS Corrispondenza per costruzione Ist. "Effeta," Sr Chiara Marchetti to the Mother General, enclosing Pio Laghi's notes, Jerusalem, March 9, 1970.

49. The Sisters of Saint Dorothy, *Cinquant'anni nella terra del Signore*, 58.

50. Bawalsa, Nadim (2022). *Transnational Palestine: Migration and the Right of Return before 1948*. Stanford: Stanford University Press.

51. Norris, "Dragomans, Tattooists, Artisans.

52. For an appraisal on the 1967 War, see Segev, Tom (2007). 1967: *Israel, the War, and the Year that Transformed the Middle East*. New York, Metropolitan Books.

53. The planimetries by the architect Yitzhak Moshe Lewkowicz are kept in the EAB, "Fatture della costruzione Effeta e sua relazione amministrativa, 1965–1971."

54. On the politically complex construction of the Basilica of the Annunciation, see Halevi, Masha (2010). "The Politics Behind the Construction of the Modern Church of the Annunciation in Nazareth." *Catholic Historical Review*, 96(1), 27–55.

55. ADS Corrispondenza per costruzione Ist. "Effeta," Sr Chiara Marchetti to the Mother General, enclosing Pio Laghi's notes, Jerusalem, March 9, 1970.

56. "*L'Istituto fin dalla fondazione ha avuto l'assistenza ai sordomuti. In provincia di Vicenza hanno una casa esemplare sotto ogni aspetto: clinico, educativo, spirituale e sociale. A Mestre l'Istituto ha una casa per l'assistenza per le sordomute che desiderano rimanere per tutta la vita accanto alle Suore da esse educate.*" ["Since its foundation, the Institute has provided assistance to the deaf and dumb. In the province of Vicenza, they have an exemplary home in every respect: clinical, educational, spiritual, and social. In Mestre the Institute has a home for the assistance of deaf-mutes who wish to remain for their whole life alongside the sisters they educate."] ADSADS Correspondence for the construction of the "Effeta" Institute, "Notes for the use of His Excellency the Delegate," [1970].

57. Ibidem.

58. ADS, Vicenza, Corrisp. S. Sede, Sr Zorzanello to Giovanni Benelli, Sostituto to the Vatican Secretariat of State, Vicenza, January 11, 1970.

59. ADS Corrispondenza per costruzione Ist. "Effeta," Patriarch Gori to Sr Zorzanello, Jerusalem, May 24 24, 1970.

60. ADS Vicenza, Corrispondenza per costruzione Ist. "Effeta," Sr Zorzanello to Sr Marchetti, Vicenza, April 30, 1970.

61. ADS Vicenza, Corrispondenza per costruzione Ist. "Effeta," "Convenzione tra la delegazione apostolica, missione pontificia, congregazione maestre di santa dorotea."

62. Ibidem.
63. Archive of the Pontifical Effeta Institute, Bethelehem (APEIB), "Fatture della costruzione Effeta e sua relazione amministrativa, 1965–1971," "Contenuto delle N. 4 casse spedite con le 3 religiose che viaggeranno con la motonave Messapia."
64. United Nations Relief and Works Agency for Palestine Refugees in the Near East (1979). *My Name is Fadwa* [Video file].
65. On this film, see Rioli, Maria Chiara (2024). *Portraying Disability in Refugeedom: Palestinian Refugees with Disability through UNRWA Photographs and Films* [unpublished manuscript]. Department of Linguistic and Cultural Studies, University of Modena and Reggio Emilia.
66. Interview with Sr Luigina Carpenedo to the author, April 24, 2023.
67. Sr Pierluigina recalls the memory of those days: "We stood in a circle and prayed with the girls hugging each other, they Allah and we God. We heard the phone ringing; it was the father of a little girl from Jericho saying, 'we are praying for you'. A psychologist told us to drink lots of water and eat sweets. When the teachers arrived, they would tell us the anguish of the night. They came from Beit Sahour, Beit Jala, and Bethlehem. One night I called the seminary because we were too afraid. We wanted an Arab man in the house. But we couldn't because there were tanks in the house." Interview with Sr Luigina Carpenedo to the author, April 24, 2023.
68. "Each child had a name tag with name, surname, identity card number, Boulos VI, 'I am deaf', in order to pass through the checkpoints." Ibidem.
69. APEIB, "UNRWA," UNRWA Students List, 2022.
70. Statutes were revised and approved in 2021. See APEIB, "Statutes and Regulations School," "Statuto del Pontificio Istituto Effeta Paolo VI."
71. For the text of the agreement, see Pope Franciscus (2016). "Comprehensive Agreement between the Holy See and the State of Palestine." In Palazzo Apostolico, Città del Vaticano (ed.), *Acta Apostolicae Sedis*. Vatican: Libreria Editrice Vaticana, 168–185.
72. Qato, Mezna (2018). "A Primer for a New Terrain: Palestinian Schooling in Jordan, 1950." *Journal of Palestine Studies*, 48(1), 16–32.

References

Ancel, Stéphane (2018). "The Ethiopian Orthodox Community in Jerusalem: New Archives and Perspectives on Daily Life and Social Networks, 1840–1940." In Dalachanis, Angelos and Lemire, Vincent (eds.), *Ordinary Jerusalem, 1840–1940: Opening New Archives, Revisiting a Global City* (pp. 50–74). Leiden: Brill.

Ari, Nisa (2021). "Competition in the Cultural Sector: Handicrafts and the Rise of the Trade Fair in British Mandate Palestine." In Sanchez Summerer, Karène and Zananiri, Sary (eds.), *European Cultural Diplomacy and Arab Christians in Palestine, 1918–1948: Between Contention and Connection* (pp. 213–246). Cham: Palgrave.

Barnett, Michael (2011). *Empire of Humanity: A History of Humanitarianism*. New York: Cornell University Press.

Barnett, Michael and Stein, Janice (eds.) (2012). *Sacred Aid: Faith and Humanitarianism*. Oxford: Oxford University Press.

Bawalsa, Nadim (2022). *Transnational Palestine: Migration and the Right of Return before 1948*. Stanford: Stanford University Press.

Becker, Judith (2008). "Conceptions of Humanity in the Nineteenth-Century German Protestant Missions." In Klose, Fabian and Thulin, Mirjam (eds.), *Humanity: A History of European Concepts in Practice from the Sixteenth Century to the Present* (pp. 107–129). Göttingen: Vandenhoeck and Ruprecht.

Bialer, Uri (2005). *Cross on the Star of David: The Christian World in Israel's Foreign Policy, 1948–1967.* Bloomington: Indiana University Press.

Breger, Marshall J. (ed.) (2004). *The Vatican-Israel Accord: Political, Legal and Theological Contexts.* Notre Dame: Notre Dame University Press.

Butturini, Emilio (2001). *Istituzioni educative a Verona tra '800 e '900.* Verona: Mazziana.

Campos, Michelle U. (2011). *Ottoman Brothers: Muslims, Christians, and Jews in Early Twentieth-Century Palestine.* Stanford: Stanford University Press.

Chatelard, Géraldine (2004). *Briser la mosaïque: Les tribus chrétiennes de Madaba, Jordanie, XIXe–XXe siècle.* Paris: CNRS.

Cohen, Hillel (2015). *1929: Year Zero of the Arab-Israeli Conflict.* Waltham, MA: Brandeis University Press.

Cozzo, Paolo (2022). *In Cammino: Una storia del pellegrinaggio Cristiano.* Rome: Carocci.

Creamer, Deborah Beth (2009). *Disability and Christian Theology: Embodied Limits and Constructive Possibilities.* New York: Oxford University Press.

Dalachanis, Angelos and Lemire, Vincent (eds.) (2018). *Ordinary Jerusalem, 1840–1940: Opening New Archives, Revisiting a Global City.* Leiden: Brill.

Dalachanis, Angelos and Tselikas, Agamemnon (2018). "The Brotherhood, the City and the Land: Patriarchal Archives and Scales of Analysis of Greek Orthodox Jerusalem in the Late Ottoman and Mandate Periods." In Dalachanis, Angelos and Lemire, Vincent (eds.), *Ordinary Jerusalem, 1840–1940: Opening New Archives, Revisiting a Global City* (pp. 118–136). Leiden: Brill.

Danan, Ariel (2010). "L'École des sourds-muets de Jérusalem: Un cas particulier dans l'histoire de l'Alliance israélite universelle." In Bocquet, J. (ed.), *L'enseignement français en Méditerranée: Les missionnaires et l'Alliance israélite universelle.*(pp. 117-124). Rennes: Presses universitaires de Rennes.

De Giorgi, Fulvio (1999). *Cattolici ed educazione tra Restaurazione e Risorgimento: Ordini religiosi, antigesuitismo e pedagogia nei processi di modernizzazione.* Milan: EDUCatt Università Cattolica.

Fabrizio, Daniela (2004). *Identità nazionali e identità religiose, diplomazia internazionale, istituzioni ecclesiastiche e comunità cristiane in Terra Santa fra Otto e Novecento.* Rome: Studium.

Feldman, Ilana (2016). "Punctuated Humanitarianism: Palestinian Life between the Catastrophic and the Cruddy." *International Journal of Middle East Studies*, 48(2), 372–376.

Feldman, Ilana (2017). "Humanitarian Care and the Ends of Life: The Politics of Aging and Dying in a Palestinian Refugee Camp." *Cultural Anthropology*, 32(1), 42–67.

Feldman, Ilana (2018). *Life Lived in Relief: Humanitarian Predicaments and Palestinian Refugee Politics.* Oakland: University of California Press.

Ferrari, Silvio (1991). *Vaticano e Israele dal secondo conflitto mondiale alla Guerra del Golfo.* Florence: Sansoni.

Freas, Erik (2016). *Muslim–Christian Relations in Late Ottoman Palestine: Where Nationalism and Religion Intersect.* London: Palgrave Macmillan.

Gallaudet, Edward M. (1881). "The Milan Convention." *American Annals of the Deaf and Dumb*, 26(1), 1–16.

Gecchele, Mario (2008). "L'abate Antonio Provolo e l'istruzione dei sordomuti a Verona." In Sani Roberto (ed.), *L'educazione dei sordomuti nell'Italia dell'800: Istituzioni, metodi, proposte formative* (pp. 345–380). Turin: Società Editrice Internazionale.

Gerd, Lora and Potin, Yann (2018). "Foreign Affairs through Private Papers: Bishop Porfirii Uspenskii and His Jerusalem Archives, 1842–1860." In Dalachanis, Angelos and Lemire, Vincent (eds.), *Ordinary Jerusalem, 1840–1940: Opening New Archives, Revisiting a Global City* (pp. 100–117). Leiden: Brill.

Guasco, Alberto (2017a). "L'istituto ecumenico di Tantur: Appunti e problemi per una storia (1963–1978)." *Cristianesimo nella storia*, 38(1), 221–246.

Guasco, Alberto (2017b). "Tantur. Un crocevia del cammino verso l'unità: L'Istituto ecumenico di Tantur tra Roma, Ginevra e Gerusalemme (1963–1978)." *Schweizerische Zeitschrift für Religions- und Kulturgeschichte*, 111, 215–227.

Haiduc-Dale, Noah (2013). *Arab Christians in British Mandate Palestine: Communalism and Nationalism, 1917–1948*. Edinburgh: Edinburgh University Press.

Halevi, Masha (2010). "The Politics Behind the Construction of the Modern Church of the Annunciation in Nazareth." *Catholic Historical Review*, 96(1), 27–55.

Hoffman, Bruce (2015). *Anonymous Soldiers: The Struggle for Israel, 1917–1947*. New York: Knopf.

Holy See, Sixteenth Ordinary General Assembly of the Synod of Bishops (2023, October). *Instrumentum Laboris: For the First Session*. Vatican: Press Office of the Holy See. https://press. vatican.va/content/salastampa/it/bollettino/pubblico/2023/06/20/0456/01015.html#en

Holy See, Sixteenth Ordinary General Assembly of the Synod of Bishops (2023, October 4–29). *A Synodal Church in Mission: Synthesis Report*. Vatican: Press Office of the Holy See. https://www. synod.va/content/dam/synod/assembly/synthesis/english/2023.10.28-ENG-Synthesis-Report_IMP. pdf

Il primo messaggio natalizio del Sommo Pontefice Paolo VI (23 dicembre 1963). (1963, December 25). *L'Osservatore Romano* (The official newspaper of the Holy See).

Katz, Kimberly (2005). *Jordanian Jerusalem: Holy Places and National Spaces*. Gainesville: University Press of Florida.

Kévonian, Dzovinar (2004). *Réfugiés et diplomatie humanitaire: Les acteurs européens et la scène proche-orientale pendant l'entre-deux-guerres*. Paris: Publications de la Sorbonne.

Lamdan, Neville and Melloni, Alberto (eds.) (2007). *Nostra Aetate: Origins, Promulgations, Impact, on Jewish-Catholic Relations*. Münster: LIT Verlag.

Löffler, Roland (2008). *Protestanten in Palästina: Religionspolitik, sozialer Protestantismus und Mission in den deutschen evangelischen und anglikanischen Institutionen des Heiligen Landes, 1917–1939*. Stuttgart: Kohlhammer.

Maggiolini, Paolo (2011). *Arabi Cristiani di Transgiordania. Spazi politici e cultura tribale (1841–1922)*. Milan: FrancoAngeli.

Mazzini, Elena (2009). "Terra Santa o Israele? Alcune Considerazioni Intorno al Viaggio Di Paolo VI (Gennaio 1964)." *Archivio Storico Italiano*, 167(4), 645–668.

Minerbi, Sergio I. (1988). *Il Vaticano, la Terra Santa e il Sionismo, 1895–1925*. Milan: Bompiani.

Morris, Benny (2004). *The Birth of the Palestinian Refugee Problem Revisited*. Cambridge: Cambridge University Press.

Norris, Jacob (2019). "Dragomans, Tattooists, Artisans: Palestinian Christians and Their Encounters with Catholic Europe in the Seventeenth and Eighteenth Centuries." *Journal of Global History*, 14(1), 68–86.

Norris, Jacob (2023). *The Lives and Deaths of Jubrail Dabdoub: Or, How the Bethlehemites Discovered Amerka*. Stanford: Stanford University Press.

O'Mahony, Anthony (ed.) (1999). *Palestinian Christians: Religion, Politics and Society in the Holy Land*. London: Melisende.

O'Mahony, Anthony (ed.) (2003). *The Christian Communities of Jerusalem and the Holy Land: Studies in History, Religion and Politics*. Cardiff: University of Wales Press.

Papastathis, Konstantinos (2018). "Diplomacy, Communal Politics, and Religious Property Management: The Case of the Greek Orthodox Patriarchate of Jerusalem in the Early Mandate Period." In Dalachanis, Angelos and Lemire, Vincent (eds.), *Ordinary Jerusalem, 1840–1940: Opening New Archives, Revisiting a Global City* (pp. 223–239). Leiden: Brill.

Paulmann, Johannes (ed.) (2016). *Dilemmas of Humanitarian Aid in the Twentieth Century*. Oxford: Oxford University Press.

Pieraccini, Paolo (1997). *Gerusalemme: Luoghi Santi e comunità religiose nella politica internazionale*. Bologna: EDB.

Pieraccini, Paolo (1998a). "Il patriarcato latino di Gerusalemme (1918–1940): Ritratto di un patriarca scomodo. Mons. Luigi Barlassina." *Il Politico*, 63(2), 207–256.

Pieraccini, Paolo (1998b). "Il patriarcato latino di Gerusalemme (1918–1940): Ritratto di un patriarca scomodo. Mons. Luigi Barlassina." *Il Politico*, 63(4), 591–640.

Pieraccini, Paolo (2006). *Il ristabilimento del Patriarcato latino di Gerusalemme e la Custodia di Terra Santa: La dialettica istituzionale al tempo del primo patriarca, mons. Giuseppe Valerga (1847–1872)*. Cairo and Jerusalem: resp. Franciscan Centre of Christian Oriental Studies and Franciscan Printing Press.

Pieraccini, Paolo (2019). "Catholic Missionaries of the 'Holy Land' and the Nahda." *Social Sciences and Missions*, 32(3–4), 311–341.

Pope Franciscus (2016). "Comprehensive Agreement between the Holy See and the State of Palestine." In Apostolico, Palazzo and del Vaticano, Città (eds.), *Acta Apostolicae Sedis* (pp. 168–185). Vatican: Libreria Editrice Vaticana. https://www.vatican.va/archive/aas/documents/2016/acta-febbraio2016.pdf

Qato, Mezna (2018). "A Primer for a New Terrain: Palestinian Schooling in Jordan, 1950." *Journal of Palestine Studies*, 48(1), 16–32.

Reiss, Nira (1991). *The Health Care of the Arabs in Israel*. Boulder: Westview Press.

Reiss, Nira (1996). "British Public Health Policy in Palestine, 1918–1947." In Kottek, Samuel S. and Waserman, Manfred (eds.), *Health and Disease in the Holy Land: Studies in the History and Sociology of Medicine from Ancient Times to the Present* (pp. 301–327). Lewiston: Edwin Mellen Press.

Rietveld-van Wingerden, Marjoke and Westerman, Wim (2009). "'Hear, Israel': The Involvement of Jews in Education of the Deaf (1850–1880)." *Jewish History*, 23(1), 41–56.

Rioli, Maria Chiara (2020). *A Liminal Church: Refugees, Conversions, and the Latin Diocese of Jerusalem, 1946–1956*. Leiden: Brill.

Rioli, Maria Chiara (2024). *Portraying Disability in Refugeedom: Palestinian Refugees with Disability through UNRWA Photographs and Films* [unpublished manuscript]. Department of Linguistic and Cultural Studies, University of Modena and Reggio Emilia.

Robson, Laura (2011). *Colonialism and Christianity in Mandate Palestine*. Austin: University of Texas Press.

Rossi, Mario (2001). *Dal canto alla parola: La musicopedagogia di Antonio Provolo*. Milano: FrancoAngeli.

Salvatici, Silvia (2019). *A History of Humanitarianism, 1755–1989: In the Name of Others*. Manchester: Manchester University Press.

Sandal-Wilson, Chris (2024). *Mandatory Madness: Colonial Psychiatry and Mental Illness in British Mandate Palestine.* Cambridge: Cambridge University Press.

Sanchez Summerer, Karène (2016). "Linguistic Diversity and Ideologies among the Catholic Minority in Mandate Palestine: Fear of Confusion or Powerful Tool?" *British Journal of Middle Eastern Studies,* 43(2), 191–205.

Sanchez Summerer, Karène and Okkenhaug, Inger Marie (2023). "The Role of Protestant Missionaries during the Great Arab Revolt in Jerusalem and South Palestine (1936–1939): Towards Humanity?" *British Journal of Middle Eastern Studies,* 52 (1), 139-158.

Sanchez Summerer, Karène and Zananiri, Sary (2021). "Introduction." In Summerer, Sanchez and Zananiri, Sary (eds.), *European Cultural Diplomacy and Arab Christians in Palestine, 1918–1948: Between Contention and Connection* (pp. 1–27). Cham: Palgrave.

Sani, Roberto and Saladini, Paola P. (2001). *Un ecclesiastico ed educatore nella Modena della Restaurazione: Severino Fabriani (1792–1849).* Rome: Città Nuova.

Scalenghe, Sara (2014). *Disability in the Ottoman Arab World, 1500–1800.* New York: Cambridge University Press.

Schianchi, Matteo (2022). "Chiesa e disabilità. Un lungo rapporto non troppo controverso." In Fontana, Alberto and Merlo, Giovanni (eds.), *A sua immagine? Figli di Dio con disabilità* (pp. 93–100). Milan: La vita felice.

Segev, Tom (2007). *1967: Israel, the War, and the Year that Transformed the Middle East.* New York: Metropolitan Books.

Shurman, Dvora (1999). "Antonio Provolo: Hero or Villain?" *Journal of Deaf Studies and Deaf Education,* 4(1), 69–72.

Simoni, Marcella (2010). *A Healthy Nation: Zionist Health Policies in British Palestine (1930–1939).* Venice: Cafoscarina.

The Sisters of Saint Dorothy (1977). *Cinquant'anni nella terra del Signore.* Le Suore M. di S. Dorotea figlie dei SS. Cuori a ricordo del loro 50° anno di missione in Terra Santa. N.p.

Sterbini, Gina Giannarosa (1988). "L'Istituto delle Suore Maestre di S. Dorotea Figlie dei Sacri Cuori, dalla fondazione alla morte del Farina (1836–1888)." In Bassani, Albarosa Ines (ed.), *Il vescovo Giovanni Antonio Farina e il suo Istituto nell'Ottocento Veneto* (pp. 455–512). Rome: Edizioni di storia e letteratura.

Stornig, Katharina (2016). "Between Christian Solidarity and Human Solidarity: Humanity and the Mobilisation of Aid for Distant Children in Catholic Europe in the Long Nineteenth Century." In Klose, Fabian and Thulin, Mirjam (eds.), *Humanity: A History of European Concepts in Practice from the Sixteenth Century to the Present* (pp. 249–266). Göttingen: Vandenhoeck and Ruprecht.

Sufian, Sandra (2002). "Arab Health Care during the British Mandate, 1920–1947." In Barnea, Tamara and Husseini, Rafiq (eds.), *Separate and Cooperate, Cooperate and Separate: The Disengagement of the Palestine Health Care System from Israel and Its Emergence as an Independent System* (pp. 9–30). Westport: Praeger.

Sufian, Sandra (2007). *Healing the Land and the Nation: Malaria and the Zionist Project in Palestine, 1920–1947.* Chicago: University of Chicago Press.

United Nations Relief and Works Agency for Palestine Refugees in the Near East (1979). *My Name is Fadwa* [Video file]. https://unrwa.photoshelter.com

Zanini, Paolo (2012). *"Aria di crociata": I cattolici italiani di fronte alla nascita dello Stato d'Israele (1945–1951).* Milan: Unicopli.

Zanini, Paolo (2017). "Vatican Diplomacy and Palestine, 1900–1950." *Jerusalem Quarterly,* 71, 120–131.

CHAPTER 7

Challenges and Opportunities for the Implementation of CRPD in the MENA Region: Insights from Iraq and Qatar

Majid Turmusani

Abstract

This chapter focuses on the implementation of the United Nations Convention on the Rights of Persons with Disabilities (CRPD) in the Middle East and North Africa (MENA) region, using the case studies of Iraq and Qatar. All ESCWA (United Nations Economic and Social Commission for Western Asia) countries of the MENA region have ratified the UNCRPD treaty and become state parties to the convention. As duty bearers, they continue to assume their obligations (legal and moral) in providing support for their citizens with disabilities. While this constitutes an unprecedented opportunity to ensure the rights of persons with disabilities in the region, such progress is being hampered by certain structural, attitudinal, and policy barriers and not least by lack of data and evidence on disability. In this chapter case studies are being presented on how disability rights are being fulfilled through inclusion practices in two countries of the region: Qatar and Iraq. In Qatar, progress has been achieved on several aspects of social and economic development and is being ranked high on the Human Development Index. The infrastructure and services are well developed in this country following universal design principles to a great extent. Inclusive technology is particularly developed in Qatar, and it targets people with disability under current e-accessibility policy (SCICT, 2011) developed under the Ministry of Transport and Communication. In Iraq, the pioneering project of USAID, "Access to Justice" program, is strategically situated to strengthen the capacity of partners (that is, civil society and government) through creating dialogue between partners and enhancing the respect for human rights.

Keywords: Disability, Iraq, Qatar, ESCWA, UNCRPD

Disability in global perspective

Disability is part of human diversity, and sustainable development can't be realized without considering the 15 percent of the world population who are considered to be Persons with Disabilities (PwDs).[1] Over the past three decades, heated debate has taken place on the concept of disability, its construct, and approaches to dealing with it. Different models of explaining and dealing with disability have emerged, such as the medical model, the social model, or the human rights model, all of which provide varying perspectives toward disability and indeed can complement one another. However, the social model of disability has particularly flourished, and its views were widely endorsed as it explains disability within the boundaries of society without ignoring the limitation of the individual. Disability from this perspective is a socially constructed and culturally produced form of oppression and the solution lies in removing discriminatory disabling barriers.[2]

The social model is often considered as synonymous to the human rights perspective on disability as it has played an instrumental role in promoting disability rights worldwide, leading to the historical international treaty on disability—Convention on the Rights of Persons with Disabilities (CRPD).[3] This marked a new era and resulted in the harmonization of national policies and programs of many countries to align them with CRPD and has also led to the introduction of a number of international declarations in favor of Persons with Disabilities, such as that on leprosy.[4] The consensus remains on the importance of mainstreaming disability into national plans of action together with making international aid policy disability-friendly (seen in articles 33, 32 of CRPD, respectively).

In 2015, the world community gathered in Addis Ababa to launch the Sustainable Development Goals (SDGs) for a peaceful and just society that leaves no-one behind.[5] SDGs explicitly include Persons with Disabilities in several of its seventeen goals and makes numerous generic references to disability as well. To ensure the proper inclusion of disability issues under various targets of SDGs, the community of Persons with Disabilities continues to step up efforts to develop specific disability indicators as part of their effective participation in the United Nations High-level Political Forum on Sustainable Development (HLPF) process.

Disability rights in the MENA region: some facts and figures

Despite the recent entry into force of the CRPD, all ESCWA countries of the MENA region have ratified the treaty and become state parties to the convention. As duty bearers, they continue to assume their obligations (legal and moral) in providing support for their citizens with disabilities.

While this constitutes an unprecedented opportunity to ensure the rights of persons with disabilities in the region, such progress is being hampered by certain structural, attitudinal, and policy barriers not least by lack of data and evidence on disability.

Disability prevalence in the Arab world, for example, varies from 0.2 percent in Qatar to 5.1 percent in Morocco. Such a low rate is being attributed to a number of factors, notably the demographics of the region that exhibit a high proportion of youth and immigrant workers.[6] That said, given the geopolitical setup of the MENA region and the continued conflict in several countries, it is likely that the rate of disability would be high due to the effect of war on the population, especially among refugees.[7] Considering the international and regional estimates of disability, it's likely that MENA countries may have used a narrow definition of disability that resulted in such a low rate.[8] An accurate prevalence requires wider definitions of disability together with due consideration to methodological issues in the collection and analysis of data.[9]

Regardless of proportion, evidence shows that Persons with Disabilities in the Arab region experience disadvantage and marginalization in education, employment, and overall inclusion, namely in rural zones where girls/women with disabilities are often doubly disadvantaged.[10] The rights of Persons with Disabilities are often restricted by lack of understanding of disability and the ability of Persons with Disabilities to lead a "normal" life, by the limited services and the widespread barriers and discrimination.

There are a number of local and global forces influencing disability rights in the MENA region. At the global level, many member states have ratified international treaties, such as the CRPD, the Convention on the Rights of the Child, and the Convention on the Elimination of All Forms of Discrimination Against Women, as well as the Ottawa Mine Ban Treaty or the Marrakesh Treaty, which have direct bearings on Persons with Disabilities.[11] Regionally, this is seen in the adoption of the Arab Charter of Human Rights in 2004, which includes articles dedicated specifically to the rights of Persons with Disabilities to health, education, and employment.[12] The Arab Decade (2004–2013) also played a role in mobilizing country efforts to develop disability policy and strategy in the MENA region.[13] Several member states have established a coordination mechanism ensuring the respect of disability rights in their respected countries known as "disability council or disability commission."[14] These bodies are charged with the responsibility of overseeing disability rights in line with the CRPD, as will be seen in country case studies, namely in Iraq.

How CRPD rights are being respected, protected, and fulfilled?

Attitudes and views toward disability and Persons with Disabilities are changing in the MENA region toward a perspective of human rights, giving Persons with Disabilities greater possibilities for integration in community life. The mobilization of the local community through different structures is a positive sign of community engagement in the inclusive development process. The interplay between the local culture, available resources, and the national legal framework has particularly influenced disability protection at the community level. This is seen in more awareness of rights of Persons with Disabilities in the local community and increased debate on fulfilment of rights. In the context of disability rights, there are three different sets of rights that are closely connected and complement one another. These are: rights promotion; rights protection, and reclamation of rights.

Rights promotion has been well debated in the region through awareness and advocacy for legal reform.[15] Rights protection, on the other hand, deals mainly with prevention of abuse or service provision. A reinforced system of social protection is possible through increasing social participation of Persons with Disabilities in the development process and its outcomes, increasing equal opportunities for services and reducing vulnerability through improved socio-economic status of family.[16] The reclamation of rights, however, can be addressed through legal means—in the context of Access to Justice (A2J) in Iraq, this being realized via legal clinics at the community level.[17]

In this section, case studies are being presented on how disability rights are being fulfilled through notable inclusion practices in two countries of the MENA region: Qatar and Iraq.

Qatar model of disability inclusion through assistive technology

Qatar has made notable progress on several aspects of social and economic development and is being ranked high on the Human Development Index. The infrastructure and services for Persons with Disabilities are well developed in the country following universal design principles.

Inclusive technology is particularly developed in Qatar and targets Persons with Disabilities under current e-accessibility policy, developed under the Ministry of Transport and Communication.[18]

While policy on disability exists to a certain extent (the 2004 law and the policy of 2011), Persons with Disabilities are actively trying to promote a rights perspective to disability and calling for a structure to be created and linked to the office of Prime Minister to take on the role of coordination and policy elaboration as well as oversight and monitoring of rights according to article 33 of CRPD.[19] Challenges facing this move include lack of legislation that is compatible with CRPD and a gap in leadership among DPOs, notably a defragmented community of Persons with Disabilities.[20] Despite the absence of disability commission in the country, Qatar continues to report on CRPD through the Universal Periodic Review (UPR) mechanism and a report being prepared by the National Human Rights Commission in collaboration with the National Coordination Committee.

Mada Assistive Technology Center

Upon the recommendation made by the CRPD committee on digital accessibility in Qatar, measures were taken to ensure the inclusion of Persons with Disabilities in Qatar in line with Qatar National Vision, QNV 2030 that sets the scene for comprehensive development that leaves no-one behind.[21] An agency was established to specifically promote and encourage Assistive Technology (AT) known as the Mada Assistive Technology Center in accordance with Law 21/2006 on private institutions for public benefits. Equal opportunities, user involvement and empowerment are at the heart of Mada's work through its AT program for enhancing outcomes in education, employment, and independent living for Persons with Disabilities.

Mada focuses on the enablement and use of assistive technology for inclusion and, as such, provides localized AT, innovates, and develops Arabic assistive technology, leads digital accessibility, provides policy and best practice in assistive technology, and raises awareness of AT and Persons with Disabilities in Qatar. The organization has strong leadership and runs as an NGO with a total workforce of forty-six competent people working on different projects under the above thematic areas.

As policy influencer, Mada is already engaged in the provision of policy advice and has played an instrumental role in the elaboration of e-accessibility policy of 2011. Such momentum to continue is so that effective disability policies are in place to bring about social change in line with QNV 2030 as well as the ideals of CRPD and SDGs. Moreover, Mada provides advice on the implementation of policy to different stakeholders, namely government agencies. For example, Mada continues to help agencies make their websites disability accessible.

As a new organization and a pioneer in the field, Mada faces challenges in achieving its mission. There are four different types of gaps that could be bridged, including issues related to the strategic directions of the organization, its scope, its delivery model, and enablers to take into consideration the enhanced role of Mada in the future.

Strategic directions

The governance model of Mada is quite comprehensive and provides different layers of oversight to ensure accountability. The role and powers of each level of governance are laid out clearly in Mada's constitution and seem to work in harmony to achieve Mada's mission. Separating powers in the governance model is important so that executives[22] are delegated enough authority to do their job in implementing the policies and decisions of the Board of Directors (BD), while the BD focuses on strategic direction, overall policy, and oversight, including financial issues. However, it's also notable that supporting such extensive governance structure may require certain secretarial work on the part of Mada, which could constitute a burden, given the current capacity and high demand on its services/products.

According to the Constitution of Mada, there are four different layers of governance regulating the organization, including the Board of Directors, the Executive Committee, the Board of Trustees, and Specialized Committees. Given the existence of the Board of Trustees (twenty-one members), this particular structure may be of great value to Mada when including Persons with Disabilities, their families, and/or their organizations (DPOs) in its membership in order to provide Mada with insights and advice on disability issues from user perspective. Activation of existing governance modalities to include DPOs on various structures such as the Board of Directors and the Board of Trustees is in fact necessary for true empowerment. Its notable that Persons with Disabilities are also employed at Mada and hold senior positions, which may allow greater opportunity for sharing a disability perspective within the organization.

Scope

According to its mandate, the main target group of Mada is Persons with Disabilities as well as organizations working with them or mainstream agencies serving everyone including Persons with Disabilities. However, it's often argued that the "disablement" has impact far beyond the person with disability and affects the whole family and the community at large. As such, families of Persons with Disabilities may be targeted at some point and be provided with AT support.

Given the lack of reliable data on the prevalence of disability and the population of Persons with Disabilities in Qatar, it's difficult to determine the size of the market and its segmentation. Using international estimates could help, but only to a certain degree. Segmentation of users is important to designate AT support to those in early childhood, schools' years, adults, and the elderly. It also helps determine the type of AT products needed and/or ICT. The existing database has updated figures covering the actual users. Available data, however, lack insights into the impact of ATs on the life of Persons with Disabilities, particularly in thematic fields of education, employment, and community.

Mada's mandate is quite comprehensive and provides an umbrella coverage for a wide range of activities. The focus on education, employment, communities, and awareness as priority areas is good and can be extended to cross-cut the TASMU framework with mechanisms for effective coordination and collaboration.[23]

Delivery model

The core strength of Mada is its capacity to provide technical advice, share models of best practices, and lead research and innovation—providing AT, in itself, is meant to be part of the above. Therefore, partnerships with other organizations, including that of DPOs, seems to be the most effective way to proceed in the future. It should be pointed out that there are capable DPOs and disability organizations with significant resources that can be leveraged by Mada.

Having forty-six staff members can be capitalized upon and their potential be fully utilized. Upon discussion with leadership and senior staff, there seems to be a strong sense of purpose and direction within the workforce and competence in using planning and monitoring tools. Perhaps performance measurement can be further enhanced with balance between quantitative and qualitative indicators as well as introducing regular internal reviews and evaluations into the life of the organization. Research and studies conducted by Mada, and other partners could also be used to inform Mada's planning and direction, including budget allocation.

The products and services provided to Persons with Disabilities by Mada have been perceived positively and with gratitude by users as well as educational and health institutions constituting Mada's partners. However, without understanding of the impact of AT on the life of Persons with Disabilities, it's difficult to get real insights into their situation and consequently the usefulness of devices and support.

Learning what DPOs say about AT provided by Mada

The consultations with DPOs/PwDs through focus group discussion as well as SWOT (Strengths, Weaknesses, Opportunities, and Threats) analysis[24] conducted centered on exploring the views on AT: levels of provision, gaps and future direction of Mada, including partnership opportunities. DPOs, namely the Association of Parents of Autistic Children, pointed out that they carried out discussion with their members on the subject and noted that the needs of people with autism vary greatly, some of which remain unmet, such as inclusive education in public schooling. Parents reported that GPS trackers were to be of large sizes and games for children could be improved. Generally, Mada is hardly known by the members and those who knew about it reported a mix of perceptions toward services. Yet, Mada's AT received by members were mostly of good quality and helped in enhancing the life of users. As for Mada's partners, namely educational institutions, AT support was greatly appreciated and used to improve play and learning outcomes. Some partners aspire for further support and follow-up, including regular visits to be made by Mada specialists to their centers.

Overall, the participants highlighted the heterogenous nature of Persons with Disabilities' needs for AT according to types of disabilities.

AT requires adaptation to suit the individual needs of each user, and this is where assessment and follow-up becomes necessary and distinguishes the services of Mada from commercial products in the market. Accessing AT products elsewhere is notably difficult and to avoid exploitation by the market when accessing commercial products, consumers suggested wider options to be available in the market and establishing direct communication with manufacturers rather than dealers in Qatar. Among high demands on AT are screen readers, mobile apps, Arabization of AT products, library collections, book recording options, e-books, Braille Note Touch system, interactive sign language options, updates, maintenance services, and accessible banking. Research on users' needs and innovation were proposed among solutions.

Enablers

Strengths, Weaknesses, Opportunities, and Threats (SWOT) analysis showed a number of strengths in the ecosystem of the disability sector, such as the existing political will, public funding to Mada, and strong leadership with a competent workforce as well as Mada's unique expertise as a hub of knowledge and innovation in the region. Opportunities included the fact that DPOs are interested in supporting Mada through partnership and collaboration, but context dictates new understanding of targeting and outreach measures. Moreover, there is potential for stepping up user research, databases and tracking systems of AT as well as enhancing innovation through supporting entrepreneurs with disabilities to develop local ATs and Arabization solutions. Equally, there is scope for enhancing the applications of AT in legal and telemedicine fields and, furthermore, for strengthening Mada's role in the Autism Strategy, as well as in the World Health Organization's (WHO's) Global Dementia Observatory and its involvement in national initiatives dealing with AT support to Persons with Disabilities.[25]

Inhibitors

While the Mada project was notably successful in maximizing opportunities and building on existing good practices, SWOT analysis exposed certain detriments, such as the lack of a national disability policy/strategy compatible with CRPD, the absence of a coordination body, the lack of monitoring mechanisms including that for AT, and the confusion over the parameters of direct services and targeting. Risk factors were centered on the turnover of skills, the limited use of a Community Based Rehabilitation approach, and centralized powers at one level of governance (that is, executives).[26]

In conclusion, Mada has an important role to play to fill the gap and provide leadership and policy influence on AT issues, namely through its awareness, research, and innovation programs. The expertise of Mada can be leveraged and can serve as a catalyst and knowledge hub that takes the organization a step further in its pioneering journey of enhancing the life of Persons with Disabilities through AT support. Despite the challenges facing the organization, Mada provides an excellent model of inclusion through ATs that can be inspiring in the region.

Iraq disability inclusion practices through access to justice and inclusive education

Across the globe, evidence shows that persons with disabilities experience hardship and discrimination in accessing justice.[27] As a pioneering project of USAID in Iraq, the Access to Justice (A2J) program is strategically situated to strengthen a partner's capacity (that is, civil society and government) through creating dialogue between partners, building capacity, and enhancing respect for human rights.[28] At the heart of the A2J mission is rights protection of vulnerable groups such as Persons with Disabilities (PwDs) whom the program works for relentlessly to facilitate their empowerment and proper inclusion into society. The program helps the government mainstreaming disability into its own program. It also assists with the process developing procedures, the writing of CRPD rights monitoring reports, and supporting the set-up of the disability commission.[29] The program equally helps civil society organizations, namely DPOs, to develop their disability advocacy strategy. The program uses a set of innovative strategies to achieve its goals, such as awareness raising, advocacy, and legal reform.

Disability legal system and Access to Justice Program

There are no reliable or disaggregated data on the population of Persons with Disabilities in Iraq. Recent statistics put the percentage of Persons with Disabilities in the country between from 3.7 percent to 8.1 percent in Iraq and much lesser in the Iraqi Kurdistan Region (IKR). These are underestimated figures considering the international estimates of 10–15 percent and the recent armed conflict in the country, which results in high casualties of landmine and terrorist attacks as well as those affected by trauma, notably among refugees and internationally displaced people (IDP). However, the Ministry of Planning in coordination with the Department of Statistics are organizing a survey on disability using Washington Disability Group Statistics with contribution from CSO/DPOs. Using WG's wider definition of disability means counting invisible disabilities and consequently having greater prevalence of disability.

The lack of investment in disability and rehabilitation by the previous regime left Persons with Disabilities poorly served and lacking effective protection. Typically, disability issues were addressed within an institutionalized framework and mandated to the Ministry of Labour and Social Affairs (MoLSA) for providing education and rehab services in collaboration with main ministries, such as Health or Education. Civil society contribution into disability issues was notably absent until recently.

The situation has changed, and an important actor of the contemporary disability sector is the organized collaboration of DPOs and the active surge of CSOs. While the disability movement is taking strength and gaining support in the country, there is still a long way to go for a recognized umbrella organization representing Persons with Disabilities and their organizations. One promising initiative toward effective networking is the advocacy network supported by A2J. This is promising work and continued capacity building for networks seems to bear fruits.

Guided by the Iraqi Constitution article 32 concerning "care" for people with disabilities, the government has recently passed legislation concerning vulnerable groups and specifically Iraqi disability Law 38/2013 and Law 22/2011 in IKR, both of which set the scene for a rights-based approach to disability in accordance with CRPD. Although Persons with Disabilities demand certain modifications to the above laws, these legislations provide some good legal protection that could be capitalized upon. Among recently passed laws that are relevant to Persons with Disabilities are: Law 20/2009 on compensations for victims of war and disabled survivors of terrorism; Law 22/2011 on education of Persons with Disabilities in school systems, including those with learning difficulties; and Law 11/2014 on social protection for vulnerable groups, including Persons with Disabilities. In IKR, there has also been a number of laws dealing with Persons with Disabilities in some way or another and these include Law 15 of the Kurdistan Ministry of Health (2007) concerning care and rehabilitation of Persons with Disabilities; and Law 12 of the Kurdistan Regional Government's Ministry of Labour and Social Affairs concerning juveniles with disabilities.

The institutional structure of service provision in Iraq is nearly identical to that of IKR. Traditionally, disability issues have been designated to the Ministry of Labour and Social Affairs (MOLSA). It is the official ministry responsible for providing services and protection for Persons with Disabilities though specialized centers, but other agencies do also provide services for this population, such as the Ministries of Health (MOH), Education (MOE), Finance (MOF), and Justice (MOJ). Typically, protection services at MOLSA are centered on services such as care, training, and rehabilitation and more recently providing easy loans for business development. At MOLSA, there are two directorates responsible for Persons with Disabilities; one deals with institutional care and is known as the directorate of social special needs and the other addresses disability issues within the wider social protection framework. Being the main department, the directorate of social special needs is responsible for wider vulnerable groups such as Persons with Disabilities, orphans, juveniles, and elderly people. They also provide care and rehab services to Persons with Disabilities, such as people with mental and/or physical disabilities as well as early detection services. As for the directorate of social protection, they provide safety nets services among which is the monthly cash transfers and identity card for orphans and juveniles. To qualify for financial support, one needs to meet a set of conditions, including a formal assessment of functional limitations determined by a specialist committee. When approved, the monthly cash transfer is offered at 105,000 IQD (approximately USD 95) in Iraq according to new regulations under Social Protection Law 11/2014 while cash transfer is offered at 150,000 IQD (approximately USD 128) in IKR.[30]

At the judicial level, there exists common institutions such as the Ministry of Justice (MOJ), tribunals, and different courts of law. MOJ plays an important role in ensuring the integrity of the judicial system: that the courts system is sufficiently developed to accommodate the needs of Persons with Disabilities during legal proceedings. Additionally, there exists a Ministry of Human Rights (MOHR) tasked with rights protection as well as a Human Rights Commission charged with responsibility of investigating violations against human rights. As for civil society, we find an active network of CSOs supporting access to justice, notably through the work of legal clinics under an A2J program. There is reportedly an increasing number of success stories in supporting Persons with Disabilities' access to justice and reclaiming their rights through such legal clinics. For example, the Amal Al-Basreyeh legal clinic helped a woman with mental health issues in her application for a monthly salary after seven years of fruitless waiting. A further example from IKR concerns the Gyanadn legal clinic that helped win a legal case concerning child guardianship of a disabled mother.

Persons with Disabilities' Advocacy Network

Persons with Disabilities' Advocacy Network is an independent group and made up of a number of partners, some of whom are supported financially by A2J. The network comprises twenty-three active CSOs, some of which have regional branches and operate in more than one city. In IKR, there are seventeen mainstream CSOs, which are increasingly taking Persons with Disabilities within their clienteles. As for DPOs, there are seven organizations exclusively serving Persons with Disabilities in IKR under the network. In Iraq, all eight CSOs under the network are active in serving disability issues. Of these, there are three DPOs and a legal newspaper specializing in disability rights and advocacy issues. Currently, A2J takes leadership in supporting the network by providing technical backup through information sharing, coordination, and capacity development of its members. This is done through monthly follow-up meetings or specialized training workshops. The network has a one-year work plan and is being supported by A2J to develop its strategic plan for two years.

The network has taken a leading role in advocating the rights of Persons with Disabilities in Iraq and making significant policy influence. Among issues on the agenda is the modification of recent disability legislation: Laws 38/2013 and that of IKR 22/2011 as well as stepping to new priorities, namely that related to inclusive education. While recognizing the Government of Iraq's keen interest in protecting the rights of Persons with Disabilities, the recently promulgated laws could be improved concerning the name of the law, its definitions and target population, available services, and articles related to rights and privilege as well as the functionality of DC.

Inclusive education practices in Iraq: the premise

According to Article 34 of the Iraqi Constitution, the right to education is guaranteed by the state. The Ministry of Education (MoE) is mandated to provide educational services to all citizens in Iraq, according to Law 22/2011.[31] For students with disabilities this takes the form of special classes. For severe cases of impairments, MoLSA provides educational services through its varied institutions: centers for persons with visual impairments, hearing impairments, physical and intellectual disabilities. There are also vocational training facilities provided. Total number of students benefiting from these facilities reaches approximately 4,000.

The work of these two ministries (MoE and MoLSA) overlaps when it comes to serving learners with disabilities. While MoE provides mainstream education under its policy on Education for All (EFA), MoLSA, on the other hand, provides care and rehabilitation for severe cases of impairments. Traditionally, MoE provided educational services to non-disabled constituents and more recently to students with mild learning difficulties. As of late 2014, legal texts allow children with disabilities to educational settings up to the fourth grade only. However, UNICEF is supporting MoE in integrating children with disabilities in the school system through resource rooms. Currently, there are 1,517 schools under this project with total students of 22,282.

Law 38/2013 has reinforced the mandate of MoE as a lead agency in providing educational services to Persons with Disabilities and its responsibility in supervising educational institutions. Accordingly, MoE is charged with providing primary and secondary education to persons with disability; developing curriculums, technical aid, and equipment; and ensuring qualified teachers to deal with students with disabilities.[32]

Law 38/2013 guarantees educational provisions for Persons with Disabilities as one of their fundamental rights. However, when it comes to Inclusive Education (IE), equal chances to learning are not determined by an improved legal framework only, but by improvement in specialized pedagogy combined with access and accessibility standards in the school system. This includes physical accessibility, teaching methods, teacher training capacity building,[33] and parents and local community awareness, and corresponds to typical components of inclusive education. It was made clear that inclusion is a process and when it comes to mild and moderate impairments, there is only one strategy for education: that is, inclusive education in the regular classroom. Moreover, it was emphasized that there is an importance of working in partnerships (interdepartmental and inter-ministerial collaboration) in order to identify and remove barriers.

The above issues were debated through a number of discussions convened to develop some consensus on "guidelines for inclusive education" strategy with the participation of key stakeholders (government, CSO/DPOs, and university).[34] Participants discussed reality and ambitions for including children with disabilities in the mainstream education system and challenges facing such a move, starting by effective identification of learners with disabilities—for example, how disability is determined and by whom, an issue that is closely linked to definitions. Currently, a medical committee is responsible for determining who is disabled, but they focus mainly on medical issues, and this again leaves a large number of Persons with Disabilities out of the definition. For example, students with learning disabilities require a multidisciplinary committee to identify and classify. Irregularities in assessing disabilities also apply to vocational training and job placements and often result in undertaking inappropriate training or placing Persons with Disabilities in jobs they can't do. Together, these affect the fulfillment of the rights of Persons with Disabilities and their full inclusion in society.

Capacity assessment of CSOs/DPOs

SWOT analysis was used to examine the capacity of CSOs/DPOs and their relationship to the A2J Network. Main issues discussed included: roles and responsibilities in partnership including process of application; organizational assessment of partners; identified gaps in capacity and feedback on priorities of work plans. During these consultations, participants also proposed a number of topics as subjects for future capacity building and training. The outcome of this analysis has been used in developing the advocacy strategy.

Strength of the disability sector and in particular A2J included issues such as the existence of human rights expertise and leadership under A2J, namely an advocacy network of local actors including functional legal clinics for defending rights through litigation, existence of disability leg-islation as well as the presence of a human rights commission and a dis-ability commission, not least the presence of DPOs. Identified challenges included the limited knowledge of effective community mobilization nec-essary for building disability movement; inadequate enforcement of the existing legal framework; absence of additional legal measures of protec-tion, such as the ratification of the Optional Protocol; prevailing negative public attitudes toward Persons with Disabilities and lack of reliable data and statistics on disability.

The analysis above was used in consolidating the advocacy strategy of Persons with Disabilities, including determining its priorities for action and modalities for implementation for the next two years. Participants endorsed the vision of strategy, focusing on the notion of inclusion as well as its mission and responsibilities. Five strategic priority advocacy issues were also endorsed: developing a legal framework to ensure rights protection of Persons with Disabilities; changing society attitudes toward Persons with Disabilities, including positive language in line with USAID policy;[35] enhancing the role of media in disability issues; effective mech-anisms for prevention of abuse at community level and a multitrack approach for accessing justice (prevention, rehab, and inclusion).

Given the exhaustive list of activities proposed for achieving the expected outputs of advocacy priorities, discussion refocused on select-ing the most important activities that are relevant to the task and that are realistic to achieve within the timeframe. For example, instead of con-ducting research at the national level to build a database, it was suggested that the Persons with Disabilities Advocacy Network could act as advisors to other agencies working in this area, such as mandated research institu-tions (that is, MoP and the Department of Statistics).

Capability to monitor the implementation of CRPD

The CRPD is a historic instrument for the promotion and protection of rights of Persons with Disabilities. If implemented adequately, it can guar-antee the empowerment and inclusion of Persons with Disabilities. CRPD has devised mechanisms for monitoring its implementation, as stated in article 33, namely concerning focal point (that is, disability council/commission). These bodies are charged with the responsibility of over-seeing disability rights and, as such, an adequate capacity for monitoring the implementation of CRPD is fundamental to rights protection of their constituents with disabilities. Such capacity includes ability to conduct research and investigation into violation of rights, ability to report on the level of implementation of CRPD, including writing official and shadow reports, and the presence of mechanisms for effective national implementation (a functioning disability commission). An example of the institutional capacity to monitor the implementation of CRPD is seen in the production of a country report that was supported by A2J in Iraq.

Technical assistance to developing CRPD monitoring report in Iraq

Iraq ratified CRPD in 2013 and enacted national legislation (Law 38/2013) to protect the rights of Persons with Disabilities. In addition to the moral obligations associated with joining international treaties, Iraq has committed itself to respecting and protecting the rights of citizens with disabilities, including reporting on measures taken to fulfill their rights.

A2J provided technical assistance in writing a CRPD official report to central and regional government in the form of training. Training focused on a comprehensive approach to rights protection, which revolves around promotion, respect, and fulfillment of rights. Attention was given to the role of disability research in monitoring the implementation of CRPD. Why discuss research issues when talking about monitoring rights? The answer is that monitoring includes a number of steps, one of which is conducting research (desk reviews as well as fieldwork to monitor the program and established services). Without research, it would be difficult to assess the impact of policy or service provision on the lives of Persons with Disabilities, to identify gaps or opportunities, and to propose solutions. Therefore, research and investigations (notably, disability research) are key in monitoring the rights of Persons with Disabilities and in writing the CRPD report.

After explaining concepts related to rights protection and good practices in monitoring the implementation of CRPD,[36] participants have worked on developing the draft report of CRPD guided by UN's Guidelines on treaty-specific documents to be submitted by state parties under article 35, paragraph 1, of the Convention on the Rights of Persons with Disabilities.[37] In addition to legal analysis, program and budget analysis were reviewed. Sources of information included: legal sources, programs and services, media, and experiences of Persons with Disabilities and society at large. Two standard parts of CRPD reports were looked at. First, the common core document, which usually contains general information about the government, the general framework for the protection and promotion of human rights, disaggregated statistics on Persons with Disabilities, as well as information on non-discrimination, equality, and effective remedies. This document also allows any reservations on specific articles. Second, a specific-treaty document containing specific information relating to the implementation, in law and in fact, of articles 1 to 33 of the Convention. Discussion focused not only on legal measures provided by the government, but also how such measures affect the full realization of the rights recognized by the Convention in terms of services.

Discussion and debate were guided by the UN principles of writing a CRPD report. Duty bearers discussed their current and future role in fulfilling the rights of Persons with Disabilities and responded to questions of rights holders from civil society, especially concerning the importance of supporting and providing services to youth with disabilities as well as to Persons with Disabilities among refugees and displaced people. A small group for drafting reports met after training and was advised by A2J team in order to verify the accuracy of data cited in the draft report that was discussed during training and compare it with UN guiding principles. They also identified missing information and its sources and assigned responsibilities for collecting such information.

Having duty bearers from several line ministries[38] and other concerned stakeholders, namely DPOs, had enriched the discussion and pointed out the importance of the collaborative framework in mainstreaming disability into development including the twin-track approach. Although governments may have already produced convention reports, such as CEDAW and CRC, technical assistance in writing a CRPD report is justified on the following grounds: techniques and methods of disability data collection and analysis, policy interpretation, and report writing skills. Therefore, the need for technical training on writing a CRPD report remains important due to: the uniqueness of the notion of disability in its construction, consequences, and measures for dealing with it; the distinctive nature of the concept of disablement that relates to functional limitations, but that is socially constructed caused by environmental barriers and discrimination; the concept of disability rights being based on planning and research and part of monitoring the implementation of CRPD; and finally the fundamental role of disability emancipatory research. The issue here is to involve Persons with Disabilities in the research process, monitoring, and evaluation as a vehicle to furthering their emancipation and empowerment.

Challenges to the implementation of CRPD (structural, attitudinal, and policy)

The ESCWA report *Disability in the Arab Region* presents a comprehensive and updated overview on the situation of Persons with Disabilities in the region. It highlights the structural and attitudinal barriers faced by Persons with Disabilities (that is, in education, employment, and community life) largely due to lack of awareness on their rights and their full potential for inclusion. The report underlines the importance of removing the multiple and multifaceted barriers, namely those related to inaccessible environment and lack of communication tools while acknowledging the fundamental role of a coordination body in monitoring the convention rights at the national level.[39]

While the newly established disability councils or commissions are still evolving and their work has not fully overseen disability rights in certain member states, they do, however, include Persons with Disabilities in disability policy formulation. For the process to be truly inclusive and empowering, CRPD has devised a number of mechanisms for monitoring the implementation of its various articles, including article 12 on A2J, article 24 on inclusive education as well as articles related to creating favorable conditions for inclusion through access to Assistive Technology as well as Information, Communication Technology, notably articles 4, 9, 20, 21, 24, 26, 29, and 32.[40] Toward that end, article 33 of the CRPD sets out three tiers of actions to ensure the respect, protection, and fulfillment of rights. It emphasizes the need for a central body at national level (a focal point, that is, disability commission) to monitor the compliance of CRPD through national laws, development plans, and programs. As such, it requires a reporting mechanism on progress made and this is to be submitted to the Committee on the Rights of Persons with Disabilities at UN–OHCHR. Currently, this role (coordination and oversight) is assumed by the different structures, such as the disability council/commission or national coordination committee on the Rights of Persons with Disabilities.

Creating an enabling and barrier-free environment, however, requires regulatory mechanisms to ensure equal rights and opportunities, but this is notably lacking in the region. Disability Monitor Initiative-Middle East sums up a number of limitations in existing policy frameworks, such as poor coordination among stakeholders; organizational weakness of disability movement; and limited evidence-based knowledge for effective interventions.[41] Data issues remain fundamental in determining the community of Persons with Disabilities as well as for planning, allocation of resources and monitoring purposes. Yet, disability data and research practices are limited in the region and rarely considered as priority.

Research agenda, disability data, and evidence-based knowledge

There are different methods of research and data collection, including two major approaches in doing disability research, namely the participatory and emancipatory paradigms. Both approaches support a move away from the traditional methods of studying persons with disabilities as respondents into greater participation and control of the research process and its production. Participation, however, does not equal emancipation, as the latter implies greater autonomy and ownership and deals generally with individual and group aspects of liberation. Participatory practices are well developed in the region, and this can set the scene for smooth transition from participation into emancipation in disability evidence-based knowledge, namely data on disability. The need for disability disaggregated data constitutes a priority directly linked to rights protection. Disability research is political by definition and can play an important role in transforming and changing the world in which it takes place. The adoption of a particular research method, for example, will influence the suggested solutions put forward to deal with disability issues (that is, influencing societal policies and provisions concerning learners with disabilities).[42]

Pertinent to this discussion is the importance of strengthening comparable data at all levels (mezzo, micro, and macro). Washington Group on Disability Statistics (WG) has the potential to provide such comparable data and can be linked to a thematic survey and national census accordingly.[43] Although known of its simple application and accuracy, WG requires considerable training being provided to data collectors on disability definitions and identification of invisible disabilities. A number of countries in MENA have already used or are planning to use WG for their next national census and, as such, it would be an occasion to use WG to obtain accurate data on Persons with Disabilities, namely for obtaining a children profile. The short set of questions of WG may be appropriate for census data. These questions concern difficulties the person experiences in doing certain activities, including difficulties in seeing even if wearing glasses; difficulties hearing even if wearing a hearing aid; difficulties walking or climbing steps; difficulties remembering or concentrating; difficulties with self-care; and difficulties in communication (understanding or being understood). These are measured on a scale, ranging from ability to perform the task to complete difficulty.

Steps forward

There exist opportunities for fulfilling disability rights in the MENA region. This includes, for example, the ongoing debate on disability and equality issues inspired by a social model and rights perspective and the good political will to advance the cause of Persons with Disabilities as well as the existing policy framework in many countries of MENA. Yet, Persons with Disabilities continue to experience hardship and discrimination manifested by repeated denial of their rights.

To redress the situation, participatory mechanisms for the harmonization of national laws and policies in line with CRPD can be advantageous. This is an important exercise involving Persons with Disabilities and their organization in policy planning and legal reform and, as such, the empowerment of Persons with Disabilities (individually and collectively) and strengthening their voice and advocacy can be instrumental to the outcomes of harmonized laws. In addition to enhancing coordination and governance practices, building capacity to ensure an effective enforcement and monitoring of CRPD rights through sound research and evaluation practices (that is, disability research) is also important. Not least the continued investment in promoting inclusive and interdisciplinary debates on rethinking disability in the MENA region. Sharing models of good practices can help toward that end.[44] Together this may help improve inclusion outcomes related to equity and non-discrimination, fulfill CRPD rights, and achieve SDGs.

Notes

1.   World Health Organization (WHO) (2010). *Community-based Rehabilitation: CBR Guidelines.* Geneva: WHO; United Nations General Assembly (UNGA) (2015, October 15). *Transforming Our World: The 2030 Agenda for Sustainable Development.* New York: UNGA.
2.   See Barnes, C. and Sheldon, A. (2010). "Disability, Politics and Poverty in a Majority World Context." *Disability & Society,* 25(7), 771–782; Fougeyrollas, P. (2010). *La Funambule, le Fil et la Toile: Transformations Réciproques du Sens du Handicap.* Québec: Les Presses de l'Université Laval.
3.   UNGA (2006, December 13). *Convention on the Rights of Persons with Disabilities and Optional Protocol.* New York: UNGA.
4.   United Nations Human Rights Council (UNHRC) (2015, July 2). *Elimination of Discrimination against Persons Affected by Leprosy and their Family Members.* Geneva: UNHRC.
5.   UNGA, *Transforming Our World.*
6.   United Nations ESCWA (ESCWA) (2018). *Disability in the Arab Region 2018.* Beirut: ESCWA.
7.   Arab Forum for the Rights of Persons with Disabilities (AFRPD) (2016). *Disability Inclusion Among Refugees in the Middle East and North Africa: A Needs Assessment of Libya, Egypt, Yemen, Jordan, and Turkey.* Washington: International Research and Exchanges.
8.   ⁸ Swedish International Development Cooperation Agency (SIDA) (2014, December). *Disability Rights in the Middle East & North Africa.* Stockholm: SIDA.
9.   WHO (2007). *International Classification of Functioning, Disability and Health: Children & Youth Version.* Geneva: WHO.
10. See Nagata, K. (2003). "Gender and Disability in the Arab Region: The Challenges in the New Millennium." *Asia Pacific Disability Rehabilitation Journal,* 14(1), 10–17; Turmusani, M. (2003). *Disabled People and Economic Needs in the Developing World.* London: Routledge; Hakim, G. and Jaganjac, N. (2005). *A Note on Disability Issues in the Middle East and North Africa.* Washington: World Bank; Axelsson, C. and Barrett, D. (2009). *Access to Social Services for Persons with Disabilities in the Middle East: Multi-stakeholder Reflections for Policy Reform.* Disability Monitor Initiative-Middle East, CBM, and Handicap International; WHO (2011). *World Report on Disability. WHO and the World Bank.* Geneva: WHO; Rioux, M. and Pinto, P. (2013). *Women with Disabilities' Rights in the Middle East: Are We Moving Forward? Regional Study on the Rights of Women with Disabilities in the Middle East.* Ramallah: Star of Hope Society; SIDA, *Disability Rights in the Middle East & North Africa;* AFPRD, *Disability Inclusion Among Refugees in the Middle East and North Africa;* ESCWA, *Disability in the Arab Region 2018.*
11. Resp. UNGA, *Convention on the Rights of Persons with Disabilities and Optional Protocol;* UNGA (1989, November 20). *Convention on the Rights of the Child, General Assembly Resolution 44/25.* New York: UNGA; UNGA (1979, December 18). *The Convention on the Elimination of All Forms of Discrimination against Women.* New York: UNGA; United Nations (1997, December 3). *Convention on the Prohibition of the Use, Stockpiling, Production and Transfer of Anti-Personnel Mines and on their Destruction.* New York: United Nations; and World Intellectual Property Organization (WIPO) (2013, June 27). *Marrakesh Treaty to Facilitate Access to Published Works for Persons Who Are Blind, Visually Impaired, or Otherwise Print Disabled.* Marrakesh: WIPO.
12. League of Arab States (2004, May 22). *Arab Charter on Human Rights.* Geneva: OHCHR.
13. ESCWA (2004). *Arab Decade for Disabled Persons, 2003–2012.* Beirut: ESCWA.
14. SIDA, *Disability Rights in the Middle East & North Africa.*

15. United Nations Children's Fund (UNICEF) (2010). *Advocacy Toolkit: A Guide to Influencing Decisions that Improve Children's Lives.* New York: UNICEF.
16. World Bank (2007). *Social Analysis and Disability: A guidance note. Incorporating Disability-Inclusive Development into Bank-supported Projects.* Washington: World Bank.
17. United States Agency for International Development (USAID) (2013). *Access to Justice Program (Facts Sheet).* Baghdad: A2J tice Program; and Access to Justice (A2J) Program (2014). *Performance Management Plan: Iraq Access to Justice Program (A2J).* Baghdad: USAID A2J Program.
18. Qatari Supreme Council of Information & Communication Technology "ictQATAR" (2011, September). *Qatar's eAccessibility Policy.* Doha: Qatari Supreme Council of Information & Communication Technology "ictQATAR."
19. Iraqi Ministry of Justice (2004). *Iraqi Law No. 2 of 2004 in respect of People with Special Needs.* Baghdad: Iraqi Ministry of Justice's Official Gazette.
20. That is said, the Association of Rehabilitation of People with Special Needs is national in its scope and cross-disability in coverage. It has 6500 members representing different types of disabilities. Their services include physical rehabilitation and employability services. The ID card is also issued by this organization, which qualifies PwDs from receiving services in Qatar such as discounted transport. As for equity organizations, such as women associations, they are being integrated within mainstream larger organizations of PwDs.
21. Qatari Ministry of Development Planning and Statistics (MDPS) and United Nations Development Programme (UNDP) (2015). *Qatar's Fourth National Human Development Report. Realising Qatar National Vision 2030 The Right to Development.* Doha: MDPS and UNDP; UNGA, *Transforming Our World.*
22. This is a four-member committee that also includes CEO whose job is focused on: directing the everyday operation of Mada, including developing annual work plans, a budget, and internal reviews.
23. Qatari Ministry of Transport and Communications (2019). *TASMU Smart Qatar Program.*
24. Sammut-Bonnici, T. and Galea, D. (2015, January 22). "SWOT Analysis." In Cooper, C.L., McGee, J., and Sammut-Bonnici, T. (eds.), *Wiley Encyclopedia of Management.* A SWOT analysis was convened by PwC with the participation of the author as part of their technical support to Mada refreshed strategy on AT.
25. WHO (2018). *The Global Dementia Observatory: The GDO Reference Guide.* Geneva: WHO.
26. See WHO, *Community-based Rehabilitation.*
27. UNDP (2004, March 9). *Access to Justice: Practice Note.* New York: UNDP; Government of Quebec (2005). *Pour une plus grande accessibilité a la justice: Rapport de groupe de travail sur la revision de Regime d'aide juridique au Québec.* Quebec: Canadian Department of Justice; Kanter, A. (2015). *The Development of Disability Rights Under International Law: From Charity to Human Rights.* New York: Routledge; United Nations Department of Economic and Social Affairs (UNDESA) (2018). *Access to Justice for Persons with Disabilities: Toolkit on Disability for Africa.* New York: UNDESA.
28. UNGA (1948, December 10). *The Universal Declaration of Human Rights, General Assembly Resolution 217 A.* New York: UNGA; United States Agency for International Development, *Access to Justice Program; A2J Program, Performance Management Plan.*
29. This is a coordination body established by the Law in both IKR and Iraq. In IKR they call it "Disability Council" and in Iraq "Disability Commission." See Turmusani, M. (2014). *101 Guide on Disability Rights in Iraq: A Tool Kit for Commissioners: USAID's Iraq Access to Justice Program*

(A2J). Baghdad: A2J Iraq; and Turmusani, M. (2015). *Access to Justice for People with Disabilities (A2J): A "Concept Paper" Prepared for The Technical Unit on Support to Civil Society, Handicap International Federation.* Luskville: Handicap et développement inclusif.

30. Based on the exchange rate in June 2014.

31. Iraqi Constitution (2005). *The Constitution of Republic of Iraq.* Baghdad: Iraqi Ministry of Justice. In Kurdistan, Iraqi Law 22/2011 also applies and guarantees education for PwDs. Equally, Law 27/2007 of Kurdistan MoE is based on non-discrimination between boys and girls in accessing education.

32. Iraqi Ministry of Justice (2013). *Law 38 for 2013 on People with Disabilities and Special Needs.* Baghdad: Ministry of Justice's Official Gazette.

33. Ainscow, M., Miles, S., and Slee, R. (2011). *Teachers for Inclusive Schools in Iraq: A Training Model for Primary Teachers in Iraq to Extend the Educational Opportunities of Disabled Children and Young People.* Report submitted for publication; United Nations Educational, Scientific and Cultural Organisation (UNESCO) (2009). *Policy Guidelines on Inclusion in Education.* Paris: UNESCO.

34. Guidelines contribute toward developing future strategy and are based on Iraqi Law 38/2013 and in line with article 24 of CRPD on inclusive education—it is not the strategy itself. The focus is placed on processes and outcomes, giving attention to principles of future strategy, its targets, and key areas as well as the implementation plan including research and monitoring issues. A standard set of components for a strategy on inclusive education is also proposed.

35. DRPI (2007). *Language and Definitions: United States Agency for International Development (USAID).* Washington: United States Agency for International Development.

36. For instance, Office of the United Nations High Commissioner for Human Rights (OHCHR) (2010). *Monitoring the Convention on the Rights of Persons with Disabilities: Guidance for Human Rights Monitors—Professional Training Series No. 17.* New York and Geneva: OHCHR; Disability Rights Promotion International (DRPI) (2014). *A Guide to Disability Rights Monitoring, Participant Version—Country Training.* Toronto: York University; and Canadian Human Rights Commission (CHRC) (2015). *The Rights of Persons with Disabilities to Equality and Non-Discrimination: Monitoring the Implementation of the UN Convention of the Rights of Persons with Disabilities in Canada.* Ottowa: CHRC.

37. OHCHR (2009, October 19–23). *Guidelines on Treaty-specific Document to be Submitted by States Parties under Article 35, Paragraph 1, of the Convention on the Rights of Persons with Disabilities.* Second session. Geneva: Committee on the Rights of Persons with Disabilities.

38. For effective protection of rights and liberties, it's important to designate a lead government agency as "duty bearers" on disability issues—this will help in identifying responsibility, accountability, and competence.

39. ESCWA, *Disability in the Arab Region 2018.*

40. OHCHR, *Monitoring the Convention on the Rights of Persons with Disabilities.*

41. Axelsson and Barrett, *Access to Social Services for Persons with Disabilities in the Middle East.*

42. Turmusani, M. (2004). "An Eclectic Approach to Disability Research: A Majority World Perspective." *Asia Pacific Disability Rehabilitation Journal,* 15(1), 1–11.

43. Altman, B. (2016). *International Measurement of Disability: Purpose, Method, and Application.* Cham: Springer.

44. Some Canadian and international innovations in disability research, policy, and practice: 1) Every Canadian Counts (ECC) is a national coalition comprising users, carers, families, DPOs, and service providers. It's set up to advocate for a comprehensive disability support system for

people with chronic and long-term disabilities. The model is based on the successful Australian experience of National Disability Insurance Scheme. 2) Réseau international sur le processus de production du handicap (RIPPH) is an interdisciplinary network on disability based in Quebec. It focuses on the role of social participation in breaking down barriers and exclusionary practices. It's distinguished by its influential policy debate and its social participation tools for measuring life habits and quality of environment. 3) The Canadian Centre on Disability Studies (CCDS) is a center of excellence on disability issues in Canada, which provides consultancy service and policy advice in research, education, and development, nationally and internationally. 4) The Canadian Disability Studies Association–Association canadienne d'études sur le handicap (CDSA-ACÉH) is a multidisciplinary, non-profit organization that promotes the exploration of disability through research, publication, artistic production, teaching, and general development. Disability Studies critically examines the interplay between disability and various policies, practices, cultural myths, and ideologies and provides a forum for the exchange of ideas and scholarship regarding disability; networking among individual members, community groups, and other academic organizations; and maintaining and building a commitment to a scholarship that is informed by an ongoing dialogue with community and consumer organizations and agencies. An essential value of the CDSA-ACÉH is the promotion of a perspective that includes people with disabilities in research and scholarship based on "Nothing About Us Without Us." 5) Appropriate Paper Technology (APT) is a cost-effective local technology that provides supplementary rehabilitation solutions for children with disabilities. It uses recycled materials to produce various products (i.e., seating and adaptations for large wheelchairs to fit smaller users, frames for Cerebral Palsy children, and others). See Hinchcliffe, A. (2007). *Children with Cerebral Palsy: A Manual for Therapists, Parents and Community Workers.* New Delhi: SAGE Publications; Westmacott, J. and Brayshaw, L. (2015). *Assistive Cardboard Equipment Using Appropriate Paper-based Technology (APT).* Glasgow: Meigle Colour Printers Limited.

References

Access to Justice (A2J) Program (2014). *Performance Management Plan: Iraq Access to Justice Program (A2J).* Baghdad: USAID A2J Program.

Ainscow, M., Miles, S., and Slee, R. (2011). *Teachers for Inclusive Schools in Iraq: A Training Model for Primary Teachers in Iraq to Extend the Educational Opportunities of Disabled Children and Young People.* Report submitted for publication.

Altman, B. (2016). *International Measurement of Disability: Purpose, Method, and Application.* Cham: Springer. 10.1007/978-3-319-28498-9.

Arab Forum for the Rights of Persons with Disabilities (2016). *Disability Inclusion among Refugees in the Middle East and North Africa: A Needs Assessment of Libya, Egypt, Yemen, Jordan, and Turkey.* Washington: International Research and Exchanges. www.wheelchairnet.org/ISWP/Resources/DPO%20Report%20FINAL.pdf.

Axelsson, C. and Barrett, D. (2009). *Access to Social Services for Persons with Disabilities in the Middle East: Multi-stakeholder Reflections for Policy Reform.* Disability Monitor Initiative-Middle East, CBM, and Handicap International. https://www.makingitwork-crpd.org/sites/default/files/2017-03/Middle%20East%20-%20Access%20to%20Social%20Services.pdf

Barnes, C. and Sheldon, A. (2010). "Disability, Politics and Poverty in a Majority World Context." *Disability & Society*, 25(7), 771–782.

Canadian Human Rights Commission (CHRC) (2015). *The Rights of Persons with Disabilities to Equality and Non-Discrimination: Monitoring the Implementation of the UN Convention of the Rights of Persons with Disabilities in Canada*. Ottowa: CHRC.

Disability Rights Promotion International (DRPI) (2014). *A Guide to Disability Rights Monitoring, Participant Version—Country Training*. Toronto: York University.

Fougeyrollas, P. (2010). *La Funambule, le Fil et la Toile: Transformations Réciproques du Sens du Handicap*. Québec: Les Presses de l'Université Laval.

Government of Quebec (2005). *Pour une plus grande accessibilité a la justice: Rapport de groupe de travail sur la revision de Regime d'aide juridique au Québec*. Quebec: Canadian Department of Justice.

Hakim, G. and Jaganjac, N. (2005). *A Note on Disability Issues in the Middle East and North Africa*. Washington: World Bank.

Hinchcliffe, A. (2007). *Children with Cerebral Palsy: A Manual for Therapists, Parents and Community Workers*. New Delhi: SAGE Publications.

Iraqi Constitution (2005). *The Constitution of Republic of Iraq*. Baghdad: Iraqi Ministry of Justice.

Iraqi Ministry of Justice (2004). *Iraqi Law No. 2 of 2004 in Respect of People with Special Needs*. Baghdad: Iraqi Ministry of Justice's Official Gazette.

Iraqi Ministry of Justice (2013). *Law 38 for 2013 on People with Disabilities and Special Needs*. Baghdad: Ministry of Justice's Official Gazette.

Kanter, A. (2015). *The Development of Disability Rights Under International Law: From Charity to Human Rights*. New York: Routledge.

League of Arab States (2004, May 22). *Arab Charter on Human Rights*. Geneva: Office of the United Nations High Commissioner for Human Rights.

Nagata, K. (2003). "Gender and Disability in the Arab Region: The Challenges in the New Millennium." *Asia Pacific Disability Rehabilitation Journal*, 14(1), 10–17.

Office of the United Nations High Commissioner for Human Rights (OHCHR) (2009, October 19–23). *Guidelines on Treaty-specific Document to be Submitted by States Parties under Article 35, Paragraph 1, of the Convention on the Rights of Persons with Disabilities*. Second session. Geneva: Committee on the Rights of Persons with Disabilities. http://tbinternet.ohchr.org/_layouts/treatybodyexternal/Download.aspx?symbolno=CRPD%2fC%2f2%2f3&Lang=en

Office of the United Nations High Commissioner for Human Rights (OHCHR) (2010). *Monitoring the Convention on the Rights of Persons with Disabilities: Guidance for Human Rights Monitors—Professional training series No. 17*. New York and Geneva: OHCHR.

Parliament of Kurdistan (2011). *Law 22 for 2011 on People with Disabilities and Special Needs*. Erbil: Parliament of Kurdistan.

Qatari Ministry of Development Planning and Statistics (MDPS) and United Nations Development Programme (UNDP) (2015). *Qatar's Fourth National Human Development Report. Realising Qatar National Vision 2030 The Right to Development*. Doha: MDPS and UNDP.

Qatari Ministry of Transport and Communications (2019). *TASMU Smart Qatar Program*.

Qatari Supreme Council of Information & Communication Technology "ictQATAR" (2011, September). *Qatar's eAccessibility Policy*. Doha: Qatari Supreme Council of Information & Communication Technology "ictQATAR"

Rioux, M. and Pinto, P. (2013). *Women with Disabilities' Rights in the Middle East: Are We Moving Forward? Regional Study on the Rights of Women with Disabilities in the Middle East*. Ramallah:

Star of Hope Society. http://drpi.research.yorku.ca/wp-content/uploads/2015/01/Regional-report_are-we-moving-forward-FINAL.pdf

Sammut-Bonnici, T. and Galea, D. (2015, January 22). "SWOT Analysis." In Cooper, C.L., McGee, J., and Sammut-Bonnici, T. (eds.), *Wiley Encyclopedia of Management*. Hoboken, NJ, 1–8. https://doi.org/10.1002/9781118785317.weom120103

Swedish International Development Cooperation Agency (SIDA) (2014, December). *Disability Rights in the Middle East & North Africa*. Stockholm: SIDA. https://www.cawtarclearinghouse.org/storage/5832/rights-of-persons-with-disabilities-mena.pdf

Turmusani, M. (2003). *Disabled People and Economic Needs in the Developing World*. London: Routledge.

Turmusani, M. (2004). "An Eclectic Approach to Disability Research: A Majority World Perspective." *Asia Pacific Disability Rehabilitation Journal*, 15(1), 1–11.

Turmusani, M. (2014). *101 Guide on Disability Rights in Iraq: A Tool Kit for Commissioners: USAID's Iraq Access to Justice Program (A2J)*. Baghdad: A2J Iraq.

Turmusani, M. (2015). *Access to Justice for People with Disabilities (A2J): A "Concept Paper" Prepared for The Technical Unit on Support to Civil Society, Handicap International Federation*. Luskville: Handicap et développement inclusif.

United Nations (1997, December 3). *Convention on the Prohibition of the Use, Stockpiling, Production and Transfer of Anti-Personnel Mines and on their Destruction*. New York: United Nations.

United Nations Children's Fund (UNICEF) (2010). *Advocacy Toolkit: A Guide to Influencing Decisions that Improve Children's Lives*. New York: UNICEF.

United Nations Department of Economic and Social Affairs (UNDESA) (2018). *Access to Justice for Persons with Disabilities: Toolkit on Disability for Africa*. New York: UNDESA.

United Nations Economic and Social Commission for Western Asia (ESCWA) (2004). *Arab Decade for Disabled Persons, 2003–2012*. Beirut: ESCWA. https://www.un.org/esa/socdev/enable/disarabdecade.htm

United Nations Economic and Social Commission for Western Asia (ESCWA) (2018). *Disability in the Arab Region 2018*. Beirut: ESCWA. https://www.unescwa.org/sites/www.unescwa.org/files/publications/files/disability-arab-region-2018-english_1.pdf

United Nations Educational, Scientific and Cultural Organization (UNESCO) (2009). *Policy Guidelines on Inclusion in Education*. Paris: UNESCO.

United Nations General Assembly (UNGA) (1948, December 10). *The Universal Declaration of Human Rights, General Assembly Resolution 217 A*. New York: UNGA.

United Nations General Assembly (UNGA) (1979, December 18). *The Convention on the Elimination of All Forms of Discrimination against Women*. New York: UNGA.

United Nations General Assembly (UNGA) (1989, November 20). *Convention on the Rights of the Child, General Assembly Resolution 44/25*. New York: UNGA.

United Nations General Assembly (UNGA) (2006, December 13). *Convention on the Rights of Persons with Disabilities and Optional Protocol*. New York: UNGA. http://www.un.org/disabilities/documents/convention/convoptprot-e.pdf

United Nations General Assembly (UNGA) (2015, October 15). *Transforming Our World: The 2030 Agenda for Sustainable Development*. New York: UNGA.

United Nations Human Rights Council (2015, July 2). *Elimination of Discrimination against Persons Affected by Leprosy and Their Family Members*. Geneva: United Nations Human Rights Council.

United States Agency for International Development (USAID) (2007). *Language and Definitions: United State Agency for International Development (USAID)*. Washington: USAID.

United States Agency for International Development (USAID) (2013). *Access to Justice Program (Facts Sheet)*. Baghdad: A2J.

Westmacott, J. and Brayshaw, L. (2015*). Assistive Cardboard Equipment Using Appropriate Paper-based Technology (APT)*. Glasgow: Meigle Colour Printers Limited.

World Bank (2007). *Social Analysis and Disability: A Guidance Note. Incorporating Disability-Inclusive Development into Bank-supported Projects*. Washington: World Bank.

World Health Organization (WHO) (2007). *International Classification of Functioning, Disability and Health: Children & Youth Version*. Geneva: WHO. https://iris.who.int/server/api/core/bitstreams/81e04699-2930-4da2-ac97-76725c7dcc07/content

World Health Organization (WHO) (2010). *Community-based Rehabilitation: CBR Guidelines*. Geneva: WHO.

World Health Organization (WHO) (2011). *World Report on Disability. World Health Organization and the World Bank*. Geneva: WHO.

World Health Organization (WHO) (2018). *The Global Dementia Observatory: The GDO Reference Guide*. Geneva: WHO.

World Intellectual Property Organization (WIPO) (2013, June 27). *Marrakesh Treaty to Facilitate Access to Published Works for Persons Who Are Blind, Visually Impaired, or Otherwise Print Disabled*. Marrakesh: WIPO.

Pan-Arab Engagements with Disability from the 1980s until Recent Times

Amany Soliman and Monika Baar

Abstract

This chapter argues that while the idea of a collective identity, shared heritage, and connected futures was always present in the Arab mindset, a momentum for joint Arab civil society action on the rights of persons with disabilities only emerged in the late 1990s. The chapter identifies the United Nations' International Year of Disabled Persons in 1981, the creation of of the Arab Organization for Persons with Disability in 1998, and The Arab Decade for Persons with Disabilities (2004–2013) as milestones in the creation of a common framework. Using archival material from the Archive of the League of Arab States, it shows how cooperation with Arab civil society toward the emancipation of people with disabilities in Arab societies emerged amid frustrations about the failure of joint action and how it intersected with massive political, security, and social challenges in the Arab world. The epilogue points to the tragic coincidence that the launch of the Second Arab Decade for Disabled Persons in 2023 coincided with a new cycle of violence in the Middle East, leading to an enormous increase in maimed bodies. It therefore concludes that disability scholars have an ethical imperative to call for the cessation and prevention of violence all over the world.

Keywords: United Nations' International Year of Disabled Persons, The Arab Decade for Persons with Disabilities, Arab Organization for Persons with Disability, Disability Scholars, League of Arab States

The International Year of Disabled Persons

During recent decades, disability has been garnering growing academic and political interest in the Arab states, which have higher rates of disability than the current global average as estimated by the World Health Organization.[1] It is evident that certain local practices and conditions contribute to these increased numbers, but this is not to suggest that all Arab peoples have been affected by the same historical and political circumstances. Although many countries in the region share a common language, religion, and culture often significant diversities exist in humanitarian contexts, socio-economic development indicators, cultural norms, political systems, and national identities. Still, a crucial common experience is that all Arab peoples have suffered some forms of coercive and violent rule through occupation and colonization and through the rule of native domestic authoritarian rulers. This included Ottoman and Spanish rule in the early modern period and British, French, Italian, and Israeli occupation in the modern era. More recently, several countries have been affected either directly or indirectly by armed conflicts of varying intensity, including the Arab-Israeli conflict, the Iraqi wars, the Arab Spring, and the Syrian and Libyan civil wars. This resulted not only in the rise of disabilities, but also in increased levels of poverty and socio-economic injustice. Moreover, colonial rule has left a lasting impact not only on material and political conditions, but also on the way authority and governance are being perceived in the Arab world: people often associate coercive governmental power with intentions of control and mistreatment.[2] Such lack of trust vis-à-vis the authorities can cause difficulties in both planning and implementing policies that could improve the lives of people with disabilities.

As some chapters in this volume have demonstrated, in the last half a century the issue of disability has been accommodated within a human rights perspective, a process that international organizations supported through numerous initiatives. This concluding chapter outlines how this process played out in the Arab world. Based on archival sources drawn from The League of Arab States archives in Cairo and on published documents it shows the ways in which political developments exerted an impact on discussions and perceptions of people with disabilities. It also shows that the development of the human rights perspective was not a teleological process, and the Convention is subject to vibrant debates up to the present day. An important milestone that catalyzed rights-based discourses was the United Nations' International Year of Disabled Persons in 1981. It represented a significant momentum in the Arab world because the proposal for this observance was submitted by the representative of the Arab Libyan Jamahirya, Mansur Rashid Kikhia (1931–1993). As a human rights lawyer, foreign minister of Libya, and later ambassador to the UN, Kikhia had worked together with war veterans and through those contacts became aware of the need to address their problems. He is credited with conceiving the idea to dedicate an International Year to this goal.[3] Lybia's initial suggestion was to observe the year in 1978. However, other member states of the UN voted in favor of 1981, in order to allow sufficient time for preparing the activities worldwide.[4]

Nevertheless, the late 1970s and early 1980s were not a favorable period in the Arab world in terms of political agreement or fraternal solidarity. Extreme polarization clouded Arab public opinion, and formal inter-state relations deteriorated due to Egypt's decision to sign a peace treaty with Israel in 1979 amid vast Arab disapproval.[5] In consequence, Egypt was suspended of its membership of The League of Arab States (LAS), the Pan Arab organization that it had co-founded in 1945 and had hosted for longer than four decades. Accusations of betrayal and aligning with the enemy against the rights of the Palestinian and other Arab peoples caused a huge rift. Egypt always inhabited almost one-third of the Arab population, and a critical mass in terms of human capital, legislators, qualified teachers, and other experts was necessary to achieve any Arab shared framework or plan. Under these circumstances it was difficult to proceed with a collective or Pan-Arab movement for people with disabilities because Egypt became boycotted by the other Arab states. This included the relocation of the headquarters of LAS from Egypt to Tunis and the appointment of a Tunisian, rather than Egyptian, person as its Secretary General.

In the late 1980s, Chedli Klibi, the Tunisian Secretary General of LAS (and its only non-Egyptian Secretary General since the League's foundation, holding office from 1979 to 1990), headed a summit meeting with Arab ministers of Social Affairs in Tunis. Klibi asserted that all Arab states should celebrate the forthcoming International Year. In his understanding, disability was an issue related to development, and he expected it to be considered with "relative" priority. Klibi referred to the escalating numbers of impairment among Arab citizens due to accidents arising in an increasingly industrialized work environment, but he also paid attention to the impact of armed conflicts.[6] He called for the integration of people with disabilities and the elimination of all forms of discrimination to become part of the strategic plans of development in the Arab world, and he reminded governments of their corresponding duties, which he expected to be fulfilled in cooperation with the private sector.

Arab states sought to address the tension around the different interpretations of human rights by issuing rights charters intended specifically for the Arab world. One of the earliest steps toward achieving Klibi's recommendations was the announcement of the Arab Charter on the Rights of the Child in December 1983.[7] This document proclaimed the equal right to development and to adequate social care for all Arab children, and it declared that discrimination on any grounds, including disability, was unacceptable. It also addressed the need for the establishment of a special system of care and education based on the principles of integration and emancipation. Moreover, it discussed the legislative framework that needed to be introduced, amended, or implemented in the Arab states to achieve these aims. While all LAS Ministers of Social Affairs signed the declaration of this Charter in 1984, the next year it was only ratified by three LAS parliaments: Yemen, Palestine, and Syria. Subsequently, Iraq ratified it in 1986, followed by Libya in 1987, Jordan in 1992, and finally Egypt in 1994. That thirteen LAS members states failing to ratify the document reveals that even a Charter that was tailor-made to suit the values and demands of the Arab world was not necessarily a general success.

Another relevant document, the Arab Charter for Human Rights, was instigated at the Beirut meeting of LAS in 1968. It took decades to prepare, draft, and revise. Its first version was accepted in 1994, and several LAS states had adopted and ratified it by 2004.[8] The question arises why this Charter was necessary when all Arab states had signed the Universal Declaration of Human Rights (1948). The reason has to do with the reservations that were maintained by these states throughout; for example, about issues related to personal freedom and criminal penalties, which they believed to be colliding with Arab religious or cultural legacy. Thus, the rationale behind the Arab Charter for Human Rights was to pay more attention to those religious and cultural differences. The Charter consists of forty-three articles with the preamble. Of these, article 34 focuses on employment, prohibiting discrimination at the workspace and guaranteeing just and safe work conditions, including for people with disabilities.[9] Article 40 is entirely dedicated to people with disabilities. It declares it to be the responsibility of Arab states to guarantee a dignified life for mentally and physically disabled persons. It also states the importance of education, including vocational education, employment (also in the private sector), self-reliance, and active participation in society. Furthermore, it declares that placing disabled people into institutions can only be used as a last resort when other options have been ruled out, and it asserts the rights of disabled people and of their closest family members or caregivers to receive social services.[10]

These ambitious desires yielded modest achievements. Three concrete results are noteworthy: the completion of the *Unified Sign Language Dictionary*, that of the *Unified Braille Dictionary*, and the formation of the Arab Organization for Persons with Disabilities in 1998. The Sign Language Dictionary was a focal project of LAS, and its completion involved intense preparatory meetings, workshops, and training sessions in the LAS headquarters in Cairo, and later in Sharjah.[11] The Common Strategy of Arab Social Work, issued in 2001, asserted the importance of normalizing and moving forward to the adoption of the unified dictionary in all LAS member states. Thereafter, Algiers hosted a training workshop on the dictionary and its implementation in August 2002.[12] By its nature the project had to exclude indigenous sign languages, yet the significant gain was the achievement of a unified version that rose above the various local dialects and idioms and could successfully facilitate intra-Arabic communication.

By facilitating the Braille Dictionary, LAS contributed to the establishment of a unified code for the Arab blind people. One of the most important steps toward achieving this aim was a workshop organized and sponsored by LAS in Amman in cooperation with Jordanian NGOs in March 2002. The workshop combined lectures by Arab experts, the explanation and presentation of the unified Arabic Braille code, field visits to institutions and schools of the Blind in Amman and other Jordanian cities, and training sessions for future educators on use of the code.[13]

The Great Hall of the League of Arab States in Cairo hosted from November 1, 1998 to November 3, 1998 the first conference that brought together Arab associations and NGOs in the field of disability, under the slogan "Towards an Arab Decade for Persons with Disabilities," an observance that was initially expected to be held from 2001 to 2010. Besides the announcement of the Decade to be launched, the conference established the Arab Organization for Persons with Disability—an umbrella NGO that brings together all the relevant Arab organizations and whose host city became Beirut.[14]

The Arab Decade for Persons with Disabilities, 2004–2013

With the outbreak of Second Intifada in 2000, addressing the needs of people with disabilities evolved into a crucial and urgent issue of Pan-Arab joint action. After almost a decade of emerging hope that peace with Israel could one day be possible, it became obvious that the conflict would not end any time soon. The gravity of the situation, combined with the pre-existing deplorable economic circumstances in Palestine, motivated LAS member states not only to address the political situation, but also to intervene om humanitarian grounds. This included both attending to the needs of the already disabled Palestinians and to the needs of those who became disabled in the violent conflict. In addition, the invasion of Iraq in March 2003 by the United States and its allies caused another massive wave of disabling injuries.

LAS's Council of Arab Ministers of Social Affairs decided to establish at least one rehabilitation center for the children who became disabled during the Intifada. Saudi Arabia and the Emirati Red Crescent offered to be the donors. In addition, a bank account was also opened to invite members of Arab civil society, individuals, and NGOs to donate for rehabilitation, with special attention to children. The Council also suggested that Arab States with sufficient human or financial capacity should host Palestinians whose injuries could not be handled in the occupied territories or sponsor their treatment and rehabilitation abroad.[15]

While the number of disablements caused by violence was sharply on the increase and LAS members were eager to address the situation in principle, they took no real steps to fulfill their promises. They requested from the representative of the Palestinian Authority to specify their requirements for the centers to be established in Rafah and Gaza, each estimated to cost approximately 2.688.000 USD. In addition to questions about accountability and transparency around the donations, the Palestinian authority also had reservations about the Saudi request to buy the land on which the centers would be established, which is a common request of donating agencies. However, Palestinians usually refrain from accepting such requests given the sensitive situation of land property in the occupied territories.[16]

Following strong pressure from activists, other Arab states had to step in to offer support. Syria paid 150.000 USD to fund the rehabilitation centers in hope of them ever seeing the light.[17] Several LAS members offered practical help rather than fundraising. Lebanon made available experts to help with legal aspects of the establishment of the centers and rehabilitation experts to work for them once they started operation.[18] Tunisia offered to receive Palestinian children in the physical rehabilitation center in Manouba and an NGO from Egypt, The Egyptian Association for the Care and Rehabilitation of the Deaf, volunteered to host and aid Palestinian injured children in Cairo.[19] The Emirati Red Crescent started establishing the rehabilitation center in Gaza in May 2003, while the Rafah Center was still struggling to see the light.[20] At the same session during which Arab Ministers failed to find a solution for the unfinished projects, they decided to organize an Arab Decade for Persons with Disabilities in the hope that this could accelerate progress. At the end, instead of the planned start in 2001, the Decade was launched in 2004.[21] LAS offered unconditional support for the Arab Decade. The General Secretariat made the commitment to dedicating most of its social funds to helping realize its agenda. The LAS Secretariat was very keen to invite observers and expert representatives, rather than official delegates of Arab States. An insight into the minutes of LAS social affairs meetings reveals the participation of the Arab Organization of Persons with Disability, the United Nations Economic and Social Commission for Western Asia (UN-ESCWA), the Arab Labor Organization, the Arab Women Organization, the Disability Bureau of the UN, and several representatives of Arab NGOs and individual activists.

The year 2006 represented a turning point in the Decade, as it marked the adoption of the United Nations Convention on the Right of People with Disabilities (UNCPRD). The Convention witnessed excessive discussions in LAS meetings and across the Arab world and it was met with objections on the same grounds as earlier human rights documents: it does not confirm to Arab cultural and legal norms and it is patronizing in its perception of human rights. These reservations motivated LAS to hold a regional conference in Algeria in 2006 to discuss the Convention and to consider adopting "national" and "local" strategies for Arab communities of disabled people. The report mentions, "We aim to suggest amendments that align with our principles and policies and do not contradict with our cultural and civilizational values."[22]

Apart from such legal debates not much happened on the ground and the Decade lacked a solid mechanism of implementation. Several projects were organized on a random basis, with no documentation or a clear follow-up strategy. Exceptions for modest initiatives that were at least documented included activities in Tunisia and Saudi Arabia aimed at the reduction of poverty. With the intention to provide an incentive for Arab NGOs, Algeria proposed to establish a prize for the best project related to the Decade under the name of the then president of Algeria Bouteflika.[23] On July 14, 2009 a national seminar was organized by the Arab Labor Organization in Cairo hosting official representatives and delegates of sixteen Arab states to discuss the gap between legislation and implementation regarding disability rights in the Arab world.[24]

The question as to what extent the UNCRPD is universal, rather than universalizing in its approach and scope, remains a contested issue until the present day. For example, as Mohammed Ghaly pointed out, a degree of tension prevails between the interpretation of the concept of legal capacity in the Convention and its interpretation from an Islamic cultural perspective.[25] This concept represents a core issue in the fundamental shift from the earlier medical understanding of disability, in which legal capacity was largely irrelevant, because it was assigned to medical and legal experts or family members, in the form of guardianship or deputyship.

By contrast, the UNCRPD's point of departure is the social and human rights model, which purports that denying legal capacity cannot be in the person's best interest and therefore acknowledging the legal capacity of every person on an equal basis in every sphere of life, regardless of whether they have a disability or not. According to this interpretation, legal capacity can help to overcome paternalistic tendencies due to its empowering effect.[26] Nevertheless, in the case of persons with mental disabilities, legal capacity on an equal basis does not align with the Islamic cultural and religious perspective. To be in accordance with divine justice does not mean to treat everyone equally in an indiscriminate way, rather, to assume the principle of proportionality: people should be assigned obligations in alignment with their mental capacities, so that they do not become overwhelmed. This implies that as a last resort guardianship can remain an option in certain situations.[27]

However, the implementation of the human rights framework is not only impeded by such cultural and religious differences, but also by the continuing prevalence of the medical approach, which results in policies that are relegated to the medicated realm in a segregated environment.[28] It is a telling sign that across the Arab countries relevant new laws omit the requirement of the "prohibition of discrimination on the basis of disability."[29]

The political uprisings that took many Arab states by storm since their start in Tunisia in 2010 were a crucial factor, at least in some of the Arab states, in the empowering of people with disabilities who could appropriate the demands for rights and justice to their own circumstances. It is unlikely that the Arab Decade for Persons with Disabilities would have seen the light had the Second Palestinian Intifada and the invasion of Iraq not taken place. The first part of the Decade focused on activism to help people with disabilities in war and conflict zones, but its pace quickly slowed down. In the second part of the Decade, the Arab uprisings gave a renewed impetus to promote political change that focused on legislation and emancipation. For example, in Egypt, the pro-democracy protests from early 2010 to 2012 appear to have been disseminating a "rights language" that could also be serviceable for disability protests. Demands addressed employment, housing, and training issues and the enforcement of the law of 2010, which established a quota of 5 percent of jobs to be offered to disabled people.[30] Even as the new government of Mohammed Morsi came to power, protests continued, one taking place in Alexandria in June 2012 and another in October 2012 in Cairo. The latter's initial demands included adequate housing and job opportunities, but after some people suffered injuries from the clashes with police, the agenda changed to demands of the freedom to protest.[31]

In 2015, two years after the Decade had officially ended, ESCWA issued a preliminary assessment. This acknowledged some achievements in the way of the creation of emancipatory organizations. It specifically referred to the successes of the disability movement in Lebanon and it also noted that Egypt was successful in the creation of strong NGOs that were well connected to the international people with disabilities.[32] In 2023, a subsequent Second Decade was launched. Plans for a United Arab Classification of Disabilities were entertained alongside the creation of an online platform to monitor and evaluate the implementation of the goals of the previous Decade at the High-Level Forum on the Second Arab Decade for Disabled Persons 2023–2032, which was held in Tunis from October 1, 2023 to October 5, 2023.[33]

Epilogue

The devastating war after October 7, 2023 rendered the topic of disability even more painfully relevant than before in the MENA region. The massacres and hostage taking by Hamas after its incursion into Israeli territory, and the ensuing Israeli military operation in Gaza that resulted in the killing of tens of thousands of people, was accompanied by temporary and permanent disablements. Their number is so high that it is extremely difficult to estimate. They are not only the result of direct injuries. Disablement is also the result of the lack of access to the health and rehabilitative infrastructure, which was largely destroyed, and of the looming famine arising from the blockade of humanitarian aid. The psychological damage resulting from the enormously traumatizing effect of these atrocities, many of which occurred in violation of international law, will haunt generations to come.

Such war atrocities, together with pollution, nuclear testing, and unhealthy and unsafe ways of production constantly produce impaired bodies and minds. Yet, discourses on the deliberate *production of impairment* rarely receive mention, let alone attention, in mainstream disability history. Conscious wounding and disabling may be deemed just as advantageous in military strategy as killing. Severely wounded people require valuable resources of treatment and care. When medical and rehabilitative provision is already extremely limited to start with and lifesaving and life-maintaining infrastructure is destroyed, the needs of those whose conflict-related direct impairments require urgent attention are typically prioritized, to the detriment of the needs of people with existing disabilities.[34] As Heba Hagrass, UN Special Rapporteur on the rights of persons with disabilities, has warned, the latter group are also at a heightened risk of loss of life, for example by being left behind because of the impossibility to flee when families or relief teams are not in the position to assist them. Simultaneously she warned that the manner of military operations on both sides violated the UN Convention on the Rights of Persons with Disabilities, Article No. 11, and the Security Council Resolution No. 2475 (2019) on protecting persons with disabilities during armed conflicts.[35]

In comparable situations, when survival only can be the utmost ambition, existing frameworks of disability studies lose their applicability. The human rights agenda, with its goals of emancipation, independent living and disability pride suddenly no longer resonate. In

Anglophone perceptions of disability, a high degree of skepticism exists toward the notion of prevention, because it implies that disability is an undesired personal tragedy. Yet, this assumption likewise requires reconsideration, as no one would doubt that disability arising from war violence is unwanted and must be prevented.[36] One of the more serviceable alternatives in this situation can be the concept of social suffering, which encompasses the collective, historical and cultural experiences distinct to a group, the "serious wounds to the body and the spirit."[37] The strategy of deliberate maiming, together with the erosion of infrastructure, can be viewed as a distinct form of cruelty, which Rob Nixon has called slow violence: "a violence that occurs gradually and out of sight, a violence of delayed destruction that is dispersed across time and space, an attritional violence that is typically not viewed as violence at all."[38] Two other relevant notions capture the essence of the tactics of "not letting people die" in a non-functioning health and rehabilitation system that cannot support their meaningful survival. Under these circumstances they become reduced to a status that Achille Mbembe calls the living dead[39] and Lauren Berlant describes as the experience of a slow death when bodies and minds experience permanent pain and exhaustion.[40]

Finally, the concept of debility, as different from disability, has been coined by Jasbir Puar in her book *The Right to Maim*, and it captures the slow wearing down of populations instead of the more concrete incident of becoming disabled. Disability "starts" at a certain point (for example, at birth or with an accident) and it is associated with certain entitlements. By contrast, debilitation is a perpetual state, and it refers to the process of a slow wearing out, which may or may not include the feeling of being disabled and is akin to some continuous condition, like chronic illness.[41]

The most crucial common denominator among these concepts is that none of them are desired conditions. It therefore appears to be appropriate to conclude this chapter and the entire volume with Helen Meekosha's reminder that disability studies scholars have an ethical mission to join forces with progressive social movements and demand the cessation and prevention of all forms of violence everywhere in the world.[42]

Notes

1.   This information can be accessed at World Health Organization, Disability (who.int)

2. Darwish, Noor (2019). "The Middle Eastern Societies: Institutional Trust in Political Turmoil and Stasis." *Silicon Valley Notebook*, 17(9). Available at: https://scholarcommons.scu.edu/svn/vol17/iss1/9

3. In 1980 Kikhia defected the government and became a peaceful opposition leader to Quaddafi. He was murdered in Cairo in 1993 where he was seeking political asylum.

4. Letter from the Libyan representative to the UN Secretary General, September 21, 1976, Archives of the LAS, Cairo.

5. On the boycott see Podeh, E. and Winckler, O. (2002). "The Boycott that Never Was: Egypt and the Arab System, 1979-1989." Working Paper. Durham: University of Durham, Centre for Middle Eastern and Islamic Studies, 1–90.

6. Speech of Chedli Klibib to the Council of Arab Ministers of Social Affairs, Tunis, December 25–27, 1980, LAS Archives in Cairo.

7. Arab Charter on the Rights of the Child, 1983, https://citizenshiprightsafrica.org/arab-charter-on-the-rights-of-the-child/

8. Al-Midani, Mohammed Amin and Cabanettes, Mathilde (Translation) and Akram, Susan M. (Revision). (2006) "Arab Charter on Human Rights 2004." *Boston University International Law Journal*, 24(2), 147–164; see LAS_Arab Charter on Human Rights_2004_EN.pdf (eods.eu)

9. Arab Charter on Human Rights | Refworld

10. Arab Charter on Human Rights | Refworld

11. Al-Ahmed, Hussameldin (2015). *Hemayat Hekouk thawy Elhtyagat Elkhasa fi Alnzima we eltashryaat alkhaligya* [Protection of People with Special Needs in Laws and Legislations of Gulf Countries], Ryadh: Law and Economics Library, 251.

12. Five-year plan to implement "Strategies of Arab Social Work: 2002–2006," LAS Archives in Cairo, 2003 Annual Report, 151.

13. Five-year plan to implement "Strategies of Arab Social Work: 2002–2006," LAS Archives in Cairo, 2003 Annual Report, 109–115.

14. See the document announcing the establishment of the Arab Organization for Persons with Disability: https://archive.unescwa.org/ar/arab-organization-persons-disabilities

15. Council of Arab Ministers of Social Affairs, LAS Archives in Cairo, November 7, 2001. ج 70/ 12 (11/10) 20. ت (8010)

16. Council of Arab Ministers of Social Affairs, LAS Archives in Cairo, December 15, 2002. ج 70/ 22 (21/20)/ 20- ق(3340)

17. Letter from the Embassy of the Arab Syrian Republic in Cairo to LAS financial office for confirmation of reception of donation, March 6, 2002, Letter no. 3/778, annexed to ج 22/07 (02/12)/ -02 ق(0433)

18. Lebanon Permanent Delegation to LAS, Memorandum no. 2065, June 2002, mentioned in ج 22/07 (02/12) -02 ق(0433), 30

19. Council of Arab Ministers of Social Affairs, LAS Archives in Cairo, December 15, 2002. ج. 70/ 22 (21/20)/ 20- ق(3340), 30–32

20. Council of Arab Ministers of Social Affairs, LAS Archives in Cairo, December 9, 2003. ج07/23 (03/12) 02 ق(0387) , 6–9

21. Ibidem, 85–103.

22. Council of Arab Ministers of Social Affairs, LAS Archives in Cairo, December 17–18, 2006. ج-07 01/26 (06/12) -05 ق(0562), 60–64

23. Council of Arab Ministers of Social Affairs, LAS Archives in Cairo, September 3, 2007. ج07-01/50 (07/09) 08(- ق(0557), 23–27

24. "Protection of Persons with Disability: Between Legislation and Implementation," Seminar organized by the Arab Labour Organization and Arab Labour Bureau in Cairo, July 14–16, 2009. Final report and resolutions (in Arabic), https://alolabor.org/wp-content/uploads/2009/07/Hemaya_N_Cairo_Cairo_14_16_07_09_Report.pdf

25. Ghaly, Mohammed (2019). "The Convention on the Rights of Persons with Disabilities in the Islamic Tradition: The Question of Legal Capacity in Focus." *Journal of Disability and Religion*, 23(3), 253.

26. Ibidem.

27. Ibidem, 269.

28. Implementation of the Sustainable Development Goals and the Convention on the Rights of Persons with Disabilities in the Arab World. Regional Report by the Arab Organization of Persons with Disabilities (AOPD), published by AODP, Beirut, 2020, 7.

29. Ibidem, 11.

30. Barnartt, Sharon N. (2014). "The Arab Spring Protests and Concurrent Disability Protests: Social Movement Spillover or Spurious Relationship?" *Studies in Social Justice*, 8(1), 67–78.

31. Ibidem.

32. "Protection of Persons with Disability: Between Legislation and Implementation." Seminar organized by the Arab Labour Organization and Arab Labour Bureau in Cairo, July 14–16, 2009. Final report and resolutions, 3.

33. Forum on 2nd Arab Decade of Disabled Persons: Call for establishment of e-platform on disability issues. tap.info.tn/en/Portal-Society/16685965-forum-on-2nd-arab

34. Berghs, Maria and Kabbara, Nawah (2016). "Disabled People in Conflicts and Wars." In Grech, S. and Soldatic, K. (eds.), *Disability in the Global South: The Critical Handbook*, Cham, Switzerland: Springer, 272–273.

35. Gaza: UN expert demands unconditional humanitarian access and relief for people with disabilities | OHCHR The report is available on the same site in Arabic.

36. Meekosha, Helen. (2011). "Decolonizing Disability: Thinking and Acting Globally." *Disability & Society*, 26(6), 670.

37. Kleiman, Arthur, Das, Verena, and Lock, Margaret (eds.) (1997). *Social Suffering*. Berkeley, Los Angeles, and London: University of California Press.

38. Nixon, Rob (2011). *Slow Violence and the Environmentalism of the Poor*. Cambridge, MA and London: Harvard University Press, 2 cited in Jones, Craig (2023). "Gaza and the Great March of Return: Enduring Violence and Spaces of Wounding." *Transactions of the Institute of British Geographers*, 48, 251.

39. Mbembe, Achille (2003). "Necropolitics." *Public Culture*, 15(1), 11–40.

40. Berlant, Lauren (2007). "Slow Death (Sovereignty, Obesity, Lateral Agency)." *Critical Inquiry*, 33(4), 771.

41. Puar, Jasbir K. (2017). *The Right to Maim: Debility, Capacity, Disability*. Durham, NC: Duke University Press, xiii.

42. Meekosha, Helen (2011). "Decolonizing Disability: Thinking and Acting Globally." *Disability & Society*, 26(6), 668.

Archival sources

Letter from the Libyan representative to the UN Secretary General, September 21, 1976, Archives of
the LAS, Cairo.

Speech of Chedli Klibib to the Council of Arab Ministers of Social Affairs, Tunis, December 25–27,
1980, LAS Archives in Cairo.

Council of Arab Ministers of Social Affairs, LAS Archives in Cairo, November 7, 2001.
0108) ت. 20 (11/10) 12 /70 ج)

Council of Arab Ministers of Social Affairs, LAS Archives in Cairo, December 15, 2002.
0433)ق -20 /(21/20) 22/70 ج)

Letter from the Embassy of the Arab Syrian Republic in Cairo to LAS financial office for
confirmation of reception of donation, March 6, 2002, Letter no. 3/778, annexed to (22/70 ج
3340)ق -20 /(21/20)

Lebanon Permanent Delegation to LAS, Memorandum no. 2065, June 2002, mentioned in 22/70 ج
03 ,(3340)ق -20 (21/20).

Council of Arab Ministers of Social Affairs, LAS Archives in Cairo, December 15, 2002.
23–03 ,(3340)ق -20 /(21/20) 22/70 ج.

Council of Arab Ministers of Social Affairs, LAS Archives in Cairo, December 9, 2003. (21/30) 32/70ج
9–6 , (7830)ق 20.

Five-year plan to implement "Strategies of Arab Social Work: 2002–2006," LAS Archives in Cairo,
2003 Annual Report.

Council of Arab Ministers of Social Affairs, LAS Archives in Cairo, December 17–18, 2006. - 62/10-70ج
46–06 ,(2650)ق -50 (21/60).

Council of Arab Ministers of Social Affairs, LAS Archives in Cairo, September 3, 2007. 05/10-70ج
72–32 ,(7550)ق -(80 (90/70).

Online sources

Arab Charter on the Rights of the Child, 1983, https://citizenshiprightsafrica.org/
arab-charter-on-the-rights-of-the-child/

Forum on 2nd Arab Decade of Disabled Persons: Call for establishment of e-platform on disability
issues. tap.info.tn/en/Portal-Society/16685965-forum-on-2nd-arab

Arab Charter on Human Rights

"Protection of Persons with Disability: Between Legislation and Implementation." Seminar organized
by the Arab Labour Organization and Arab Labour Bureau in Cairo, July 14–16, 2009. Final
report and resolutions (in Arabic)
https://alolabor.org/wp-content/uploads/2009/07/Hemaya_N_Cairo_Cairo_14_16_07_09_Report.
pdf

The establishment of the Arab Organization for Persons with Disability, https://archive.unescwa.org/
ar/arab-organization-persons-disabilities

Implementation of the Sustainable Development Goals and the Convention on the Rights of Persons with Disabilities in the Arab World. Regional Report by the Arab Organization of Persons with Disabilities (AOPD), published by AOPD, Beirut, 2020

Gaza: UN expert demands unconditional humanitarian access and relief for people with disabilities | OHCHR The report is available on the same site in Arabic.

World Health Organization, Disability (who.int), accessed on March 14, 2024.

Printed sources

Al-Ahmed, Hussameldin (2015). *Hemayat Hekouk thawy Elhtyagat Elkhasa fi Alnzima we eltashryaat alkhaligya* [Protection of People with Special Needs in Laws and Legislations of Gulf Countries], Riyadh: Law and Economics Library.

Al-Midani, Mohammed Amin and Cabanettes, Mathilde (Translation) and Akram, Susan M. (Revision) (2006) "Arab Charter on Human Rights 2004." *Boston University International Law Journal*, 24(2), 147–164; see LAS_Arab Charter on Human Rights_2004_EN.pdf (eods.eu)

Barnartt, Sharon N. (2014). "The Arab Spring Protests and Concurrent Disability Protests: Social Movement Spillover or Spurious Relationship?" *Studies in Social Justice*, 8(1), 67–78.

Berghs, Maria and Kabbara, Nawah (2016). "Disabled People in Conflicts and Wars." In Grech, S. and Soldatic, K. (eds.) *Disability in the Global South: The Critical Handbook* (pp. 269–283). Cham, Switzerland: Springer.

Berlant, Lauren (2007). "Slow Death (Sovereignty, Obesity, Lateral Agency)." *Critical Inquiry*, 33(4), 754–780.

Craig, Jones (2023). "Gaza and the Great March of Return: Enduring Violence and Spaces of Wounding." *Transactions of the Institute of British Geographers*, 48, 249–262.

Darwish, Noor (2019). "The Middle Eastern Societies: Institutional Trust in Political Turmoil and Stasis." *Silicon Valley Notebook*, 17(9). https://scholarcommons.scu.edu/svn/vol17/iss1/9

Ghaly, Mohammed (2019). "The Convention on the Rights of Persons with Disabilities in the Islamic Tradition: The Question of Legal Capacity in Focus." *Journal of Disability and Religion*, 23(3), 257–278.

Kleiman, Arthur, Das, Verena, and Lock, Margaret (eds.) (1997). *Social Suffering*. Berkeley, Los Angeles, and London: University of California Press.

Mbembe, Achille (2003). "Necropolitics." *Public Culture*, 15(1), 11–40.

Meekosha, Helen (2011). "Decolonizing Disability: Thinking and Acting Globally." *Disability & Society*, 26(6), 667–682.

Nixon, Rob (2011). *Slow Violence and the Environmentalism of the Poor*. Cambridge, MA andLondon: Harvard University Press.

Podeh, E. and Winckler, O. (2002). "The Boycott that Never Was: Egypt and the Arab System, 1979-1989." Working Paper. Durham: University of Durham, Centre for Middle Eastern and Islamic Studies, pp. 1–90.

Puar, Jasbir K. (2017). *The Right to Maim: Debility, Capacity, Disability*. Durham, NC: Duke University Press.

About the Authors

Monika Baar holds a Joint Chair in the Department of History and the Robert Schuman Centre for Advanced Studies at the European University Institute in Florence. She holds undergraduate degrees in History, Literature, and Linguistics from Eötvös Loránd University (ELTE), Budapest, and MA degrees in History from the Central European University, Budapest, and in Slavonic and East European Studies from the School of Slavonic and East European Studies (SSES), London. She completed her doctorate in Modern History at the University of Oxford under the supervision of Robert Evans in 2002. She has held positions in the Max Planck Institute for the History of Science, the University of Essex, the University of Edinburgh, the National Europe Centre, the University of Canberra, the Graduate Institute, Geneva, the University of Groningen, and Columbia University, among others. Among her publications are *Historians and Nationalism: East-Central Europe in the Nineteenth Century* (Oxford Historical Monographs, Oxford University Press, 2010), "Vegetables of the World Unite!: Grassroots Internationalization of Disabled Citizens in the Post-War Period," forthcoming in Jessica Reinisch and David Brydan (eds.), *Europe's Internationalists: Rethinking the History of Internationalism* (Bloomsbury, 2021) and "International Days at the United Nations: Expanding the Scope of Diplomatic Histories," *Diplomatica. A Journal of Diplomacy and Society* special issue on UN Observances, 2019:2.

Gildas Brégain is a researcher of the National Center of Scientific Research, hosted at the High School of Public Health in Rennes, France. His research interests focus on transnational disability history, public policy, social movements, and life experiences. After conducting research on Argentina, Brazil, and Spain, he completed a post-doctoral fellowship about the blind on colonized Algeria (early twentieth century–1962). His current research project encompasses three cultural areas, Latin America, North Africa, and Europe. He has published several articles on policies to assist the war-disabled, the blind, and the civilian disabled in certain countries of the French Empire, particularly in North Africa. His most recent book is *Pour une histoire du handicap au XXe siècle. Approches* *transnationales (Europe et Amériques)* (Presses universitaires de Rennes, 2018).

Riham Debian is currently a tenured Associate Professor for Cultural Studies at the Institute of Applied Linguistics and Translation, Alexandria University, Egypt. Her research interests span the fields of Translation, Gender and Cultural studies with a specific focus on intercultural communication and international relations—the purview of Cultural Communication and Diplomacy.

Heba Fawzy El-Masry is an associate professor of translation studies at the Department of English Language and Literature, Faculty of Arts, Tanta University, Egypt. She obtained her PhD from the University of Warwick in 2018. Her research papers include "'Trumpslation Analysed: Constraints and Interpreter Strategies in the Simultaneous Interpretation of Donald Trump's Unscripted Speeches into Arabic" (2022) and "Translation as an Ideological Tool: An Analysis of Rasha Ṣādiq's Feminist Translation of Rosalind Miles's Who Cooked the Last Supper? The Women's History of the World" (2024).

Imene Zoulikha Kassous, PhD, is a dedicated youth advocate and researcher focused on autism representation in the Global South. She wrote a letter to editors discussing autism and the Global South (https://tinyurl.com/gsaut). Imene was awarded an International Society for Autism Research Cultural Diversity Internship to investigate the experiences of mothers of autistic females in Algeria.

Maria Chiara Rioli is Associate Professor in Contemporary History at the University of Modena and Reggio Emilia, Italy. She is Co-Coordinator of the EU-funded project ITHACA—Interconnecting Histories and Archives for Migrant Agency. Previously she was Marie Skłodowska-Curie Global Fellow at the universities of Ca' Foscari in Venice and Fordham in New York, and project manager, Digital Humanist and Post-doctoral Fellow of the ERC Starting Grant project "OPEN JERUSALEM—Opening Jerusalem Archives: For a Connected History of 'Citadinité' in the Holy City, 1840–1940." Among her publications: *A Liminal Church: Refugees, Conversions and the Latin Diocese of Jerusalem, 1946–1956* (Brill, 2020).

Amany Soliman is an associate professor of modern and contemporary history and the director of the Mediterranean Studies Institute at the Faculty of Arts in Alexandria University in Egypt. She joined the ERC project "Rethinking Disability" as a non-resident postdoctoral fellow in 2017, as she was based in the Netherlands-Flemish Institute in Cairo. Soliman obtained her PhD from Alexandria University in 2010. Prior to her work in Alexandria University, Soliman worked as a researcher in the Library of Alexandria (Bibliotheca Alexandrina) and as a lecturer at the Arab Academy for Science and Technology. Soliman is a member of the editorial advisory board of Cambridge Core Journal *Medical History* since 2019. She is currently the Executive Director of International Relations at the Faculty of Arts, Alexandria University. Her publications include "Refugees of the Eastern Mediterranean in the aftermath of the Great War: History Lessons to a Complicated Present" (*Mediterranean Review*, 2017) and "The Rise of Egyptian Nationalism and the Perception of Foreigners in Egypt 1914–1923," in the volume *First World War and Its Aftermath* (ed. by T.G. Fraser, Ginko, 2015).

Majid Turmusani, PhD, specializes in disability inclusive development. In 1999, he completed his PhD in Disability Studies from the University of Leeds, UK. He has extensive international experience, including work in the following countries: Jordan, Yemen, Iraq/Kurdistan, Qatar, Afghanistan, Myanmar, Bangladesh, Rwanda, Togo, Guinea, Kosovo, UK, and Canada. Having worked for large-scale organizations such as the UN, the World Bank, the international non-governmental organizations (INGOs), academia, and governments, he has developed skills in critical and analytical thinking, strategic planning, monitoring, and evaluation. Often, he worked on the management of community based rehabilitation, inclusive education, access to justice, and disability rights. Dr Turmusani has taken an active part in the negotiation process for the development of the UN's Convention on the Rights of Persons with Disabilities (CRPD) and sustainable development goals (SDGs) as well as in their implementation, monitoring, and evaluation. He has actively published work, including three books and dozens of articles and chapters in books. For more information on the publication, please see the profile at LinkedIn: https://www.linkedin.com/in/majid-turmusani-phd-34704430

Bouchra Yahia graduated cum laude from the Radboud University Nijmegen with a master's degree in Arabic and Islam. Throughout her studies, she focused on the role of Islam in everyday life, particularly within political and social contexts. As part of this exploration, she wrote her thesis on Islamic psychology, examining its concepts and practical implications, especially for Muslims living in the West. In 2019, she was selected to present her thesis at the "Rethinking Disability" conference in Cairo hosted by Leiden University. She is currently working at the Dutch Migration Office in the Netherlands.

www.ingramcontent.com/pod-product-compliance
Lightning Source LLC
Chambersburg PA
CBHW051956270326
41929CB00015B/2678